WEALTH OF PEOPLE

A New Framework for Economics

WEALTH OF PEOPLE

A New Framework for Economics

PARITOSH M. CHAKRABARTI

Om Books International

First published in 2024 by

Om Books International

Corporate & Editorial Office
A-12, Sector 64, Noida 201 301
Uttar Pradesh, India
Phone: +91 120 477 4100
Email: editorial@ombooks.com
Website: www.ombooksinternational.com

Sales Office
107, Ansari Road, Darya Ganj,
New Delhi 110 002, India
Phone: +91 11 4000 9000
Email: sales@ombooks.com
Website: www.ombooks.com

ISBN: 978-81-19750-59-7

Printed in India

10 9 8 7 6 5 4 3 2 1

To the memory of
Gavin Sinclair

Contents

Preface ix

Introduction xix

1. Structural Components of Modern Political Economy: Terms and Concepts 1

2. Origins of Modern Economics and the Socio-economic Climate 28

3. The Leading Economic Theories: An Introduction 48

4. The Leading Economic Theories: A Critical Analysis 71

5. The Laws of Nature: Thermodynamics 121

6. Work and Energy: Where Thermodynamics and Economics Meet 144

7. The Framework of a New Economic Order 176

8. Healthcare and the New Economic Framework 229

9. Brave New World Dream 257

Appendix 1: Some Historical Dates, Book 1 to 4 276

Appendix 2: Historical Dates of People and Events Mentioned in the Memoir 278

Appendix 3: Summaries of Books 1, 2 and 4 284

Bibliography 288

Index 293

Preface

In December 1999, I was honoured with a bronze plaque for excellence in entrepreneurship at the Global Bengali Conference held in Kolkata, India, by Mr Jyoti Basu, the chief minister. The famous Bengali writer Sankar, who wrote a story about financially successful Bengalis abroad, highlighted my life's history in a commemorative book, entitled *Smarak Grantha*.[1] During the conference, Sankar approached me with a proposal to write my biography, which he said was relatable and would inspire young Bengalis.

At about the same time, Dr Surabhi Banerjee, the pro-vice chancellor of Calcutta University, whom I had first met in connection with my endowment of a chemistry chair at the university, also approached me about writing my biography. Dr Banerjee, also a well-known writer, had previously written Basu's biography.

I declined both requests. I didn't think that I was such an example-setting person that someone would want to read

1 Ed. Sunil Gangopadhyay (a legendary literary figure in Bengal), Saraswati Press, Kolkata, 1999.

my biography. There existed better examples of financial, academic, and business successes, I thought. So writing a simple biography didn't interest me much. It would have been an act of self-propaganda, which I have always avoided. What I thought could be worth writing about, however, were some deep-seated experiences that I'd had during the course of my long life. They might inspire new research to advance matters of societal interest. Such thoughts and experiences, of course, intertwined intimately with my life, so they wouldn't have the same impact if they were detached from my life history. Lessons of broad human interest can come alive only when we glean them from the real-life experience of the person describing them. If I had to write about myself, I thought, the subject had to be greater than myself. Hence the thought arose of writing a memoir rather than a simple autobiography.

Initially, I thought of writing my memoir as one book with several chapters. As the writing progressed, however, I came to understand that the material wouldn't fit neatly into one book. The memoir had four themes: (1) an autobiography; (2) the creation of PMC Group, which could serve as a model for twenty-first-century corporations; (3) economics and the creation of a new economic framework; and (4) a treatise on religion, truth, morality, and the purpose of life. The topics were so diverse that a single reader might not be interested in all of them. So, at the suggestion of a few friends, I decided to write my memoir as a series of four books, with each book covering one of the four themes.

The first chapter of the first book opens with my childhood, much of which was spent moving from one place to the next, and describes my turbulent life until I was twelve years old. The last chapter of the fourth and final book explores life's purpose, which, I conclude, transcends one's own life. In between, I use anecdotes from my own life as a jumping-off point to investigate a broad range of topics, including economics, science, and history.

In presenting the narratives, particularly of Books 1, 2, and 4, I had to dig deep into my memory. What came forth were shards of experiences pertaining to the unusual events I encountered and the special people I met throughout my life. The events evoked both ends of the emotional spectrum and everything in between—happiness and sorrow, pleasure and pain, sex and celibacy, peace and turmoil, health and sickness, faith and scepticism, morality and sin, right and wrong, good and evil, science and superstition, commitment and evasion, universality and provincialism, honour and disgrace, pride and shame, wealth and poverty, and success and failure.

The negative experiences seemed, at the time they were unfolding, to accentuate the hardships of life, but when viewed in the aggregate and along with the positive experiences I have enjoyed, they represent an arrow pointing towards the better end of the spectrum. My belief in that arrow provided me the motivation to move forward in life, even in the face of adversity. When we lose faith in that arrow, we fail. My faith in that arrow carried me from humble beginnings to today's abundance. In my role as one of the fifty richest people living in New Jersey and as a thoughtful philanthropist, I have engaged in such diverse endeavours as instilling a soul in a corporation, developing a new economic framework, and establishing a theory of truth. My faith in that arrow has given me a philosophical view of life that is both retrospective *and* prospective, and it has led me to present this view in a treatise on religion, truth, morality, and the purpose of life.

*

In this book, I examine two principles of science—the second law of thermodynamics and Darwinism—that deal with equality and inequality. The first principle, one of the fundamental laws of physics that rule the infinitely vast inorganic universe, strives to achieve equality in death, figuratively at the graveyard of entropy. The second tries to maximize inequality in "survival of the fittest", with the law of the living world that represents the tiniest corner of the tiniest part of the universe.

I show how politicians, egalitarian philosophers, and economists, heedless of those laws, fell into error while designing rules for human society. I show that both these principles of science can help us to design a process for reaching the ultimate truth about the goal of humanity. The laws of science, however, cannot reveal the goal—the "products" or the "ends" as philosophers call it—of the process. Such products reside in a unique set of rules—the rules of morality—that make us human. I discuss some of the debates over equality that, for decades if not centuries, consumed the egalitarian philosophers. I hope my discussion will give their followers a new perspective. These principles of humanity, enshrined in the process and the products, run through all four books but feature most prominently in this book and in Book 4, *The Highest Reality* (Prabhat Prakashan, 2024).

Whenever we present thoughts and theories based on our own experience and inquiries, our personal biases influence our discussions. These biases concern our tendency to emphasize the evidence that supports our propositions and to minimize that which opposes them.

Biases also influence where we draw the line between right and wrong, between truth and non-truth. The lines aren't always sharp. They are often more like transition zones between one way of thinking and another, each representing various shades of grey. Even so, we often view things as black or white, and our biases inspire us to adopt clear-cut positions as a result. Although I have endeavoured to present reasoned arguments, I must confess that in each case, I started with my personal beliefs and convictions rather than with a clean slate.

For instance, I have strived to never act purely from self-interest. So it's natural that I don't quite agree with Adam Smith's thesis that self-interest is the exclusive—if not the primary—source of collective interest. Similarly, I don't believe that the scientific method is the gold standard for determining what is true or false. I have argued that our morality differentiates humanity from the rest of the physical world. Science, which represents the rules that the physical world follows, is amoral. Accordingly, I have argued that those who would have science dictate their lives are greatly in error. Thus it shouldn't come as a surprise that I define truth in two dimensions: scientific and moral (or spiritual). I place moral truth above scientific truth and have made the point that science, to be helpful, must always follow a moral guide, lest it bring an end to humanity.

With these books, I hope to reach educated men and women who possess a keen sense of judgement, intellectuals who can make up their own minds about the substance of an argument. Only such people can be agents of change. Just as we can't ask clerics, nuns, and bishops to reform religions, we can't ask a modern economist to tell us in plain language what they want to communicate. As Deirdre McCloskey put it, "Most journals of economics nowadays look like journals of applied mathematics or theoretical statistics … technical economics are no longer even superficially accessible to laypeople." Yet to have any impact on decision makers, we must explain everything as simply as possible—even complex thoughts concerning economics, science, technology, and religion.

*

In Appendix 3 I have summarized Books 1, 2, and 4. To wrap up this preface, I'd like to provide a quick look at what follows in the pages to come.

This book, Book 3 in the series, provides a discourse on replacing today's existing economic theories and arrangements. The seed of this book was planted during the latter part of my career at PPG Industries and continued germinating while I built PMC Group. It took more than thirty years for my thoughts to bloom. During that time, I discussed them with many business leaders and academics and during the many lectures I delivered at universities, research institutions, and national conferences. Those lectures, however, were mostly on managing technology and corporate growth models; they invariably involved factors that made an economy grow and thrive. Naturally, my interest moved to growth models of economics and then to a new economic framework.

The book starts as a primer on modern economic states by introducing essential economic terms, beginning with a definition of money and money supply, and ending with a commentary on stock market crashes. It discusses the terms and concepts behind central banks' monetary policies, international financial transactions, credit and credit creation, the role of gold in an economy (many countries, including the United States, still hoard large reserves of gold in their treasuries), the role and function of the International Monetary Fund (IMF), and so forth.

I then trace the origin of modern economic theory and the political and socio-economic climates in which the various theories arose. Next, I introduce the most significant modern economic theories: the Smith–Ricardo–Mill–Malthus doctrine; the demand-side macroeconomic theory that Keynes introduced in the aftermath of the Great Depression, communism, and socialism; and several morality-based theories. I then follow with a critical analysis of the leading theories, emphasizing why socialism and communism are impotent as economic arrangements and why capitalism has become an immoral force.

Regarding the latter, I present a set of forceful arguments about how and why capitalism, despite its success in creating national wealth, has become immoral. These arguments include the following: (1) capitalism has overemphasized the role of capital, (2) capitalism has reduced labour to the level of the inanimate raw material of production, (3) the unfettered growth of monopolies has led to innumerable negative consequences, (4) Wall Street has hijacked the term "technology", (5) the funding of government inefficiencies and excesses, paid for with annual increases in debt, makes the US economy look like a Ponzi scheme, (6) big corporations can raise debt unfairly in comparison to small corporations, and (7) various mixtures of capitalism and socialism are even more dangerous.

While pondering the subject of economics, I was dismayed to find that the mainstream economic arrangements—capitalism on one end and communism on the other—focus on either maximizing wealth creation at the national level or equitably distributing wealth among the workers. The first leads to the concentration of wealth in a few hands, while the second, although it has achieved better distribution, fails to generate much wealth. Worse, all extant economic theories are based on the theories of just a few people, such as Adam Smith and Karl Marx.

Worse still, the economic theories are not based on immutable principles. I found that, although economists like to refer to their discipline as "economic science", no science is evident in their theories. The validity of a scientific theory depends on its reproducibility, but in economic theory, there is no such thing as reproducibility. The committee that awards the Nobel Prize in economics honours radically opposite theories. I became convinced that a better and more consistent theory must exist—one that can achieve wealth creation *and* an equitable distribution thereof. I searched for clues of such a theory in nature and found my answer primarily in the laws of thermodynamics.

The final part of the book explores developing a new framework of economics that uses a process based on the irrefutable principles of the laws of thermodynamics. I begin by discussing several key concepts of thermodynamics. Then I draw a link between thermodynamics and economics, pointing out parallels between various economic and thermodynamic terms. The discussion of the thermodynamic principles and terms gets a little technical, but I have tried my best to describe them in as simple language as possible.

Of course, the laws of nature are amoral; they adhere to no moral code. Any economic arrangement, however, must not only be consistent and reproducible but also morally acceptable. Science concerns natural phenomena, but morality belongs to humans—the only living species on Earth that has a conscience. Thus, as we seek guidance from nature for how to function, we must also seek guidance that serves our moral principles. I discuss morality in detail in Book 4, *The Highest*

Reality, while in this book, I address it only briefly in connection with the proposed economic arrangement.

I was inspired to ponder and eventually develop an alternative economic arrangement because of the absence of any better system. The current arrangements swing from capitalist instincts, which eventually lead to immoral excesses, to socialist instincts, which eventually bring forth misery because of socialism's inherent impotence, necessitating a return to capitalism. Socialism and communism were created in reaction to the capitalist excesses of monarchy, aristocracy and owners of capital, and the recent rise of socialist sentiment in capitalist countries is similarly a reaction to the surge of capitalist excesses.

I begin each of the first eight chapters of this book with a personal anecdote that relates the contents of the chapter to real-life experiences, which hopefully has the effect of turning dry subjects into enjoyable reading. Chapter 8 of the book summarizes the new framework's essential features, which include distributing a certain proportion of economic output—the part derived from the use of the common pool of technological progress—equally to every member of the society as a right, not as help for the needy or in the form of welfare programmes. The surplus economic output will go to the hard-working and entrepreneurial people in accordance with their contributions. The new framework minimizes government's role, restricting it to providing only those common functions that benefit all equally and that individuals cannot discharge on their own. It recommends replacing the federal income tax with value-added taxes on the consumption of goods and services. If a country were to adopt the tenets of the new framework, it would eliminate inheritance tax and reinforce the right to private property as the key to wealth creation. The reader will learn why this framework, even without an inheritance tax, will prevent wealth from ever accumulating in the hands of a few.

The framework recommends banking reforms that would enable small corporations to raise debt with the same leverage ratios and at the same interest rates as large corporations. To eliminate any undue advantage of one nation over another, the framework recommends eliminating the reserve status of any currency. Currently, the US dollar enjoys that status, and it gives the US borrowing power that other nations don't have. All currencies should be anchored to a collection of products and services that are common to every country in much the same way that stock-market indexes such as the Dow Jones Industrial Average are anchored to a collection of common stocks.

Finally, the book recommends transitioning to the new system by initiating a "movement" approach and discourages violent or revolutionary means. The latter necessarily entails the rise of dictators and autocrats, something we must avoid if the framework is to serve the purpose for which it is proposed.

Introduction

To believe your own thought, to believe that what is true for you in your private heart is true for all man—that is genius.

—Ralph Waldo Emerson

In 1997, at the initiative of Dr Gavin Sinclair, a professor at Purdue University, I was invited to give the keynote address at a session on innovation at the National Conference of Agribusiness, hosted by Purdue. The session was titled "Strategic Orientation", and I began my talk with a scathing condemnation of the way big corporations are run today. Big corporations, I told my audience, have turned capitalism into an immoral force, and I started PMC Group to protest that immorality (the story of how I did that can be found in Book 2 of this memoir series). I then discussed the strategy I adopted at PMC Group.

The talk was well received, and a few days later, I received a kind note from Professor Michael Boehlje, the convenor and a professor of economics at Purdue:

Dear Dr Chakrabarti,
Your comments and observations on the innovation strategy and how you are using a technology platform to grow PMC Group into a Fortune 500 company in the next decade were stimulating and provocative. I had a number of people come to me after your sessions and make very complimentary comments about your observations; maybe the best way to describe the essence of many of them is to paraphrase one who said, "Wow! I got enough good ideas from this session to pay for my time and conference fees many times over."

I personally found your ideas on the follower's advantage and know-when and know-how stimulating and expect to use them in discussions with my students and others in strategic planning and thinking. It is a real pleasure to see someone from the business community with your philosophical perspective moving forward to implement that perspective and having such success in doing so.

Sincerely,
Michael Boehlje, Professor
November 21, 1997

After the conference, I joined several of its same attendees, including faculty members from Purdue's economics department, for an informal reception. The discussion turned to economic theories.

"Unless the basic economic theories are replaced by something better," I told the group, "a full-fledged assault on the issue of immorality won't be possible."

Gavin, already aware of my thoughts on the matter, raised an eyebrow. "Can you elaborate?"

"The main frameworks of economic theories grew from certain ideas—like those of Adam Smith and Karl Marx—about human nature and at a certain juncture of socio-economic development in England and Europe," I responded, "and as such, they carry with them the personal biases of the originators of those theories. For a framework to be unbiased and sustainable, it must have the rigour of a scientific process. Today's economic theories don't have that."

I went on to suggest that the laws of thermodynamics could be used as a template to create a robust economic model. Most listening thought my ideas were intriguing, but they couldn't quite grasp the connection between economic and thermodynamic terms—largely, they said, because they didn't have the scientific training. Gavin, who had a degree in chemical engineering from Purdue University and a PhD in economics from Carnegie Mellon University, was the lone exception.

A few days later, Gavin called to tell me that my audience thought I would do a great service to the economic community if I were to write a book on my thoughts.

"Talking about a subject is one thing," I replied, "but writing a book on it is quite another."

Indeed, if I were to write such a book, I told myself, I would want it to be of interest not only to professional economists but the educated public at large. I would have to outline the major economic terms and concepts of today, explore the socio-economic conditions that birthed today's leading economic theories, analyse the pros and cons of each major development and show how they came to be, explain how a new model would have to be built on certain scientific templates, describe the templates and why they are important, and so on and so forth. Finally, I would have to make clear that science is amoral, but humans belong to a moral society. Any theory we propose must therefore be developed with scientific rigour while marshalling the laws of ethics and morality. Making all of that easy to follow for a reader with a secondary education would be no easy task.

"I don't think I have the time," I told Gavin. "But I will keep your request in mind."

Unfortunately, Gavin died of cancer in 2001, well before I could write the book. Two decades later, when I began writing my memoir series, I knew from the outset that I would dedicate this book to the memory of Dr Gavin Sinclair.

*

Today's economic arrangements are based on flawed systems. Put in the simplest of terms, communism and socialism are impotent, and capitalism is immoral. Anything in between contains a mixture of impotency and immorality. In this book, I will propose a new economic arrangement that is free from the deficiencies of communism, socialism, and capitalism.

Two issues have concerned economists since modern economic systems first arose. The first is the creation of wealth, which is generally measured at the national level, such as by the aggregate wealth of a nation. The second is how this wealth is distributed among stakeholders of the economy, such as aristocrats, the bourgeoisie (capitalists), the proletariat (workers), and other individuals within a nation. Of course, equitable distribution without wealth creation is an empty approach because in such a system everyone loses. A successful economic system would create optimal wealth *and* distribute it equitably.

Most economists argue that capitalism is unrivalled in its capacity to create wealth. The father of this order is Adam Smith. But the chief criticism aimed at capitalism is that it is immoral (we will discuss later whether Smith intended for it to be so). Indeed, a critical analysis of naked capitalism will reveal that it is the economic equivalent of social Darwinism—i.e., survival of the fittest. Thus my term for naked capitalism: economic Darwinism.

As I will argue repeatedly throughout this book—and in fact, throughout all four books of my memoir series—scientific laws are amoral, but human laws are based on moral principles, something uniquely human without parallels anywhere in the universe. If economic Darwinism is about survival of the strongest, morality is about protection of the weakest.

Something that is amoral is oblivious to morality, but something that is immoral involves an agent deliberately choosing immorality over morality. The distinction is subtle but substantive. When a hurricane gathers strength, for example, it is oblivious to its destructive power as it carves a path through poorly built residences and poor neighbourhoods. A hurricane is guided by the laws of nature, nothing more. It is amoral. On the other hand, when a powerful man uses his power to extract more wealth by deceiving the poor, he acts wilfully against human morality. He is immoral. The result of both is the destruction of the poor. The difference lies in the absence of will in the first case and the presence of wilfulness in the second.

Although capitalism began as an amoral system, it has become immoral. In the chapters ahead, I will track capitalism's immorality to two sources: (1) the elevation of money to the centre of economics and its singular status as all-powerful capital, and (2) the flawed distribution of wealth. The latter allows corporations to become monopolies, to become "too big to fail". Such an imbalance can't be remedied by raising taxes on corporations or the wealthy; fundamental changes are needed.

Karl Marx, who was born about twenty-eight years after the death of Adam Smith, was among the first to attack the immorality embedded in capitalism. He didn't question the basic principles that made capitalism a successful production machine, but he criticized the distribution of the fruits of the economy among its constituents. The capitalist system, he argued, had been used by those with the levers of power against those without them. Therefore capitalism, as practised, benefited mostly the aristocracy (the bourgeoisie) and by extension the modern capitalist class. He believed that on moral grounds, the fruits of any economic system, particularly those of an industrial economy, should belong to the working class, whose labour was embedded in the products they made. Marx outlined his vision in *The Communist Manifesto*. Alas, moral reasoning notwithstanding, communism proved to be a practical disaster, for it was unable to create wealth. Wherever it took hold, it led to a basket of failures. Why? Because communism is based on a flawed understanding of how wealth is created.

The world has tried to cope with the problems presented by these two extreme economic philosophies by providing various compromise between them. But, as I will argue later, the compromises have proved no better than the original systems.

*

My ultimate purpose with this book is to propose a new framework for a better economic system—one based on the scientific principles and processes that ushered in the Industrial Revolution, and one that results in more equitable distribution.

I'm not an economist by training, so I have made it my business to understand the basic concepts behind the prevailing economic theories and share what I have learned with the reader. To understand a theory, I intuitively realized, you must first understand the person or people behind it. So I studied the lives of economists, their cultural origins, and the circumstances that led to their theories. The reader will be able to walk in my footsteps and at the same pace I employed while surveying a broad history of economic theories. Of course, to understand economics, we must familiarize ourselves with common economic terms, defining them as clearly as possible so that we can follow the economic developments that have occurred over the past three centuries. And in this journey, we're not alone. John Maynard Keynes, one of the most renowned economists of the twentieth century, was untrained in economics yet managed to deliver the economies of the West from the ruins of the Great Depression.

I have kept this book as free as possible from confusing details, lest the reader mistake the wood for the trees. As long as we can grasp the big picture, we can feel safe leaving the details to others. As Nobel laureate Muhammad Yunus once wrote of Nicholas Georgescu-Roegen, a professor of economics at Vanderbilt University:

> He taught me there was little need for memorizing economic formulas. Far more important was to understand the underlying concepts that drive them to work. He also taught me that things are never as

> complicated as they seem. It is only our arrogance that prompts us to find unnecessarily complicated answers to simple things.[2]

In the same spirit, I have kept mathematical formulas to a minimum.

2 Yunus, 1999 p. 19.

1

Structural Components of Modern Political Economy: Terms and Concepts

In the winter of 1977, I vacationed in India as an executive at GAF Corporation, which would later become International Specialty Products (ISP) and still later, a division of Ashland Chemicals. My rapid rise in the corporation—from a group leader to the director of chemical research within a short five-year period—was unprecedented in GAF's history. I considered my promotion the result of the goodwill and support of many of my colleagues in marketing, sales, and other departments. By providing a steady stream of innovative products and services to aid them in exceeding their own goals, I had demonstrated a genuine interest in helping them, thus earning their reciprocation. As my colleagues flourished in their respective departments, so did I in my department. I never felt discriminated against and always believed that when I genuinely tried to help someone, I received genuine help in return—often much more than I had given.

Thus, I came to India confident that when someone unselfishly tries to help another person, the effort is invariably appreciated. My faith in the goodness of human nature inspired me to start a chain reaction geared towards the alleviation of poverty during my vacation. I decided to perform a pilot experiment of trust. I would start with a handful of poor people, which conventional wisdom suggested would be the least trustworthy. I had conducted a similar experiment in education earlier in life, and although the experiment had faltered and eventually failed, I was convinced I had designed a better model this time around.

There is no supermarket in India. At least, there was none in 1977. Likewise, few homes boasted refrigerators. People relied instead on the local bazaar, a place where every family could shop in the morning for fish, meat, vegetables, fruits, and spices. Individual farmers and traders brought fresh produce and displayed it on the concrete floor for customers to inspect. A few permanent stalls featured dry goods like rice, wheat, spice, salt, and sugar. Some vendors sold green coconuts. They would cut open the face of the coconut and sell you the juice, which you could drink on the spot or take home for later consumption. Others sold freshly milled sugar-cane juice and date juice. There was no such thing as a fixed price, particularly when it came to buying perishable items. Every sale had to be negotiated. As a result, the bazaar was a noisy place, full of hundreds of buyers and sellers haggling over the price of this or that.

Kolkata's large bazaar on College Street positively hummed, producing a chorus of bargaining that could be heard blocks away. It opened every morning at six o'clock, and by the time it closed five hours later, it looked like a disaster zone. Workers swept away the foul debris and washed every inch of the place to make it ready for the next morning.

After I arrived one morning, I spotted a trader selling *maan-kachu*, a popular vegetable in Bengal known for its large esculent stems. The trader, a thinly built man about thirty-five years old, stood roughly five feet and eight inches tall—the typical height of a working-class male villager in India. He wore only a lungi—a cotton garment that features a chequered red-and-green pattern and a cylindrical shape—which hung like a skirt from his lower waist, just below his navel. He had lifted and tied the lower end of the lungi so that it formed a folded skirt just above his knees, and he kept whatever money he had in a knot at the end of the garment. A *gamchha*, a piece of loosely knit red fabric about four feet long, hung from his bare shoulder and served as a towel of sorts to wipe sweat from his body. Like many of his fellow traders, he was barefoot.

His torso showed signs of malnutrition—I could count his ribs—and his chest was slender. He was dark-skinned, most likely due to constant exposure to the sun. Caked dirt and mud could be detected in the cracks in the skin around his heels. He had a long face, a sharp nose, and an unruly beard. Yet his face radiated serenity, revealing no malice towards the society that was perhaps responsible for his poor condition. He seemed resigned to his fate and was courteous towards his customers, addressing the men as *dada* and the women as *didi* (elder brother and elder sister, respectively), which showed respect towards them regardless of their age.

I approached with my experiment in mind and asked him how much he wanted for one maan-kachu. He had five for sale.

"Five rupees," he said.

I countered with three rupees, and after several rounds of negotiation, we finally settled on a selling price of four rupees.

"How much profit will you make selling this *kachu* to me?" I asked after handing him the coins.

"I bought them for three rupees each in the village," he answered, "so by selling this one for four, I make a profit of one rupee."

A gross margin of 25 per cent. At GAF, we expected 36 per cent.

"If I can sell all five at four rupees each," the trader continued, "I will make a profit of five rupees. With this money, I can buy rice and spices to feed my family."

"If the maths is so simple," I replied, "why not trade ten, fifteen, or twenty every day?"

"Credit." He frowned. "I can only buy five kachus on credit. If I want more, I must pay in cash, which I do not have."

I thought for a moment. "I would like to make you a proposition. I will lend you one hundred rupees. I want you to buy thirty kachus and use the other ten rupees for transportation in order to bring the larger load to the market. I will come back in three days to collect the one hundred rupees plus one rupee in interest. If you make a standard profit, you will be making a profit of thirty rupees, so paying one rupee in interest on top of the principal should not be a problem."

"That is fairer than any deal I could imagine," he said, furrowing his brow. "But how can I prove that I will not disappear with the money?"

"It's called trust," I said. "I trust you to give me my money back."

"Do you need witnesses?"

"No. If I asked for witnesses, it would not be trust. I trust you will keep your honour, since I am trying to help you unsolicited." I handed him one hundred rupees and turned to leave. "What is your name?"

"Ratan."

Ratan means "jewel" in Bengali. Perhaps his parents had named him Ratan when he was a newborn baby because he was like a priceless gem to them. Or perhaps they had hoped that the name would change his fate, that he might grow up to be a rich man someday.

"I will see you in three days," I said.

*

I returned to my brother-in-law's apartment, where we were staying, and narrated the morning's events to him.

My brother-in-law, Mrinal, was a sales executive for an engineering firm. "You do not know the poor people in India," he said. "The trader will never show up again. He will be selling his kachu in another market."

"I hope to prove you wrong," I replied.

On the third day, I returned to the same stall where the trader had sold his kachu. He wasn't there. I surveyed the area one last time and, seeing no trace of him, turned to leave.

Just then, a man ran to me. "Ratan told me to tell you to wait a couple of minutes. He will be here soon. He had to go to a bigger spot in another part of the bazaar because he had so many kachus."

True to his word, Ratan arrived a few minutes later, clean-shaven and dressed in a *neema*, a short-sleeved cotton shirt that reached his lungi. Now he kept his money in his breast pocket, not in a knot in his lungi. He was all smiles. "Here," he said, handing me 110 rupees—a 10 per cent return in three days (more than 1,200 per cent annually).

Perhaps he will fulfil his parents' dreams, I thought.

"You were supposed to give me only one hundred one rupees," I said.

"What you did for me, no money can compensate for," he said, still smiling. "It is not about the money but the trust that you placed in me without even asking for my home address or how to find me."

I placed my hand on Ratan's shoulder in appreciation. "I have another proposition for you. Since you have returned the trust I placed in you, I will give you all of the money as a gift—but under one condition. You must use that money only for additional business and reinvest your profit so that you can do more business. If you do, you will be a medium, if not big, businessman. You will have enough capital to expand your operations and sell on a larger scale."

"But what about you?" he asked, shaking his head. "You will be the only loser in this arrangement."

I smiled. "You do not know what return you have already given me: the pleasure of freeing someone from poverty. I would like to do the same for nine more people."

Ratan walked with me as I gave one hundred rupees each to nine more people. By the time I was finished, a crowd of vendors and customers had gathered around me in disbelief.

"How can I see you again so that I can repay my debt?" the vendors asked.

"You won't see me again," I answered. "But there is a way each of you can rid yourselves of the burden of debt if you want. When you think you have made enough money, select ten poor people and do the same for them that I have done for you. And when they ask how they can repay you, extract a similar commitment from them. The process will unfold like a chain."

My previous endeavour to start a chain reaction in education, as described in the first book of my memoir, had faltered, primarily because I left India to pursue postdoctoral studies. This time, I was confident that the chain would succeed. The first experiment had required people to donate their time; this one required only a one-time donation of money, which is easier to spare than personal time, especially as you become more successful.

*

Since meeting Ratan at the bazaar in Kolkata decades ago, I have given modest amounts—from $1,000 to $10,000—to many individuals in exchange for similar promises. My wife and I revived the education chain, providing Chakrabarti Foundation scholarships to many college students in the US and abroad. Though we were mostly satisfied with the results, a few exceptions disappointed us. For instance, a handful of recipients didn't even recognize us later, and in some extreme cases, recipients spoke ill of us. The latter seemed to think that acknowledging our help somehow reduced their own capabilities. But these were exceptions, and the exceptions didn't exceed the proportion of bad debts we incur routinely in business when "capable" debtors don't pay their dues despite signed legal documents.

As a result of my experiences, I formulated a maxim: *trust accorded is returned by trust*. This maxim is not only statistically true but is unequivocally true for people of all stripes, rich and poor. If I had to qualify it, I would say that the maxim holds truer when the initial recipient of trust is a poor person.

When established maxims exist, you can be guided by them. When they are absent, you need to formulate one. This is what I did. And my wife and I have since been guided by my maxim in all our philanthropic work. My maxim found further confirmation in the work of Dr Muhammad Yunus, the father of microfinance, founder of Grameen Bank, and winner of the Nobel Peace Prize in 2006 (see Chapter 2).

Though I was able to help a few people with my initiatives, I was naïve to think that the chain would work. Though the plan looked praiseworthy, it wasn't sustainable. The small donations that I made to ten people in the Indian bazaar in 1977 and the scholarships that followed have changed lives, but to expect the recipients to carry on the chain by donating some of their wealth to others was unrealistic. For one thing, people rarely think they're rich enough to give some of their wealth to others. Indeed, the spirit of giving isn't in everyone. For another, even if the first group I gifted had been motivated enough to pay it forward, the motivation and the message almost certainly would have been lost before the next group could repeat it. Without a strong leader to guide the recipients, the chain was unsustainable.

I could have collected the money from those who succeeded and used it to fund the next layer, and so on. But that would have required a significant effort to create and manage the system. Professionally, I was a scientist, an educator, and a business leader, not an economist or social reformer. So I took the easy way out to satisfy my inner need to help others and assumed a philanthropic role. The same inner need motivated me to found PMC Group as a model corporation—one with a soul.

We still continue our philanthropic efforts, which is better than doing nothing. In fact, my wife and I have now included educational and cultural institutions as recipients of larger gifts, ranging from $100,000 to $2 million. For these larger gifts, we insist on associating our names with them, hoping that the names will motivate others in the future to give.

Our work exists within the framework of a system infinitely larger: the economy itself. It's to this topic that we turn now. In the decades since that trip to India in 1977, I have become convinced that our economic system has failed the plurality of our population. We need a new framework that lifts everyone, narrows the gap between rich and poor, and offers equitable outcomes to all. Before we can hope to change the world, however, we must first understand it—not as we wish it to be but as it is.

Money, Money Supply, GNP, GDP

Money lies at the centre of modern economic orders. The concept has been used from its inception to mean an operating system for transactions of goods and services. Beginning with the barter system, it has undergone continuous evolution, though not of intent but of form. *Webster's Dictionary* defines it in broad terms as a medium of exchange and a measure of value. If you try to read books to understand the exact definition and/or nature of money, I assure you that you will be thoroughly confused. Physicist and Nobel laureate Richard Feynman once said, "I think I can safely say that nobody really understands quantum mechanics." The same can be said of money. As Lawrence Ritter and William Silber wrote in the book *Money*, "Only two people can understand international finance."[1] We can leave quantum mechanics to the physicists. As for money,

1 Ritter and Silber, 1984, p. 5.

we need to find a way for ordinary people like us to understand it. One way of doing so is to narrow its definition.

For the purpose of this discussion, I will employ the definition used by the Federal Reserve Bank (the Fed), the central bank of the United States. Congress created the Fed on 23 December 1913, after the Federal Reserve Act was passed to provide the country with an independent agency to design and manage its monetary policies for long-term stability. It's meant to be independent of all government agencies, including the US Treasury. However, the Fed turns its earnings over to the US Treasury, after expenses.

According to the Fed's definition, money—or more accurately, money supply—is the measure of the Gross National Product (GNP), which is alternatively called the Gross Domestic Product (GDP). And GNP/GDP is defined as a nation's combined outputs of goods and services. There is, however, a subtle difference between GDP and GNP. GDP is calculated on the basis of a nation's composite goods and services, whereas GNP is calculated on the basis of goods and services of a nation's residents. To be sure, GDP/GNP doesn't include the federal government's transfer payments, such as Medicaid, Medicare, Social Security, federal business subsidies, and other welfare payments. Transfer payments are called Personal Consumption Expenditures (PCE).

Money can take the form of paper notes issued by a government or by an authorized bank or financial institution. The Fed divides the money supply into three classes: M1, M2, and M3. The classification is based on the liquidity of financial instruments. Briefly, M1 represents currency and checking accounts. It covers the most liquid of all financial assets and is considered a measure of an economy's *highest form of liquidity*. M2 includes M1 plus savings accounts, money market accounts, time deposits/certificates of deposit (CDs), and money market mutual funds. The parts of M2 that are not M1 have *intermediate liquidity*. M3 includes M2 plus time deposits of more than $100,000 at all depository institutions, including institutional money market funds, short-term repurchase, and similar instruments. Parts of M3 that are not M2 have the *lowest liquidity*. Economists consider M3 to be an estimate of the entire money supply of an economy.

Velocity of Money Supply

The velocity of money supply is defined as the turnover rate of the more liquid forms of money supply (M1 or M2). It is a measure of the number of times one dollar is used to purchase final goods and services included in GNP. Velocity = GNP/(M1 or M2).

Monetary Policies

The primary job of every central bank is to administer the country's monetary policy with the following objectives in mind:

- High employment
- Price stability—at or near a certain rate of inflation (in the case of the Fed, 2 per cent)
- Economic growth
- Balance of payment equilibrium

Economists don't agree on how to accomplish these goals and can be divided into two main groups:

Monetarists

Also known as quantity theorists, monetarists believe that all economic problems can be solved by properly managing the liquidity of money supply. Historically, support of the monetarist policy has come from economists like David Ricardo, John Stuart Mill, and Irving Fisher. The face of this group has been Milton Friedman (1912–2006; Nobel Prize 1976).

Proponents of monetarism assume that there is a concrete link—and if I'm interpreting it correctly, a *reversible* link—between money supply and GNP. Monetarists argue that the link is expressed in the predictability of the velocity of money supply. The Fed can increase public liquidity (M1 or M2) by purchasing government securities in the open market. When this is done during a recession, the monetarists argue, the public uses the excess liquidity to buy goods and services, thus driving up GNP until the velocity of money supply reaches its normal value. An increase in GNP also increases employment, because it requires labour to make additional goods and services. However, if money supply is increased when the economy is near full employment, the increased liquidity produces the unfavourable effect of higher prices. By the same token, the Fed selling government securities in the open market decreases liquidity, which can drive the GNP lower because the public purchases less until GNP drops to a point where velocity of money supply returns to normal. This purported direct link between velocity of money supply and GNP, monetarists contend, is quite rigid. Thus monetarists assert that the Fed can fine-tune the economy and solve recessions, inflation, high unemployment, and labour shortages simply by controlling liquidity.

Milton Friedman, however, added a twist to monetarism when he argued that an *expansionary* monetary policy raises interest rates while a *contractionary* monetary policy lowers them. Friedman justified his conclusion as follows: "An increase in money supply may initially lower interest rates if the liquidity is spent in financial assets. But that is only the beginning. Once GNP responds to the increased money supply, the transactions for money will increase, thereby driving interest rates upward."[2]

Keynesians or Fiscal Policy-mongers

This group believes the opposite of what the monetarists believe. John Maynard Keynes (1883–1946) developed his "demand-side" macroeconomic theory during the Great Depression of the 1930s in his attempts to correlate the effect of total spending in the economy with GNP output, employment, and inflation. He recommended massive government intervention, i.e., government spending and lowering taxes to stimulate demand and pull the economy out of recession. At the time, his policy recommendation was hugely successful. A strong supporter of the Keynesian policy has been Massachusetts Institute of Technology's Robert Solow, who earned the Nobel Prize in economics in 1987.

Keynesians question the validity of the monetarists' assumption that the link between money supply and GNP is smooth and robust. When the Fed increases liquidity by buying government securities in the public market, Keynesians contend, the public might simply hold the excess cash for a

2 Ibid., 1984, pp. 42–43.

rainy day or invest it in the stock market, with the net result being that liquidity remains at the previous level and the velocity of money supply remains unchanged. The purchase of stocks, however, will reduce interest rates and increase the creditworthiness of the public. Lower interest rates will prompt businesses to invest to produce goods and services, and this will increase GNP and lower unemployment. So, according to the Keynesians, there will be a significant time lag between liquidity infusion and GNP increase and job creation, and not all liquidity will necessarily be used. A decrease in liquidity at times of low unemployment will likewise work in the reverse way, causing GNP to decrease and prices to increase—with a time lag, of course.

The Keynesians recommend active government participation during times of economic crisis. According to Keynesians, leaving the economy to cure itself with the Fed's money supply could destabilize the private sector. The "animal spirit" of private corporations will discourage capital investment at times of recession in order to raise GNP, and vice versa. The result will be wild fluctuations in unemployment. Only government intervention in the form of spending and tax policy changes can change economic outcomes quickly, according to the Keynesians.

Econometric Models

Because neither of these policies produces consistent results, a third group, the econometric models, has emerged to add empirical data to the two abstract policy models, creating computer-generated models. Two such models that are commonly mentioned are the Federal Reserve-MIT-Penn Model (FMP Model) and the St Louis Fed Model that uses the monetarists' model as its starting point.

The President's Policy Decision

Each president of the United States, depending on his preference for the policy models and the state of the economy he inherits, hires an economic advisory group that aligns more or less with his policy preferences. No one, of course, adopts purely one ideology or the other. Instead, a president's policy is inclined towards monetarist or Keynesian policies. For instance, the Eisenhower and Reagan administrations generally followed a modern version of "supply-side" monetarist policy. On the other hand, the policy adaptations during the presidencies of Kennedy and Johnson were mostly Keynesian. The administrations of Nixon, Ford, and Carter were mixtures of both. The Obama administration, facing the Great Recession of 2008, adopted a primarily Keynesian policy and used a massive dose of government spending to bring the economy back to life. Despite the policy's emphasis on speed, however, the recovery was slow—among the slowest in history. Maybe the massive dose of government spending was not massive enough.

Since in most democratic countries, the term of the presidency or his/her equivalent is of limited duration—four years in the US—a major time lag between policy implementation and results is rarely acceptable, because it has political implications. The Trump–Pence administration claimed credit for "near complete employment numbers" during its first two years, with Trump asserting that those numbers were the result of his economic policies—primarily a supply-side policy of reducing taxes and removing regulatory barriers. The prior administration of Obama–Biden, meanwhile, pointed to the delayed effect of their huge infusion of government spending as the cause. When it comes to economic conditions, the public generally gives credit or fixes blame to the administration that is in power. We have yet to see the effects of the Trump–Pence administration's efforts to combat COVID-19—one of the most massive peacetime government spending projects ever—or the continuation of the same with even higher spending during the Biden–Harris administration.

Does Gold Have Any Role in Monetary Policy?

During the era of the gold standard, which began in the mid-nineteenth century and lasted more than a century, the gold reserve of a country determined its money supply. In other words, nations fixed the value of their money to their reserve of gold. This resulted in fixed foreign exchange rates, not floating rates. The Nixon administration permanently severed the relationship between money supply and gold holdings in 1971. Since then, no country has used gold as the medium of exchange.

The central banks of most countries still hold stockpiles of gold as reserve funds. The total amount of gold held by nations is now estimated at 33,800 tonnes. The top six central banks hold two-thirds of the reserve. Their shares are as follows:

US	8,113 tonnes (24 per cent)
Germany	3,371 tonnes (10 per cent)
International Monetary Fund (IMF)	2,815 tonnes (8.3 per cent)
Italy	2,452 tonnes (7.3 per cent)
France	2,436 tonnes (7.2 per cent)
Russia	1,910 tonnes (5.7 per cent)

If there's no official connection between gold and money supply, you might ask, why do the central banks still hold so much gold on behalf of their governments? The primary reason is to maintain a hedge or insurance policy against possible financial disasters like hyperinflation or a drastic fall of their currency. In such cases, the country can sell its gold reserve and support its currency by buying it back in the open market. Other reasons cited by the various central banks are to maintain liquidity reserve, to provide a safe-haven asset, to manage the balance of payment deficit by selling gold from the reserve, to make a profit (since gold prices have usually outpaced inflation), and to preserve a nation's creditworthiness.

International Balance of Payment: Foreign Exchange Rates

While considering monetary policy options, a country cannot cast a blind eye towards the impact of a potential policy on international trade and international balance of payment. The international balance of payment of a country is an accounting record of all trade across its national borders. In essence, it is the difference between a country's inflow and outflow of money. A surplus means that a country exports more than it imports. Obviously, a long-term rise in the trade deficit is bad for a country, for it increases inflation and lowers the standard of living—unless, of course, a country can make up for the deficit by other means or can wield oversized financial muscle.

There are three types of such balance of payments: a *current account payment*, which measures the import and export of goods and services plus net income and transfer payments; a *financial account payment*, which measures the increase (surplus) or decrease (deficit) in the flow of money through investments in real estate, business ventures, and so on; and a *capital account payment*, which measures financial transactions that don't affect income, production, or savings, such as the international transfer of trademarks, copyrights, or mining rights.

Since at least the 1990s, the US has been running a steadily increasing current account deficit. In 2018 alone, the account deficit of the US was $491 billion and it increased by another $7.4 billion in 2019 to $498.4 billion, the largest in the world. The US can get away with such huge deficits because the US dollar is still considered the "safe-haven" currency in the world. But this can't go on forever. Sooner or later, the country will have to learn to live within its own means. The solutions are not pretty. One way to bring exports and imports into balance is to drastically reduce the buying power of the US population. The Fed could do this by tightening the money supply and increasing interest rates, which would lower the price of domestic products, reduce wages, and increase unemployment—all recipes of a deep recession, voluntary or otherwise. Such an approach would perhaps lead to other problems. Higher unemployment or wage reduction would make wealth inequality even worse than it is today. Moreover, the US economy is so big that if it dipped into recession or depression, it would drag the rest of the world with it. An opposite approach—namely, increasing the price of foreign goods and services by imposing trade barriers and tariffs—would lead to tit-for-tat reaction by other countries, ensuring that the whole world loses.

Another, presumably less painful, approach would be to create flexible or floating foreign money exchange rates. Freely floating exchange rates that depend on the supply and demand equation could solve many of our balance of payment problems. Market forces would lower the value of the US dollar and make foreign goods and services more expensive for Americans and American goods and services less expensive for foreigners. This would increase the export of US goods and services and reduce the import of foreign goods and services. The result would nonetheless be a reduction in the standard of living among Americans.

Still another approach would be to bring down the price of American goods and services through the relentless infusion of superior technology in production—something I will explore later while discussing the role of technology on GDP output.

International Monetary Fund (IMF) and the World Bank

The IMF and the World Bank are the twin pillars of an international effort to bring financial order to international monetary structure. The renowned Depression-era economist, John Maynard Keynes, was the founding father of both institutions.

The IMF was established on 27 December 1945, and is headquartered in Washington DC. Its goal is to provide a basket of financial initiatives to improve the economies of the 190 member countries and to reduce global poverty—often with funds drawn from the World Bank. One of its initial goals was to maintain fixed exchange rates among the currencies of the member states, but this has since given way to floating exchange rates, with not much help sought from the IMF.

The World Bank was established July 1944, boasts a membership of 189 nations, and, like the IMF, is headquartered in Washington DC. The goals of the IMF and the World Bank are complementary, but they often overlap. The main function of the World Bank is to provide financing, financial advice, and finance-related research services to developing nations, with a focus on reducing poverty.

The IMF and World Bank borrow their funds primarily from member nations and derive their income from investments in financial markets and interest charged to loans given to the borrowing nations.

The Fed's Inflation Target and Interest Rates

The Fed tries to maintain inflation at a target rate of 2 per cent. Since inflation and interest rates move in tandem, setting too low an inflation rate will also make interest rates too low. This will rob the Fed of one of its options—namely, easing interest rates—to combat a recession when it hits. Furthermore, allowing interest rates to remain too low increases people's expectations of low interest on an ongoing basis. On the other hand, letting inflation go up too much hurts people by increasing expenses in essential consumable items like food, energy, and shelter. The Federal Open Market Committee (FOMC) considers 2 per cent inflation ideal for keeping both expectations and options in balance. Moreover, some inflation is necessary to keep pace with GNP growth in an expansionary economy.

Credit and Credit Rating

Credit is an essential component of business finance and personal finance. Business operations depend on using both equity and borrowed money. The better a business uses borrowed money, the better its profit or return on its equity. Suppose a business sets a target of 12 per cent return on equity. It will be easy to achieve that goal if it can use a bank loan at 3 per cent or issue corporate bonds with 3 per cent interest to leverage financing its business operations. The ability to access such low-cost funds, however, depends on the company's credit rating. Similarly, an individual's ability to finance the purchase of a car or house will depend on his or her credit rating.

Credit, of course, is the ability to borrow money (or access goods or services) in return for a promise to pay it back with interest on a predetermined schedule. This generally depends on the ability of the borrower to pay back the borrowed money and their willingness to do so on time. Credit ratings depend on both. Whether working with individuals or companies, the rating companies analyse the borrower's net worth and the history of their debt payments to determine credit ratings.

Since the financial institutions make money by lending it, they offer lower interest rates to entice creditworthy customers. Thus, rich people and big corporations can borrow money at lower interest rates than poor people and small businesses.

Stocks and Bonds

Stocks and bonds are financial assets. They are not counted in the money supply, but they can influence GNP and money supply. The value of a stock does not always depend on its fundamentals. It has a sentimental component—expectation of growth or decline. The composite of such sentimental values determines the stock market index, which in turn can influence production of goods and services and therefore, GNP and money supply.

The latter relationship—namely, the influence of GNP on stocks and bond markets—means that the prices of the broad stock and bond indices can also be influenced, at least partially, by active management of the money supply by the Fed. As already mentioned, when the Fed intervenes in the economy and decides to increase money supply, consumers will not always use all of it to purchase goods and services. They might then use what is left to buy financial assets like stocks and bonds. The proportion of money supply that goes into boosting the GNP will depend on the exact status of the economy at the time. During a serious depression, the higher amount—perhaps nearly all of it—will go to boost GNP. At other times, up to a significant proportion of it will go to the purchase of stocks, raising their value. This can happen directly or in two stages, but with the same end result. In the step-wise method, the excess cash first goes into the "safer" bond market, but this will drive demand and soon make the bond market price higher, making stock prices more lucrative. Thanks to the lure of a better return from stocks, greed replaces the safety of bonds.

Notwithstanding the above analysis, the price movements of the stock index can elude even the experts. This is because besides fundamentals, many factors can influence the stock market. Such unpredictability is a blessing in disguise. Were it not the case, the market would become highly predictable, and high predictability would play unfairly into the hands of predators. The factors that make the stock market unpredictable include the following:

1. The stock market is forward-looking. Any announcement of new technologies—even before they occur—will raise stock prices. When I was at PPG, I concluded a large long-term contract with the Scripps Research Institute in order to enter the biotech market, the darling of Wall Street at the time, with new products. After the news was published in the *Los Angeles Times* and in other leading journals, PPG's share price went up significantly within a short period.
2. The pendulum effect: Anything that has a *sentimental* value reacts excessively in one direction or the other on positive or negative news. This often leads to wild fluctuations in the stock market until price catches up with reality.
3. Stock market bubbles: Bubbles are created when the prospect of something big happening is built into stock valuation before it happens. Bubbles grow when these expectations foster a herd mentality. Consider the case of

biotechnology, one of the major technological advances of the 1980s. The euphoria of the technology superseded reality. Turning these technologies into commercial realities required massive speculative investments—in science, regulatory skills, commercial development capabilities, marketing, and general management. Those who could do so eventually succeeded. But the euphoria was so big that those who couldn't afford to get into the big game bought into companies that were literally formed "by a scientist and a mouse". No wonder these fringe companies that mushroomed eventually failed and the biotech bubble burst. Another bubble, the dot-com bubble, burst a decade later. The problem with bubbles is that they are bound to burst sooner or later.

4. The stock market reacts to speculation on how the Fed will manage the money supply in the near future or on the policy expectations of an incoming president.
5. The stock market often falls victim to tricks engineered by financial experts that can deceive lawmakers and the central banks.
6. The stock market can go through wild fluctuations within a short span of time due to computerized trading. Computers execute both buy and sell transactions of the same stocks literally within seconds based on changing sentiments of investors. The goal is to make an instant profit for the traders, who make money only if a trade is executed.
7. Control of the stock market by institutional investors and the gradual disappearance of long-term individual investors is becoming an issue of great concern. The interests of these two groups don't align. The institutional brokers never lose money. They charge their client a fee

when they execute a trade—buy or sell—irrespective of whether the transaction proves wise. Moreover, when the market provides a reward, they take a share of the gain, but when the market produces a loss, they don't share the loss. This attitude invariably leads to many wasteful transactions and an underperforming market.

8. Still another problem is the complex securitization of financial assets in the form of derivatives. Sophisticated Wall Street firms hire PhD mathematical physicists, called quants (quantitative analysts), to develop derivatives. Such securities often become so complex that only a handful of people understand their underlying value, but on the surface, they look attractive. For example, the securitization of mortgages in the 1980s and '90s eventually yielded "toxic assets". The value of these derivatives increased from $1 trillion in 1987 to $11 trillion in 1995.[3] To grow their size, banks provided subprime mortgages to millions of people without good credit and then sold them in lumps to those who securitized them. When the subprime mortgages defaulted, the entire derivatives market collapsed. Lehman Brothers, the fourth largest investment bank and a pioneer of the derivatives market, was the first to fail and filed for bankruptcy on 15 September 2008, triggering a cascade of events that resulted in what is now known as the Great Recession of 2008. At PMC Group, we had just completed the acquisition of the $175-million oleochemicals business from Chemtura before all hell broke loose in the financial market. If we had waited only a few more months before closing the

---

3 Greenspan and Wooldrige, 2018, p. 381.

transaction, the credit and financing necessary to close the deal would have disappeared.

A Commentary on Stock Market Crashes

The history of the stock market is full of crashes, big and small. Economists are skilled at analysing such events—such as the Great Depression or the Great Recession—once those events are safely in the rear-view mirror. But rarely can they tell us in advance what will happen. If they could, we would've avoided countless economic disasters.

Theoretical economists base their theories on human behaviour, forgetting that human behaviour is influenced by circumstances. How people behave in economic matters depends on their own life experiences and when they make economic decisions. Experiences vary from country to country and within each country, from one socio-economic strata to the next. Countless other factors make people behave differently. My father, who lived through the Great Depression, always preferred to purchase land and gold and to save money in deposit accounts at the post office—something that no longer exists but that is similar to today's treasury bonds. He didn't buy anything on credit. For him, if he couldn't afford to buy something with cash, it wasn't worth buying.

This propensity to save still dominates in India, where cash transactions are commonplace. After Prime Minister Modi banned banknotes of denominations of 500 rupees and higher to thwart black-market money, he realized what a hardship he had imposed on the common people, most of whom didn't have bank accounts or know about credit cards.

To theoretical economists, saving and holding cash is bad for the economy, but if they want to formulate an economic law based on human nature, they can't ignore the majority of the world's people, most of whom live outside the Western world. Even when such people move to Western countries, they carry with them their old habits. The empirical economists, those who base their conclusions on the analysis of historical data, are somewhat better, but they also forget that in economic matters, history is seldom a reliable predictor of the future. The problem with economic theories—the purpose of which is to codify some process—is that they aren't based on natural principles or scientific facts. You can't compare the subjective quality of information used by Adam Smith to the objective statements made by someone like Charles Darwin.

Concluding Remarks

The discussion above is an oversimplification of economic fundamentals, but it lays the groundwork for what I plan to explore later: the immorality of today's capitalistic economic policies. How wealth is defined, how it's distributed to a country's stakeholders, how strong nations extract advantages from the economy unavailable to weaker nations—all will come under my scrutiny. My goal is to present a framework for establishing a robust economic arrangement that is based not on a subjective view of human nature, but rather, on objective principles widely applicable to nature. But first, let me describe the work of some of the prominent economists whose theories have shaped the world we know today.

2

Origins of Modern Economics and the Socio-economic Climate

Sufiya Begum scratched out a living in 1976 by weaving bamboo stools. She lived in a dilapidated mud hut in the poorest corner of Jobra, a small village in Bangladesh. She was twenty-one.

To make one stool, Sufiya bought the bamboo canes required—no more, no less—from a trader for five taka, the Bangladeshi equivalent of twenty-two US cents. Mind you, she didn't have five taka. She had to borrow the money from the same trader as part of an arrangement in which she would sell the stool back to him for an agreed-upon price. Each stool took an entire day to craft, and at the end of the day, Sufiya made one-half of one taka, or two cents, from her labour. The trader would then turn around and sell the stool for a much higher price in the open market, and the process would begin anew the next day, with Sufiya borrowing five taka to buy the bamboo canes she needed to make a single stool. The trader took no risks but pocketed all but 0.5 taka of the profits. Sufiya, for her part, couldn't cut out the middleman—the trader—because she had no credit. The only way she could have amassed the money on her own would have been to borrow it from a loan shark, who would have charged 10 per cent interest per week and an astronomical 500 per cent or more per year. In other words, Sufiya was stuck, with no hope of upper mobility.[1]

I read about Sufiya's plight decades later, in 2006, after Dr Muhammad Yunus, a Bangladeshi, won the Nobel Peace Prize in tandem with Grameen Bank, a microfinance organization Yunus had founded in 1983 to help people escape poverty. I knew little about Yunus when I first read about his accomplishment in the newspaper, but as I dug into his history, I discovered that we had much in common. He was born in 1940 in Chittagong, a district in East Bengal, now Bangladesh. I was born the same year in Moulmein, Burma, now Myanmar, about a thirty-minute plane ride away, and was the son of parents from East Bengal. We shared the same mother tongue—Bengali—and began our respective careers as teachers.

Our similar approach to helping the poor connected us further. In 1976, a year before my experiment at the bazaar in Kolkata, Yunus carried out a similar test in Jobra, where he lent forty-two people like Sufiya twenty taka each, interest-free, and instructed them to buy their own bamboo canes and sell their products in the open market for a much higher profit. In his experiment, however, he required the borrowers to return the money they had borrowed. He was an economist, after all, and knew that philanthropy alone might not suffice. At the same time, he understood that the poor were unfairly disadvantaged when it came to borrowing money and starting

1 Yunus, 1999, p. 48.

a business. "It seemed to me the existing economic system," he wrote, "made it absolutely certain that Sufiya's income would be kept perpetually at such a low level that she would never save a penny and would never invest in expanding her economic base."[2]

Yunus's experiment was a grand success. The borrowers returned his money—with interest. He hadn't documented the loans, but no one defaulted. Trust had prevailed. The germ of an idea, meanwhile, was born: microfinance. Poor people couldn't succeed because of their lack of creditworthiness. What was needed was an institution willing to grant small loans to poor people without credit. Through 2003, Grameen Bank provided 3.8 billion dollars' worth of microfinancing to 2.4 million families in rural Bangladesh, and the concept spread to the rest of the world.

Yunus studied economics at Vanderbilt University in Tennessee and was the chair of the economics department at Chittagong University when he began his project in 1976, but he proposed no new economic theory in winning his Nobel Peace Prize. He did, however, introduce two new concepts to economics: microfinance and microcredits. He also changed the definition of creditworthiness. "Nothing in the economic theories I taught reflected the life around me," he wrote, later adding, "The brilliant theorists of economics do not find it worthwhile to spend time discussing issues of poverty and hunger."[3]

Grameen Bank has improved the fortunes of many poor people in Bangladesh, but the country remains among the poorest in the world. Although it boasts the world's eighth

2 Ibid., p. 49.
3 Ibid., pp. viii, 35.

biggest population, its per capita GDP ranks only 166th. The gap between rich and poor continues to widen. As the country makes economic progress, an increasing amount of the national wealth is being concentrated in the hands of a few. Before we can understand why such a disparity exists—and why it continues to grow—we need to go back in time and look at the origins of modern economic theory and how the socio-economic climate shaped them.

*

A nation's economic system—also called its political economy—has a twofold purpose: (1) to increase national wealth and (2) to ensure a fair system of wealth distribution among its people. Individuals, corporations, and government each play a role in achieving these goals, but achieving both simultaneously has thus far eluded economists. The result? Two competing economic frameworks: capitalism and communism. Adam Smith and Karl Marx, the two men most associated with those two extremes, wrote *The Wealth of Nations* and *Das Kapital*, respectively. Only one book in the world has been read more: the Bible.[4] John Kenneth Galbraith summarized the conflicting views succinctly:

> In the United States ... economists divide today between classicists (the overwhelming number) and institutionalists, between those committed to the inevitable and constant equilibrium and those who, with much less claim to scientific precision, accept a

4 Galbraith, 1987, p. 62.

> world of evolution and continuing change. One source of institutionalists' ideas is … in the worlds of Hegel—and of Marx.[5]

Even though Smith and Marx established the boundaries of economic thought, no boundary is razor-sharp, and no individual or individuals can be fully credited for the existing boundaries, which, like those in other disciplines, are necessarily blurry and can be traced to many contributors. John Maynard Keynes, meanwhile, didn't push the philosophical boundaries of economic theory like Smith and Marx did. Instead, he focused on tactical approaches to righting an economy during the Great Depression. Other pioneers in economic thought include the egalitarian economists—moral philosophers-turned-economists whose main concern has been the injustice in our economic distribution system. Among them, Amartya Sen (b. 1933) won the Nobel Prize in 1998 for his work on welfare economics.[6]

Before we propose a new economic model that meets the twin goals of wealth creation *and* equitable distribution, let's take a look at the three giants—Adam Smith, Karl Marx, and John Maynard Keynes—and the socio-economic climates and other factors that informed their thinking.

---

5 Ibid., p. 129.

6 For a comprehensive list of egalitarian economists, see Sen, 1988, p. 32.

Why Study Socio-economic Climate? Why Study Biography?

People, including philosophers and economic theorists, do not work in isolation. Each of us is a product of our time, and our thoughts are reflected in our environment. No ideas, however radical or mundane, originate on their own. They evolve from the ones that preceded them. The radical thinkers, however radical they may be, stand on the shoulders of the giants that preceded them. Frank H. T. Rhodes, president of Cornell University, made the same points, only more forcefully, in his 1986 report, "Leaders Create Leaders". He wrote:

> Our experience with presidential scholars suggests that the best training for leadership comes from watching those you respect as leaders. It is perhaps too much to claim that great scholars always produce great scholars, yet a study several years ago of fifty-five Nobel Prize winners living in the United States found that thirty-four of them worked in earlier years with forty-six other Nobel laureates.

Extraordinary leadership, Rhodes argued, is born not when the conditions are just right but when everything has gone wrong. "Yet it is always from the crisis of an era—not from its times of gentle breezes and calm seas—that the greatest leadership emerges," he wrote. "It is the time of crisis that the Lincolns and the Churchills of history emerge."

In the same report, while focusing on the importance of studying the lives of individual leaders, Rhodes added, "One can make a convincing case that there is more to be learnt about leadership from reading Plato's *Republic* and Melville's *Billy Bud*, from reading Machiavelli's *The Prince*, and speeches of Kennedy and Churchill, than from the most comprehensive and weighty management texts."

The leaders that shaped our economic policies were influenced by *their* leaders and were the products of their time. Thus their seminal works reveal the biases and prejudices of the era and culture that birthed them. To understand their views fully, we must study the socio-political climate that nurtured them, particularly if we are to reject their theories and propose a new one with more universal appeal, which I plan to do.

The Cradles

There must be something special in the British air. Adam Smith (1723–90) and Karl Marx (1818–83) wrote their most important works in Great Britain, although only Smith was born there (Smith was born in Scotland, whereas Marx was born in Germany). British-born John Maynard Keynes spent his academic and productive years in England. Even Amartya Sen, the most contemporary voice on welfare economics, did his seminal work while employed at Trinity College in Cambridge, England. To be sure, none of these luminaries were confined to the geographical limits of their birthplaces or where they worked; they travelled extensively and wrote for a global audience. But the influence of their environment was undeniable.

Revolutionary thoughts often arise in unpredictable ways. Indeed, protests against injustice often come from the privileged classes, not just victims of injustice. Karl Marx, who championed the causes of the oppressed working class (the proletariat), was born in an affluent family and could have flourished among his fellow bourgeoisie. Similarly, a prince raised in an opulent lifestyle and protected from harm isolated himself for years to contemplate the cause of human suffering and emerged as Gautama Buddha, the founder of Buddhism, the world's most peaceful religion and among the largest creeds. We can never fully understand Buddhism unless we study the history of ancient India and Nepal, the tiny nation to the north, where Gautama Buddha was born in 563 BCE.

Meanwhile, the famine of 1943, a devastating famine in Bengal, left a dark impression on Amartya Sen, then only nine years old, and sowed the seeds of his theories as a welfare economist. Of course, those that passionately teach certain values don't always practise them. Adam Smith, for example, taught the folly of mercantilism but ultimately served as the commissioner of customs in Scotland. Let's take a look at the socio-economic and political climate of Britain and Europe and how those forces influenced Adam Smith, Karl Marx, and others whose economic and political theories were destined to dominate modern economic thought.

Britain

From the 1670s to the 1780s, Britain fought a series of wars against France—the empire's "perfidious enemy", as British admiral George Rodney put it. France fought either directly against Britain or indirectly in support of Britain's other foes. Those wars included the Nine Years' War (1688–97), the War of Spanish Succession (1701–14), the War of Austrian Succession (1740–48), King George's War (1744–48), the Seven Years War (1756–63), and the American War of Independence (1775–83), in which France intervened in 1778. These wars were largely fought to protect and/or expand the imperial powers' hold on the colonies outside Europe. There was, however, a period between 1715 and 1738 when Britain and its colonies enjoyed both peace and strong economic growth. Though France boasted more land, a bigger economy, and a larger population, England emerged victorious in most of the wars, aside from the American War of Independence.

The wars cost blood and treasury, but each side was determined to protect its colonial interests while thwarting the other's expansion. Britain found a clever way to fund the wars by incurring national debt—a novel approach at the time—thus sparing its citizens from additional taxations. The government borrowed from the rich merchant class and made payments only on the interest, and the merchants were only too happy to lend the money to the government since they too had a stake in the wars. The merchants believed that their economic future depended on procuring cheap raw materials from the colonies and exporting the value-added finished products back to them. Such a notion could be traced to mercantile capitalism, which held that the global economy was static and that the health of any national economy could be measured by the net positive export of its goods and services. For instance, when Robert Clive defeated Siraj ud-Daulah, the nawab of the powerful Indian state of Bengal, in 1757 and imposed British rule, British citizens greeted the news favourably, for Bengal now could become another colony to fulfil Britain's economic ambitions. In short, Britain found a way of indirectly funding the wars by extracting income from the colonies.[7] Thus, the merchant class took a

---

7 James, 1994, pp. 51–53, 58, 71, 81; Garraty and Gay, 1972, pp. 627, 633.

front seat when negotiating with government, while ordinary labourers took a back seat.

Not surprisingly, panic overtook Britain when it lost the American War of Independence. Since the birth of the American colonies in 1607, Britain had exported manufactured products like fine woolen cloth, glass, shoes, hats, bales of canvas, and pewter and brass utensils to the New England cities and had imported from the colonies raw goods like wheat, rye, preserved beef, pork, herrings, and large quantities of tobacco. Over time, exports of the finished products to the American colonies soared, but imports—some of which Britain re-exported to other colonies—remained steady. By 1700, these re-exports alone constituted 30 per cent of Britain's foreign trade. From the mercantile point of view, the loss of the colonies in North America was a devastating blow to Britain's economic prospects. This reaction, however, was more psychological than actual, and the country soon recovered from the shock. In *The Wealth of Nations*, Adam Smith proposed an alternative economic arrangement—based on free trade and the free market—which became known as capitalism, helping Britain recover from its psychological nadir. Smith became an immediate celebrity in both countries, each of which adopted his economic policy. England still prized its remaining colonies but under capitalism's new economic model viewed them as protected markets in an expanding economy,[8] and the importance of the trading class to political operatives remained undiminished.

France was not as successful as Britain in financing the wars between the two nations. The Seven Years War, which began as a struggle to claim military supremacy, grew into a

8 James, 1994, pp. 27, 119–20.

larger conflict of global scale, engulfing many other countries, particularly the Spanish Empire. Losing the war proved a devastating blow to France's economy. The American War of Independence, during which France had fought with the freedom fighters against Britain, further drained the French treasury. By the end of the eighteenth century, France found itself on the brink of financial bankruptcy, which led to turmoil among the aristocrats and nobles, who wanted to form a new constitutional government of the people, by the aristocracy, for the aristocracy. The result was the French Revolution. Louis XVI was executed in 1793, and a constitutional monarchy replaced the *Ancien Regime* (old regime) of hereditary monarchy.

Napoleon Bonaparte rose to power during the revolution and became emperor of France in 1804. A brilliant military leader, he successfully waged a series of wars against the European nations until his army suffered a devastating blow in its failed efforts to invade Russia in 1812. As part of Napoleon's plan to conquer England, a joint expedition by the French and Spanish navies led to the Battle of Trafalgar (1805), but the mighty British navy decisively pushed back the French and Spanish fleets. This battle would establish the overwhelming supremacy of British naval power for the next hundred years.[9]

While Napoleon was busy making gains in land battles on the eastern front, Britain used its superior naval power to occupy several French colonies. The British Empire's colonization efforts were so effective in the nineteenth century that it controlled a fifth of the world's land and one quarter of the world's population, and English became the most widely spoken language in the world.[10]

9 Garraty and Gay, 1972, pp. 765, 774–89.
10 James, 1994, p. xvi.

With power came reflection. The Englishmen faced a difficult question: Was the colonization of foreign land morally justifiable? John Milton provided them a satisfying answer. The colonial lands, he argued, "... were full of natural resources but their people never realized this fact". Therefore, it was morally justified for the "superior people of Britain" to help those people use and replenish their resources.[11] Ironically, because Britain considered its people superior, it became committed to just laws and freedom of expression, all of which later made it possible for Karl Marx to find an audience. After being driven away from his native continental Europe, Marx expressed his contrarian views while in England, a country whose economic order he hoped to destroy.

During the eighteenth century, England's big cities were dirty and overpopulated. A century later, most of the British people were poor and worked in the mines. Only a minority of rich merchants and aristocrats lived in elegant mansions and country houses.[12] The glaring contrast between rich and poor would not escape the attention of people like Karl Marx, Friedrich Engels, and their left-wing predecessors.

As the nineteenth century and the Victorian Age came to a close, the British Empire remained formidable. A ten-year period under the optimistic Edward VII (1901–10) followed, and it seemed the honeymoon would never end. But a series of events presaged the end of English hegemony. First came the rise of the Liberal government (1906–14), which would eventually lead to England's welfare state. Next came World War I (1914–18), which drained the country of its economic resources. Then came the Irish War of Independence,

---

11 Ibid., p. 12.

12 Garraty and Gay, 1972, p. 746.

followed by the partition of Ireland in May 1921. Britain's sense of invincibility absorbed one final, devastating hit after America's exuberant stock market bubble burst, leading to "Black Tuesday", the famous crash of 29 October 1929. The Great Depression spread like wildfire across the world, robbing every nation of its self-confidence and accelerating the socio-economic upheavals already forming. While economists scrambled to figure out how things had spiralled out of control, England's John Maynard Keynes (1883–1946) devised an economic policy response that rescued the world from the immediate crisis. Recovery from the Depression would not, however, end the political upheaval that had already begun. It would take another world war to finally dismantle the British Empire, beginning with the loss of India, its Crown jewel among the colonies, in 1947. The emergence of a New World Order would disproportionately favour the United States and give its capitalism an aura of invincibility.

Europe

After the inevitable dissolution of the Holy Roman Empire in 1806, the German-speaking countries of Europe split into more than three hundred little kingdoms, each with its own king. Realizing that such a structure was unsustainable, particularly in view of Napoleon's repeated invasions of most of Europe, the Congress of Vienna decided in 1815 to combine the fragmented kingdoms into a German Federation comprising thirty-nine German-speaking kingdoms. These kingdoms, although still small in comparison to the other countries of Europe, entered into a military alliance to defend each other in case of a foreign invasion, but they lacked well-developed economic plans and legal systems, which resulted in widespread injustices, mass poverty, and the persistence of serfdom.[13] Karl Marx was born in the new German Federation in 1818, just three years after its inception and about twenty-eight years after Adam Smith's passing, and it was here where Marx spent his formative years.

Infighting among the poorly organized German kingdoms led to the dissolution of the German Federation in 1866. In 1871, after winning the Franco-Prussian War, Otto von Bismarck, the prince of Bismarck and duke of Lauenburg, forged the northern German states into the German Empire, to be led by Prussia, and assumed the role of its chancellor. Although this arrangement remained intact until the beginning of World War I, the empire was besieged with an undercurrent of anti-Semitism, as was, to a lesser extent, the rest of Europe.

A Short Biography of Adam Smith (1723–90)

An economist first and a moral philosopher second, Adam Smith was born in 1723 in Kirkcaldy, Scotland, the son of Adam Smith Sr and Margaret Douglas. Adam Smith Sr was an advocate-solicitor before becoming the comptroller of customs in Kirkcaldy. The junior Adam Smith attended Burgh School of Kirkcaldy, where he learned Latin, mathematics, history, and *belles-lettres* (essay writing). At fourteen, he studied moral philosophy under the well-regarded Francis Hutchinson at the University of Glasgow—an experience he would remember as one of the most enjoyable and rewarding of his life. In contrast, he reportedly teetered on the edge of a nervous breakdown at Balliol College in Oxford, where he completed his graduate studies.

---

13 Garraty and Gay, 1972, p. 743.

During his early professional career, Smith delivered public lectures at the University of Edinburgh on rhetoric and belles-lettres. He became a professor of moral philosophy at the University of Glasgow in 1751 and stayed there for thirteen years, serving as the head of the department during the last few years of his tenure. In recognition of his extraordinary scholarship, the University of Glasgow conferred upon him the title of Doctor of Laws (LLD) in 1762.

To expand his understanding of economic principles on a global level, Smith travelled extensively in Europe, and to support himself during his travels, he tutored private students, including Henry Scott, the young duke of Buccleuch and the grandson of the enormously wealthy Charles Townshend. The Royal Society of London granted him a fellowship—one of the highest honours that could be conferred upon an academician—in 1773 for his accomplishments in research. And over the course of his career, he met and befriended philosophers Voltaire and David Hume and the legendary American polymath Benjamin Franklin, all three of whom influenced Smith's moral and economic theories.

Scotland appointed Smith the commissioner of customs in 1778. The prestigious and profitable job seemed at odds with Smith's economic theories, which were critical of the mercantile economic system. Five years later, Smith received the Royal Charter, making him a founding member of the Royal Society of Edinburgh, and from 1787 to 1789, he served as the University of Glasgow's rector.

Smith was a brilliant thinker, an outstanding theorist, and a prolific writer. Among his most noteworthy works were *The Theory of Moral Sentiments* (1759) and *The Wealth of Nations* (1776), the latter a monumental and enormously influential theory of economics that cemented his reputation as the father of classical economics and of capitalism.

Smith never married. He died on 17 July 1790, leaving a treasure trove of ideas that would keep economists busy for centuries. He remains the most revered and influential of all economists, and his ideas continue to be debated.

A Short Biography of Karl Marx (1818–83)

Activist philosopher. Revolutionary socialist. Left-wing economic theorist. Father of *The Communist Manifesto*. Author of the famous *Das Kapital*. Karl Heinrich Marx, one of the most influential thinkers and writers of the nineteenth century, was born on 5 May 1818, in Trier, Prussia, which belonged to the German Federation. He was the son of Heinrich Marx and Henrietta Pressburg.

Heinrich practised law and had inherited several vineyards. He belonged to Prussia's upper middle class, if not the upper class. Born a Jew, he later converted and was baptized in the Evangelical Established Church, but in practice he was a non-religious liberal and took part in the uprising against the Prussian monarchy and its constitution. He taught Karl at home until Karl was twelve years old and then sent the boy to Trier High School, which was dominated by left-wing teachers. Because of the school's anti-government faculty, it soon became the target of police raids. In 1835, when Karl was seventeen years old, he was transferred to the University of Bonn, where he joined a radical poets' club, took part in anti-government activities, and succumbed to heavy drinking. When Karl's grades deteriorated, his father transferred him to the University of Berlin, where Karl matriculated in law. While at Berlin, Karl was indoctrinated in the radical arm of Hegelian philosophy and developed a strong inclination towards left-wing political views. He pursued his doctoral work at the University of Berlin but, fearing that his PhD thesis, "The Difference Between the Democritean and Epicurean Philosophy of Nature", would be rejected by the university's conservative faculty, submitted it at the liberal University of Jena, where he received a PhD in 1841.

In 1843, at the age of twenty-five, Karl Marx married Jenny von Westphalen, his sweetheart of several years. Jenny came from a prosperous Dutch Jewish family, which later founded Philips Electronics.

After receiving his PhD, Marx became a journalist and wrote fiction on the side. The revolutionary and anti-government tone of his writing saw him driven from one place to another—from Cologne to Paris, from Paris to Brussels—and then out of Brussels.

In August 1842, Marx met and befriended the German socialist Friedrich Engels, and the two remained friends until Marx died. Engels owned several income-producing properties in England and provided financial assistance to Marx whenever Marx experienced dire financial conditions. The two friends collaborated to publish *The Communist Manifesto*, a political pamphlet, in February 1848. Having been denied residence in mainland Europe, Marx moved a year and a half later to London, where he stayed permanently and produced most of his life's work, including *Das Kapital*.

To sustain his livelihood while in London, Marx worked as a journalist for the *New York Tribune*, but much of his financial support came from Engels. Born rich and having married into wealth, Marx championed the labour class like no one had before him and died poor and distressed in London on 14 March 1883, at the age of sixty-four. Jenny, his wife of thirty-eight years and the mother of their seven children, had passed away two years earlier. Marx's philosophy, thoughts, and theories—collectively known as Marxism—are still very much alive. As an alternative to capitalism, Marxism inspires class warfare and violent uprisings of the proletariat against capitalism and the bourgeoisie in many corners of the world. It will continue to do so until a more equitable socio-economic arrangement can be found.

A Short Biography of John Maynard Keynes (1883–1946)

John Maynard Keynes was born in the upper crust of the British middle class in Cambridge, England, in June 1883, the son of John Neville Keynes, an economist and lecturer of philosophy, and Florence Ada, a social reformer. Keynes was born the same year Karl Marx died and a little less than a century—ninety-three years to be exact—after Adam Smith passed.

A brilliant student with a penchant for mathematics and a flair for moral philosophy, Keynes attended elite Eton College, where he earned a scholarship, and later King's College of the University of Cambridge, where he received a bachelor's degree in mathematics. Although he would become the most celebrated economist of his time, he received no formal education in economics. He did, however, attend informal lectures on the subject. As an aside, the fact that a non-economist like Keynes would go on to become a world-renowned economist has given me courage to venture into the field, offer a critique of the current economic order and suggest a new.

When Keynes was born, the British Empire was at the height of its power, but he witnessed a series of crises that shaped his views forever: America's bank failures of 1907 and the global economic downturn that followed, World War I and the drain on England's resources, the recessions of 1920 and 1921, the Great Depression of 1929–39, and the beginning of the dismantling of his country's great empire.

Keynes worked as a clerk at the India Office (1906–08), an editor at the *Economic Journal* (1911), a member of the Royal Commission on Indian Currency and Finance (1913), an aide to Lloyd George, the Chancellor of the Exchequer (1914), a senior official at the Treasury of Britain (1915), a financial representative of the British Treasury at the Versailles Peace Conference (1919), and a leader of the British delegation and chairman of the World Bank Commission (1944). Recognition for his work included King's Birthday honours (1917) and decoration as an officer of the Belgian Order of Leopold (1920). His publications remain his main legacy, with the following the most noteworthy:

- An article in the *Economic Journal* (1909) about the effect of the 1907 global economic downturn in India.
- His first book, *Indian Currency and Finance*, published in 1913.
- *A Treatise on Probability* (1921), which provides the philosophical and mathematical underpinnings of the probability theory as it applies to economics.
- *A Treatise on Money*, published in two volumes in 1930, in which he advanced the thesis that high interest rates can cause unemployment to rise by making savings exceed investment.

- *The Means to Prosperity* (1933), which argued many of the things that were to be fully vetted in his later publications on Keynesian economics.
- His most famous book, *The General Theory of Employment, Interest, and Money* (1936), provided the foundation of modern macroeconomics. Here he outlined the basic tenets of Keynesian economics, which diverged from classical economics and was credited with rescuing the Anglo-American economy from the Great Depression.

Keynes was openly gay for several years, but in 1925, at the age of forty-two, he wed Lydia Lopokova, a Russian ballerina. The couple had no children, and Keynes died of ill health on 21 April 1946, in Firle, England, at the age of sixty-two.

Concluding Remarks

As we've seen thus far, individual biographies and the broader socio-economic climate have greatly influenced today's most influential economic theories. To explore the former helps us understand the latter. But how have these theories evolved over time and how have they shaped the world? Let's find out.

3

The Leading Economic Theories: An Introduction

In *Conversations with JOV*, a novel by Bengali writer Ramkumar Mukhopadhyay, the narrator shares a story with JOV, his dinner guest.[1] The story is about a dacoity—an armed robbery by a gang—and is set in the village of Baital.

As midnight fell on the village, the narrator recounts, dacoits descended on the zamindar's (landowner's) house. In the glow cast by hundreds of flambeau torches, the villagers could see countless clubs, bludgeons, axes, hatches, and spears dancing in the air. The deafening roars of the dacoits filled the air, waking nearby villages. Birds fled their nests and took to the night sky. The mahogany entrance gate flew open, and hundreds of the zamindar's security guards, each wearing a black headband,

1 Mukhopadhyay, R., *Conversations with JOV*, September 2021, monthly *Krittibhash*, p. 190. Prajatney Pratibhas, Kolkata, India.

confronted the dacoits, who wore red headbands. Clubs struck clubs, bludgeons struck bludgeons, swords struck swords, and spears flew like lightning. The fighting raged for two hours before the leader of the security guards surrendered and the dacoits entered the inner compound of the zamindar's home.

Two young widowed sisters of the zamindar stood with their hands raised, stopping the dacoits in their tracks. "You may take everything," they said, "but you must not hurt our zamindar brother."

The leader of the dacoits, noticing the likeness of his two daughters in the zamindar's sisters, felt his heart melt as he stared at their tender faces. "Mothers," he said, "our people are hungry for want of food. They want a full meal to eat. If they are fed, we will give up dacoity and won't take anything or hurt anyone."

At the direction of the sisters, the cooks began to prepare a feast, firing up a dozen cooking furnaces in the courtyard. Hundreds of meals were prepared, and the dacoits ate heartily before daybreak.

JOV, having listened silently to the story thus far, tells the narrator it's time for him to go.

"Ah," the narrator says, "but the story is not over."

"What else can there be?" JOV asks.

"The real story has not yet been told," the narrator answers before continuing with his tale.

When they were only nine and ten years old, respectively, the two sisters were married to two wealthy zamindar families of nearby villages. But when their husbands died of cholera a short time later, the sisters returned to their village to live with their brother, unable to inherit any property of their husbands' estates because they had no children. After feeding the dacoits, they went to court and told the judge that they had just adopted a hundred children and wished to claim their husbands' estates. The court approved their wishes, and from that day on, the dacoits lived with the zamindar and his sisters. Now law-abiding citizens, the former dacoits threw themselves into voluntary work.

After the narrator announces the end of the story, JOV stands up to leave. Halfway out of the door, he stops, turns, and asks his host a pivotal question: "What do you think costs less—maintaining the security guards and installing a police force in every village or feeding the hungry and making them part of a productive workforce?"

With the question hanging in the air, JOV leaves.

The story above is a work of fiction, but it reminds me of a real episode in my childhood, related in Book 1 of my memoir, when armed dacoits invaded our ancestral house. Moreover, it contains within it much wisdom and truth. How a society allocates its resources is a direct reflection of its values. Guards and security fences, it turns out, don't always constitute the best defense against theft. Indeed, when we wall ourselves off from the rest of the world, we unwittingly make ourselves less safe. Equity, opportunity, and inclusion, on the other hand, have the potential to turn criminals into contributors and enemies into friends.

*

We turn now to the three economic theories that have provided the frameworks for all others: industrial capitalism, which is called the classical tradition; communism, which is called the institutional tradition; and Keynesian economics, otherwise known as the demand-side macroeconomic tradition.

The Classical Tradition: The Smith–Ricardo–Mill–Malthus Doctrines

It might come as a surprise to the average reader that the term "classical economics" was coined by Karl Marx, who, while trying to dismantle its structure, called it "vulgar economics". The classical tradition is also called the industrial capitalist tradition to distinguish it from the mercantile capitalist tradition, the economic framework it replaced. Some economists also call it the neoclassical tradition, a more sophisticated term, with the prefix *neo* implying that the doctrine applies even to current situations without substantive change.[2]

The father of classical economics, of course, was Adam Smith. In *The Wealth of Nations*, he posited that when individuals or corporations own their property (private property) and work towards maximizing their individual interests, an "invisible hand" works to maximize the wealth of the collective—i.e., the nation. The principle of laissez-faire attributes a minimal role to government and instead relies on market competition to shape the economy. In the purest form of capitalism, individual freedom is emphasized, and the government's role is largely limited to providing defence, maintaining law and order, and protecting private property. When used in the real world, capitalism has managed to maximize national wealth, as intended, but historically it has been unsuccessful in achieving a fair distribution of wealth among the people. The US has championed capitalism while modifying it over time. As I will contend later, while I agree with the key concepts of a minimal role of government, a certain part of national wealth ought to

2 Sowell, 1977, p. 4; Galbraith, 1987, p. 90.

belong equally to all citizens of a nation, and the government should be responsible for ensuring the said distribution.

Smith's theory contained three basic tenets:

1. The broad force that motivates economic life is self-interest. "It is not from the benevolence of the butcher, the brewer, or the baker," Smith wrote, "that we expect our dinner, but from their regard to their own interest. We address ourselves not to their humanity but to their self-love." He then uses the metaphor of an invisible hand guiding the market for the public good.
2. The market will determine prices and the distribution of profit to labourers (wages) and those who own capital (return on capital).
3. The state can use certain policies to support and enhance economic progress and prosperity.

Although Smith articulated the first tenet very well, he left the second and third incomplete. David Ricardo (1772–1823), John Stuart Mill (1806–73), and Thomas Robert Malthus (1766–1834) filled in the gaps, which is why Smith's industrial capitalism is often called the Smith–Ricardo–Mill–Malthus Doctrines. Before writing *The Wealth of Nations*, Smith had been a prominent professor of moral philosophy. Unfortunately, by leaving his theory incomplete, he left room for capitalism to evolve into an immoral force.

The neoclassical order appeared to be a quantum improvement over the old system it was replacing: mercantilism. Indeed, mercantilism discouraged competition and encouraged monopolies. It created a dominant merchant class that partnered with the state to colonize foreign lands by establishing business interests as a first step (the British East

India Company, for example, paved the way for the British occupation of India). It discouraged free trade and the import of foreign goods, thus inhibiting innovation and the subsequent price reductions that improve citizens' quality of life. It held the misguided notion that precious metals (gold and silver), not goods and services, are the source of national wealth. And it exploited family-centric production of goods and services at predatory prices, thus delaying factory-based mass production.

The classical economic tradition paved the way for the Industrial Revolution, which began in the last third of the eighteenth century and unleashed the creation of enormous wealth in the West. But when it came to the matter of wages, Smith suggested only that they should equal the cost of sustaining labour.

Ricardo supported Smith's position but also added his own interpretation. In his subsistence theory of wages, which he called the Iron Law of Wages and outlined in *On Principles of Political Economy and Taxation*, he argued that wages should consist only of what would be required "to bring the worker into being as a worker and sustaining him in the job". To him, a more serious matter was return on capital to the capitalist that supported the factory. This included not only shares of the "excess value" (profit) but also generous payment for the machines and equipment used in production. With the combined returns on capital and equipment, the rich enjoyed a period of exuberant and ostentatious excess, while labourers were pushed into the lowest rung of the value chain.

As concerns about the misfortune and miserable conditions of labour under the new system of industrial capitalism surfaced, Malthus doubled down on Smith and Ricardo's position towards labour. In *An Essay on the Principle of Population* (1798), Malthus argued that the employer—the capitalist—was not the architect of the misfortunes of the poor. "The miseries of the workers, the ineluctable slide toward bare subsistence, were their own doing," he wrote, "the result of their uncontrollable commitment to procreation." Mill, a noted economist who worked for the British East India Company, made a similar argument. In his *Principles of Political Economy* (1848), Mill attributed the poverty of labourers to "on the one hand, an immutable physical law of diminishing returns to labour as more and more workers were added to the productive apparatus, and on the other, the relentless procreative impulse of the masses" and "irresponsible sexual behaviour".

Smith's successors, it seemed, held a rather dim view of labour. But noted welfare economist Amartya Sen reminds us that Smith was a professor of moral philosophy at the University of Glasgow and that he never spoke out against public support of the poor.[3] Commenting on Sen's interpretation of *The Wealth of Nations*, John M. Letiche of the University of California, Berkeley, wrote, "An accurate interpretation of Adam Smith, [Sen] demonstrates, does not lend support to believers in, and advocates of, a narrow interpretation of self-interested behavior either in ethics or in economics."[4]

A secondary and yet important contribution of Malthus was that he voiced concern that the classical capitalist tradition had the potential to create massive and uncontrollable overproduction of goods, which in turn would lead to deep recession or depression and a subsequent rise in unemployment. In taking such a position, he differed from his contemporary, Jean-Baptiste Say (1767–1832), who predicted in his *Traite d'Economie Politique* (1803) that Smithian economics

---

3 Sen, 1988, pp. 2, 25.

4 Ibid., p. xi.

can never lead to underproduction or overproduction. Say's view, expressed in what today is known as Say's Law, was that the proceeds received by workers, capitalists, and landlords from the sale of products would be spent to buy back the products, thus establishing an equilibrium (pari passu) between production and sales. Should local shortages or overproduction appear, they would be brief, forming a wavelike business cycle rather than changing the fundamental premises of the law. Say's Law did not hold up over the long term, and Malthus's concerns proved correct (see the discussion on John Maynard Keynes and the Great Depression below).

Socialism and Communism

As the classical economic tradition replaced the old mercantile one, criticism against the new order grew. Although the new system had spurred economic progress, it also perpetuated a lopsided distribution of income, leading to class divisions in which a minority of "highborn" aristocrats dominated a majority of "lowborn" workers and commoners. The criticism came initially from a new, informal school of thought called socialism, which called for society to control the means of production, distribution, and trade. Socialism proposed shifting the control of economic power from factory owners and other industrialists to the public. Under such a system, individuals could still own property, but the resources of industrial production would be communally owned by the public, i.e., by a democratically elected government. By insisting on a democratic process, socialism advocated for making peaceful changes within the political structure rather than overthrowing the existing social order.

Karl Marx and Friedrich Engels considered socialism too weak. Human history, Marx contended, should be viewed through the lens of class war and the ongoing struggle between the bourgeoisie and the proletariat. The bourgeoisie were the industrial capitalists who owned private property and the capital of business and industry. The proletariat, on the other hand, consisted of the vast majority of working-class people, from wage labourers to "the physician, the lawyer, the priest, the poet, the man of science", and didn't own private property or capital. In *The Communist Manifesto*, Marx and Engels called for the elimination of private ownership of property through violent uprisings.

Not surprisingly, communism roiled the world. Less than forty years after Marx's death, the Russian Revolution (1917) toppled the tsar and eventually led to the Soviet Union and the adoption of communism by several other governments, including China, Cuba, North Korea, Laos, and Vietnam. The basic tenets of communism can be summarized as follows:

1. The rejection of classical economics and an unchanging relationship between employer and worker, between land, capital, and labour. Marx maintained that socio-economics are in a constant state of flux and continue to evolve through class warfare caused by the inherent injustice of the existing orders.[5]
2. The elimination of private property.[6] Power is derived from possession of private property, Marx argued, and since feudal times has belonged to aristocrats and landowners.

5 Galbraith, 1987, p. 128.
6 Ibid., p. 133.

3. The banning of religion. Marx argued in *Critique of Hegel's Philosophy of Right* (1844) that religion, morality, and idealism are "distortions of what is genuinely human".

Keynesian Economics: A Demand-Side Macroeconomic Theory

The rise of Keynesian economics is deeply entwined with the Great Depression, which challenged some of capitalism's assumptions. The Anglo-American countries and much of Western Europe had weathered countless booms and busts, somehow always managing to emerge from each crisis largely unscathed. Their dependence on capitalism and the principle of laissez-faire were confirmed by the steady rise of national wealth, particularly in the US, which, after gaining independence in 1776, had adopted a Constitution in 1789 that mirrored the same set of principles Adam Smith had proposed in 1776 in his *General Economic Theory*.

But in 1929, the stock market collapsed, and the ensuing panic spread like wildfire, soon engulfing the entire free world. By 1933, the global domestic product had shrunk 15 per cent, international trade had fallen by more than 50 per cent, and unemployment had risen to 23 per cent in the US and up to 33 per cent in many poor countries. Prices everywhere dropped as people lost income, and price deflation touched every market, including food. As demand fell in the US, crop prices fell by roughly 60 per cent. Various countries imposed protectionist policies, but their frantic attempts to escape the situation backfired and created a domino effect of negative consequences, including depressing international trade further.

As economists searched for answers, some turned to the Soviet economy, which was the only communist one in the world. Having isolated itself from the rest of the world since the Russian Revolution, the Soviet Union contributed very little to international trade and thus breathed a sigh of relief when the depression virus stopped at its gates. Could socialism or communism save the rest of the world?

Before any such revolution could take hold in the West, John Maynard Keynes came to the rescue of the Western economy. In *The General Theory of Employment, Interest, and Money* (1936), he presented his diagnoses of the crisis and his solution to the problem. Keynes contended that microeconomics' bottom-up, laissez-faire approach lacked the tools to deal with recession and depression. His top-down macroeconomic prescription, which came to be known as Keynesian economics, was simple: let government step in and do so in a bold way.

While the classical tradition maintain that supply determines demand, Keynes argues that the supply-siders' argument rests on a faulty assumption that when a supply shortage dampens demand, prices and wages will fall and adjust accordingly, thereby establishing a new equilibrium. But such thinking, Keynes counters, is backward. On the contrary, when demand sinks, firms cannot reduce wages promptly. As a result, demand remains low, unemployment rises, and recovery is difficult. His prescription is to proactively increase demand so that supply will adjust itself. Such a proposal flips the equation and asserts a different relationship between supply and demand.

Keynes maintains that the private sector is incapable of increasing demand. Why? Because the private sector won't invest more in business to create demand when demand is already low. Only the government can increase demand by increasing federal spending to fund public projects and/

or welfare. More money in the hands of consumers means higher purchases of goods and services and a higher GDP. Only then will the private sector increase investment to meet higher demand. Employment too will rise, further increasing aggregate demand and causing a multiplier effect that accelerates economic growth.

Keynes's solutions helped inspire US president Franklin D. Roosevelt's New Deal, an unprecedented federal spending programme, and produced positive results. But in supporting government's increased role in managing the economy, Keynes drew criticism from many, with his detractors calling him a socialist in disguise. Yet a closer look at *The General Theory of Employment, Interest, and Money* reveals that what he proposed was not socialism but "managed capitalism". Nevertheless, the stigma lingered. Intended or not, Keynes's emphasis on the increased role of the government, although meant to be used only in times of crisis, gave the socialist-minded liberals an opening to argue for federal control of every phase of public life, crisis or not.

Morality-based Economic Theories: Rawls and Sen

As the world experimented with various modifications of the three major economic arrangements explored above, a group of ethicists was developing a purely morality-based approach to welfare economics. Moral considerations, they contended, should provide the sole basis of any economic arrangement, and it ought to be possible to devise such an order strictly from philosophical ideas. Most of these ethicists agreed on one thing, namely that the immorality of existing economic arrangements lay mostly, if not solely, on the way resources—materials, wealth, and opportunities—are distributed among people. They sought egalitarian principles that would ensure the equal treatment of everyone.

Since the ethicists' theories were based entirely on philosophical reasoning, there was no way to verify the truth of the assertions. Moreover, the personal beliefs of each ethicist invariably influenced their opinion of what exactly constituted a just economic arrangement. Let's take a moment now to look at two such theories.

A Theory of Justice

John Rawls's *A Theory of Justice*, published in 1971 and considered a classic of political philosophy, equates justice with fairness. Rawls describes fairness as an equal right to equality of opportunity, which implies a need to raise the prospects of the least advantaged in society. His theory suggests that a just society should be governed by two basic principles of justice: first, guaranteeing the fundamental individual liberties of speech, association, and worship, among others; and second, ensuring that social and economic equalities are arranged to offer the greatest possible benefit to the worst off in society while upholding the equality of opportunity—i.e., ensuring equal distribution of wealth. The resulting socialist arrangement guarantees a welfare state able to provide a minimum income to anyone, eliminate monopolies, encourage savings to benefit future generations, and command obedience when dictating rule of law regarding matters of equity.[7]

---

7 Kukathas and Pettit, 1990, pp. 36, 47, 51, 53.

Rawls arrives at his conclusions by imagining a contractual arrangement between rational people. In this hypothetical scenario, or Original Position (OP), a group of people set out to choose from several economic and political arrangements the one that will best balance their rights, liberties, opportunities, power, income, and wealth. But they do so from a "veil of ignorance"—in other words, nobody knows what their socio-economic status is or what position they might occupy in the new arrangement. Being rational people, they will vote unanimously in favour of an arrangement that guarantees liberty, equality, and happiness for everyone. Such an arrangement, Rawls contends, must also be a just one. He goes on to argue that when people are assured that everybody will be treated equally under the law, they will agree to comply with it.[8]

Robert Nozick (1938–2002), a fellow philosopher and Harvard professor, levelled one of the biggest critiques at *A Theory of Justice* by arguing a point I agree with and will expand on later: "Rawls is mistaken in assuming that goods come into the world unowned and await distribution on the basis of justice."[9] My second criticism is that the reproducibility of Rawls's approach is assumed, not demonstrated. To be robust, such a process must have scientific rigour and must demonstrate reproducibility. My third criticism is that to produce any economic value, you need polarity—namely, a gradient between a source and a sink in much the same manner that a higher concentration of energy at a source and a lower concentration of energy at a sink is needed for energy to produce work (see Chapter 6). In Rawls's theory, the agents all start with the same amounts of resources, such as wealth. Thus there is no gradient in his arrangement, which

8 Ibid., pp. 19–25.
9 Ibid., pp. 90–91.

means such a system can never generate new wealth. It will soon become "equality at death"—a thermodynamic concept I will explore later. My fourth criticism is that Rawls's theory contradicts the classical utilitarian theory of Jeremy Bentham (1748–1832). The utilitarian theory, clarified by Bentham's student John Stuart Mill, describes a moral act as something that produces a high level of happiness and pleasure. There is no such assumption of pleasure in Rawls's *A Theory of Justice*. Perhaps Rawls isn't interested in whether an action generates pleasure or pain. His chief focus, according to his own definition, is on whether it's fair and just.

The Social Choice Theory

Amartya Sen, a prominent developmental economist who combined ethics and Smithian self-interest, rejects the assumptions behind Rawls's OP theory. Using examples, he shows that the test of impartiality proposed by Rawls can be passed by a biased person. Rather than trying to select one absolute truth, Sen suggests using a comparative approach to select several alternatives. Such an approach, which he proposes in The Social Choice Theory, might eliminate some of the problems faced by those seeking absolute solutions. We shouldn't be given only one just arrangement, Sen argues, but several alternatives to choose from. "Just as when determining the relative heights of Mount Kilimanjaro and Mount McKinley," he says, "knowing that Mount Everest is taller than both is an entirely redundant fact."[10] The comparative approach might not give us one perfect solution, but reality can never

---

10 Roger, 2020, p. 3.

be realized in perfection. A firm believer in the democratic process, Sen was wise to remind his readers that democracy is, after all, about freedom of choice.

Sen, who earned the 1998 Nobel Prize in economics, put himself at odds with canonized philosophers like Thomas Hobbes, John Locke, Jean-Jacques Rousseau, and Immanuel Kant, whose ideas informed Rawls's theories. Interestingly, Sen dedicated his book *The Idea of Justice* (2009) to Rawls—testimony to his respect for the ethicist.

Sen suggests that rationality is conventionally defined by a twin process of (i) maintaining internal consistency of choice and (ii) seeking maximization of self-interest.[11] He traces the origin of economics to two logical sources: ethics and engineering. And he returns to the Socratic question, "How should one live?"—a question that Bernard Williams also argues is the central motivation of ethics.[12] But I would argue that if we are to seek a just economic arrangement, it can't be based on two different arrangements (one ethics-based and the other engineering-based). There can be only one just economic arrangement. Any just economic arrangement must be arrived at via a scientific approach—Sen might have meant "science" when he said "engineering"—and modifying the final arrangement to fully comply with ethical laws. For a process to have credibility, it must be reproducible and shouldn't depend on morality, the definition of which varies over time and among cultures. The latter is evident given how ethicists disagree on how to define ethics, despite agreeing on the "grand fairness test".

Sen criticizes internal consistency of choice as an ill-conceived method of demonstrating rationality. "If a person

11 Sen, 1988, p. 12.
12 Ibid., pp. 2, 3.

does exactly the opposite of what would help achieve what he or she wanted to achieve," he writes in *Consistency as a Criterion for Rationality*, "and does this with flawless internal consistency, the person can scarcely be seen as rational, even if that dogged consistency inspires some kind of astonished admiration on the part of the observer."[13]

Like Rawls, Sen searches for the origin of the right kind of economic arrangement in ethics. Unlike Rawls, he understands the process involved in the creation of wealth. Accordingly, in The Social Choice Theory and companion works, Sen tries to find the source of ethics in capitalism based on the Smithian concept of self-interest. In support of his contention, Sen insists that Smith was not an immoral person. Indeed, in *The Theory of Moral Sentiments* (1759), Smith posits that "virtue consists in benevolence".[14] It seems that, while writing the book, he still held the views of his teacher Professor Francis Hutcheson, who wrote, "It was benevolence only which could stamp upon any action the character of virtue." But the person who wrote *The Theory of Moral Sentiments*, I would argue, was not the same person who wrote *The Wealth of Nations* seventeen years later. By then, Smith was openly critical of Hutcheson and was extolling the virtues of self-interest. Capitalism, I will argue later, is immoral. But that doesn't mean Smith suddenly became immoral. Nobody argues that. And we recognize that his sense of morality remained unshaken even when he wrote *The Wealth of Nations*, in which he condemned the East India Company for its shameless greed in buying cheap and selling dear: "Such a council [of merchants] can command

---

13 Ibid., p. 13.

14 Cannan, 1994, p. ii.

obedience only by the military force with which they are accompanied, and their government is necessarily military and despotic."[15]

Regardless, Sen's attempt to confer morality upon self-interest is grossly misplaced. The morality of a person need not be confused with the morality of their theories. As mentioned earlier, although Smith sought to demolish mercantilism with his theory, he nevertheless took the job of the office of the commissioner of customs in Scotland, a job that protected and promoted mercantilism. Perhaps Smith didn't have the courage of his convictions. But such speculation misses the point. Ricardo, Mill, and Malthus completed Smith's work and, as I will soon argue, exposed its fundamental immorality in the process.

Let's recognize capitalism for what it is: a scientific notion of rational behaviour that, as its supporters like to contend, leaves no room for moral arguments. Sen's attempt to find morality in self-interest is akin to searching for water in a desert. But my criticism isn't of Sen so much as it is of the source of his justification. Sen's implicit recognition of capitalism as a preferred means of wealth creation and his admiration for Smith and Mill is well placed (Sen was a recipient of the Adam Smith Prize in 1954 and the Charleston-EFG John Maynard Keynes Prize in 2015). Rather than trying to find morality in capitalism, Sen would have done better to suggest safeguards to protect capitalism from the greedy and render it a moral force, as I will attempt to do in the pages that follow.

Nature—and by extension science that expresses the workings of nature—by definition is devoid of morality, which applies only to humans. We occupy a unique place within the

---

15 Ibid., p. 689.

unfathomable vastness of the expressed physical universe. We have free will and can act with motive. The rest of the universe has neither free will nor the ability to act with motive, but as I will argue later, it possesses an arrow imparted by the laws of entropy. Sen errs again when he claims that internal consistency can't be a condition of rationality and as such, of an economic theory.[16] The exact opposite is true. If an economic theory is a model based on the principles of science, it will have internal consistency, for science is ruled not by free will but by the immutable and reproducible laws of the physical world. This brings me to another point that the microeconomics of capitalism, although silent on the subject of morality, has been used by the greedy to harm the less advantaged and thus has become an immoral force.

While I have criticized some of Sen's assertions, I nevertheless recognize his talent and scholarship. His intimate knowledge and understanding of modern economic arrangements became apparent when, while a student at Cambridge in the 1950s, he won nearly every award available to students of economics. A graduate of first rank with Tripos from Cambridge, he became, at age twenty-seven, the youngest full professor at the Delhi School of Economics. He later served as a professor at the London School of Economics, master of the Trinity College at Cambridge, and professor of philosophy and economics at Harvard. He won the 1998 Nobel Prize in economics and in 1999 was awarded India's highest civilian award: the Bharat Ratna. Who can criticize the achievements of this scholar extraordinaire and one of the most revered economists in the world? His seminal work, *Development as Freedom*, for which he was awarded the Nobel Prize, shaped the world, and he helped

16 Sen, 1988, p. 13.

identify and remedy several ill-fated concepts in economic policy in developing nations.

*

My thesis in this book begins with my reasoned rejection of the very foundation upon which modern economic arrangements rest. I'm not a formally trained economist and thus don't know the intricate details of the voluminous literature that has grown around the established economic theories. When we condemn a high-rise building as being unsafe and demolish it, does it matter whether we have an intricate knowledge of every compartment in the complex? No. The only thing that matters is that we have a plan for a stronger foundation to replace the old one and a sturdy framework to place atop our new foundation. We can then leave it to others to fill in the details. This is this book's purpose: to demolish the old foundation that has grown dangerous to society so that we might provide a new, morally and functionally sound foundation to build upon.

National Economics

Modern democratic nations aren't necessarily run with strict adherence to any particular socio-economic philosophy and instead, largely conform to the principles proclaimed in their constitutions. Each constitution defines the rights of the people and the government, and each is a living document. In its original adoption, it declares the general principles by which the country is to be run, and as social conditions change with the passage of time, the same changes are accommodated in the constitution by introducing amendments.

The United States of America declared independence from the British in 1776, and its Congress ratified its Constitution with seven articles in 1788. It came into operation in 1789. Since then, twenty-seven amendments have been added—the first ten, the Bill of Rights, on 15 December 1791, and the last one, compensation for senators and representatives, on 7 May 1992. Even with these amendments, legal experts and regular citizens alike struggle to determine the constitutionality of various government actions. Such decisions ultimately fall to the judiciary. In the US, the Supreme Court is ideologically divided. Conservative justices believe in interpreting the constitution as it is written. If Congress wants to change those instructions, they contend, it must do so by passing new laws that explicitly state what the people want. Liberal justices, meanwhile, believe that no law can fully explain its purpose in writing. They believe that their job is to interpret the laws based on their intents, the spirit behind them, and not strictly what is written. A constitution, in other words, is not an ironclad document. In democratic countries, it can be changed or modified by the people through their elected representatives by introducing new amendments and new laws.

Adam Smith published *The Wealth of Nations* in 1776, the same year the US issued its Declaration of Independence. The emphasis on individual freedom is prominent in both documents, and not surprisingly, the US adopted the capitalist framework at its inception, leaving mercantilism behind. An alternative to the capitalist model didn't arrive until seventy-two years later, when Marx and Engels published *The Communist Manifesto* in 1848, and the USSR became the first communist nation in 1917, when Vladimir Lenin led the people's revolution to overthrow the tsarist regime.

In the US, economic policies evolved from president to president within a broad capitalistic framework. As part of the New Deal, President Franklin D. Roosevelt incorporated Keynesian policy recommendations—socialist programmes, as critics called them, because they used government-directed public works, farm subsidies, welfare payments, and other measures—to salvage the economy. The various policies, which were enacted between 1933 and 1939, helped the US escape the Great Depression but didn't meet Keynes's expectations, who would have preferred they go much further. Roosevelt had to balance the budget, but Keynes recommended a deficit budget, with the size of the deficit matching the size of the problem. The US economy didn't fully take off until it committed to the "war spending"—off-balance-sheet spending on war supplies that made the economy roar and resulted in better than full employment—of World War II. For the first time in US history, a female workforce emerged to trigger economic recovery and growth during and after the war.

Although his demand-side approach worked well during recessions and depressions, Keynes presented it as a theory of general applicability. But once government uses its power to create new programmes, those are all but impossible to rescind. No country can achieve prosperity by spending more than it earns and continually running a deficit budget. As time passed, Keynes's approach began to lose favour and was officially rejected in Great Britain when Margaret Thatcher, the leader of its Conservative Party, became prime minister in 1979. A similar fall from grace occurred in the US when Ronald Reagan assumed the presidency in January 1981. During the Great Recession of 2008, President Obama embraced Keynesian policies, and similar policies have been in place in the US ever since. The American policy of deficit spending is made possible by its almost limitless borrowing power, but it has gone far beyond what Keynes prescribed and has become not only an economic concern but a moral one as well.

Concluding Remarks

Now that we've taken a brief look at today's leading economic theories, it's time to dig deeper. In analysing the various theories and exploring their strengths and weaknesses, we will be forced to return to the same stark truth first introduced in Chapter 2: no current system has managed to successfully balance the objectives of increasing national wealth *and* ensuring a fair system of wealth distribution among its people.

4

The Leading Economic Theories: A Critical Analysis

I met a Kabuliwala—a name we gave the nomad Afghan men—when I was five years old. He announced his arrival by ringing a bell as he walked. Upon realizing that ours was the biggest in the village, he stopped at our house and sat in the outer courtyard. We lived in our ancestral home in the village of Silaur, now in Bangladesh. The women of the village—young and old, rich and poor, about fifty or more—came and sat down beside the Kabuliwala, surrounding him.

More than six feet tall, the Kabuliwala boasted a fair complexion and wore a pair of pleated trousers and a baggy, long white shirt—a salwar kameez—the kameez nearly reaching his ankles. He struck an imposing figure beside the dark and relatively short Bengali men of the village. The Kabuliwala had brought with him colourful glass bangles of different sizes to sell. The women loved them, and most, including my mother, bought some. He offered to sell them on credit to those without money and told them that he would be back in two weeks to collect. But the poor women didn't buy on credit; they knew no one could avoid paying a Kabuliwala his legitimate dues.

When the man left, my mother told me that the Kabuliwalas came from a faraway country called Afghanistan and that they were very hardworking people. She told me that "Kabuliwala" meant "people of Kabul", the capital of Afghanistan. The Kabuliwalas, she told me, were very honest people. They didn't deceive anyone and always kept their word, and they expected the people they met to be honest as well. She told me a story about a man who borrowed some money from a Kabuliwala and told him that he would repay with interest in four weeks. When the Kabuliwala returned in four weeks to collect his money, the family members of the man informed him that he had died. The Kabuliwala asked the man's family members to honour the deal, and when they refused, he went to the graveyard and started to dig up the dead man's grave. Seeing this, the family members and the other villagers rushed to him and gave the man his money.

"Everybody knows how serious the Kabuliwalas are," Mother told me, "which is why no one buys anything on credit from them."

After hearing Mother's story, I stood in awe of the courage of the Kabuliwala, whose ruthlessness and cold-hearted nature struck fear in me.

Later, when I was about ten years old, I read a story, "Kabuliwala", written by Rabindranath Tagore, a novelist, short-story writer, and poet who won the Nobel Prize in literature in 1913. The story was about a Kabuliwala who sold things on the streets of Kolkata. The Kabuliwala met the poet in his house, and the poet, who believed in the essential sameness of human emotions, no matter a person's region or ethnic class, talked to the Kabuliwala about the family he might have left behind 1,700 miles away. The Kabuliwala had left a little girl back home, and he admitted that he missed her every day, particularly when he saw other little girls playing with their parents. But he had to travel to faraway countries to earn a living for his family. I read the moving story of love and emotion over and over, tears forming in my eyes every time I finished it. Behind the strong and imposing figure of the Kabuliwala, I saw the same tender heart—a heart full of parental love and emotion—that children who live with their parents take for granted.

*

Fast forward to 2005. By now, I was an established businessman and owner-founder of PMC Group of Companies, a global enterprise headquartered in the US. PMC Group had just bought ICI's rubber chemical business in India. Along with this acquisition came not only the manufacturing complex of rubber-processing chemicals but also a garden house, called the Bose House, on the banks of the River Ganga. The house had once belonged to the family of Subhas Chandra Bose, the legendary freedom fighter. As I read the history of the Bose House, I learned that Subhas had used the house as a stopover while evading the watchful eyes of the British government. From there, he proceeded to Afghanistan, and with the aid of the friendly Afghan people, escaped to Europe to continue India's freedom movement. Subhas Bose was a hero to me, as he was to most Indians. The kindness the Afghan people showed him demonstrated the goodness of their hearts and their love of freedom, leaving a deep impression on me. Afghanistan has always been a friend of India. Religious differences—the Afghans are Muslims, while about 80 per cent of the citizens of secular India are Hindu—never stood in the way of the friendship of the two countries.

Four years earlier, on 11 September 2001, I woke up early for a nine-thirty meeting with KKR Private Equity in New York City. The meeting was to take place on the forty-second floor of KKR's office on Fifty-Seventh Street. KKR, which was eyeing acquiring PPG's chemicals portfolio, knew that before starting PMC Group, I had been PPG's chief technical officer and was on the shortlist to become its CEO and thus was in a position to help them. They were thinking of acquiring PMC Group as a first step and hiring me. As KKR's CFO put it, I could be a corner drugstore or be part of something big like Merck.

Although I had no intention of selling out to KKR, I thought it wise to get involved in the acquisition of PPG's chemicals business. So, after leaving my headquarters office on Chestnut Street in Philadelphia, I decided to take a Greyhound bus to avoid traffic. As the bus approached the Lincoln Tunnel, someone said that the World Trade Center was on fire. The rest of us looked out of our windows and spotted the smoke and fire. We lost sight of the building as the bus took a turn to enter the tunnel, and my thoughts returned to the impending meeting.

After exiting the bus, I took a taxi to the KKR building. When I arrived for my appointment, we learned that the second tower of the World Trade Center had also collapsed, the first having already collapsed a few minutes earlier. All tall buildings in the city, we were told, could be at risk of aeroplane attack. We hurriedly evacuated the building, and soon the city was sealed off, with no one allowed to enter or leave.

The unprovoked attack by Islamic radicals rattled Americans to their cores. The country, in the mood for revenge, was ready to punish the perpetrators. We soon learned that the architect of the attack was a wealthy Arab, Osama bin Laden, who was hiding in Afghanistan under the protection of Mullah Omar, the leader of the Taliban, which ruled Afghanistan at the time. On 7 October, the US began the war in Afghanistan, invading the country with the stated objective of dismantling al-Qaeda and denying Osama bin Laden a safe haven by removing the Taliban from power.

Now, more than twenty years and a trillion dollars later, the US has left Afghanistan with the Taliban's help, and the country is once again under Taliban rule. It's easy to judge history with twenty-twenty hindsight, but we have to ask ourselves the following: Was it morally right to invade Afghanistan? Was it worth the cost?

Of the nineteen hijackers responsible for the 11 September attack, fifteen came from Saudi Arabia, two from the United Arab Emirates, one from Lebanon, and one from Egypt. No one was from Afghanistan. The US didn't attack Saudi Arabia. We couldn't afford to, for our economy depended on its oil. Later, when we learned that Osama bin Laden was hiding in Pakistan, we didn't ask Pakistan to hand him over because we knew Pakistan was knowingly hiding him and would move him to another location if it suspected we knew as much. We didn't invade Pakistan to deny bin Laden safe haven. We couldn't because Pakistan possesses a nuclear arsenal.

In this way, we had attacked the weakest and poorest country in the region simply to satisfy our lust for revenge.

Granted, Mullah Omar was a bad person, but was it morally justifiable to punish the entire country for just one man? Couldn't we have removed both bin Laden and Mullah Omar without invading the country?

When we discovered that bin Laden was hiding in a Pakistani residence, we landed in his compound with surgical precision and killed him without any loss of American lives. Surely our military had possessed the capability to do the same back in Afghanistan. But we had wanted to make a show of dramatic revenge. We had felt compelled to invade the whole country.

Could the trillion dollars dedicated to the Afghanistan war have been better spent? As JOV might have asked the narrator in *Conversations with JOV*, "What would have been cheaper: helping and educating the Afghan people or making them our enemies, as we did, by trying to destroy them?"

The population of Afghanistan was 21.6 million in 2001. Its per capita GDP was $180, compared to $40,000 in the US. One trillion dollars meant $46,000 per Afghan—255 times the income of the average Afghan. Had we sought Amartya Sen's counsel, he would have told us that you cannot fight every injustice with the same vigour. You must choose the abject injustices and try to remove them first. If we had provided food, education, sanitation, infrastructure, and education for the Afghan people, we would have spent much less money and would now have a friend in Afghanistan.

How can we build an economic framework that won't allow such situations to develop in the first place? To answer that question, we must first explore in depth how the current economic systems are failing us.

The Case Against Communism and Socialism: They Are Impotent

The communist Soviet Union that existed from 1922 to 1991 collapsed from hunger and a lack of economic productivity. The ghost of that union—the form of Russia that exists today—is a military nuisance but no longer an economic force. Only five nations still call themselves communist: China, Vietnam, Laos, North Korea, and Cuba.

As mentioned earlier, communism originated from socialist theories. Socialist countries, however, feature multiparty political systems and try to achieve their socialist agenda without violence. Like communist countries, socialist countries boast strong social safety nets and government ownership of key industries and infrastructure. But socialist countries allow ownership of private property. Some of the socialist countries that exist today are Venezuela, El Salvador, Nicaragua, Zambia, Angola, Ecuador, Bolivia, Barbados, Portugal, and Greece. They suffer from the same miseries as the communist countries, and their economies are in shambles.

At the root of communism's and socialism's failure is the inability to accept that polarity—not necessarily extreme polarity—is critical for wealth generation. Much creativity is lost when citizens aren't allowed to create economic polarity, with some becoming providers of resources and others becoming receivers. A lake can't run a hydroelectric plant. You need a dam or a waterfall. Calm weather can't turn a windmill. You need the wind to blow. Static electricity can't power a light bulb. You need an electrical current to flow from a higher to a lower voltage. For actions to take place, you need polarity. Thus, you can't create products and services unless wealth flows from someone with higher wealth to others with lower wealth. Yet too powerful a waterfall can destroy a hydroelectric plant, too strong a wind can shred a windmill, and too big a voltage difference can produce a violent thunderbolt. Similarly, too big a gap between the haves and have-nots can lead to a violent revolution.

Monopoly is also detrimental to the creation of wealth. Communism, as I mentioned earlier, is a giant monopoly with resources and levers of power concentrated in a single source: the government. If too much polarization and wealth disparity are detrimental to the creation of wealth, so too is the absence of both. Without the creation of wealth, equal distribution becomes an empty gesture.

Communism's elimination of private property destroys the incentive to work, and its one-party political system stifles individual freedom. Although socialism allows multiparty political choices, such choices are limited when the government owns the means of production. If people's needs could be reduced to sex and hunger alone, communism or socialism might have worked to some extent. But our fulfilment requires food for the soul, not just the body. Communism bans religion. By banning religion, it denies us one of our most important needs: spiritual growth.

Communist and socialist countries, having found that their economic systems failed to generate enough national wealth, have been slowly adopting capitalist tools within their state-controlled frameworks. China, for example, changed its constitution in 2004 to allow private property and a few market-driven initiatives. Laos began to allow private ownership in 1988. Likewise, Vietnam in recent years moved towards a market economy and supplanted some of its socialist ideas with capitalism. I will discuss these mixed systems later in this chapter.

The Case for Capitalism

Most economists have praised capitalism as superior to other economic arrangements. The proof, according to capitalism's supporters, lies in the economic data. The countries of the capitalist West have consistently outperformed their communist and socialist counterparts in the East and in Latin America.

The United States, which adopted the capitalist framework from its very inception, did splendidly well in creating national wealth. Although its share of global GDP has declined, it still remains high both in absolute terms and on a per capita basis. Thus, from 2015 through 2020, although America's share of the global population declined from 4.35 per cent to 4.27 per cent, its share of global GNP barely budged, dropping from 16.41 per cent to 15.93 per cent—astronomically high numbers when compared to those of the rest of the world. We can debate whether capitalism alone was responsible for making US national wealth the envy of the world or whether other factors—such as the wars that devastated other nations—were also responsible for creating such vast differences. But even when other factors are taken into consideration, the great success of the US economy stands out as a unique phenomenon and an arresting fact.

Capitalists are correct in assuming that unless there is a polarity in wealth distribution, there will be no incentive to work. They also remind us that the incentive to work lies at the root of generating a higher quantity of work and that this quantity is what determines the products and services an economy produces. Incentive is dramatically improved, as Adam Smith told us, when the government adopts a laissez-faire approach.

An important feature of capitalism is its clearing mechanism that lets sick companies go bankrupt and either fade away or re-emerge reorganized and reinvigorated. In stark contrast, socialist and communist governments tend to protect sick companies. Protecting the sick is a virtue and a moral imperative in society, but when it comes to commercial ventures, protecting the sick is a sin. Unless concrete plans exist to make sick companies healthy, spending resources to keep them alive can only drag down the rest of the economy.

The Case Against Capitalism: Capitalism Has Turned Immoral

Capitalism has failed in two ways: (i) in how the economic inputs (labour, technology, and capital) are weighed, and (ii) in how the fruits are distributed among the stakeholders. This failure is not necessarily an economic failure but rather a moral one.

But what is meant by moral or ethical? Philosophers define moral or ethical acts in different ways. Socrates tells us that morality can be found by seeking an answer to the following question: "How should one live?" Bernard Williams argues that such a question is central to the study of ethics.[1] As explored earlier, John Rawls contends that a moral arrangement assures that social and economic equalities are so structured as to "offer the greatest possible benefit to the worst off in society". John Stuart Mill describes morality as something "that gives a high level of happiness and pleasure from an action". Francis Hutcheson,

1 Sen, 1988, p. 2.

the professor who taught moral philosophy at the University of Glasgow and included Adam Smith among his students, tells us, "It was benevolence only which could stamp upon any action the character of virtue." A two-word definition of morality—*non sibi*, Latin for "not for self"—guides many Western intellectuals in their pursuit of morality in whatever they do. Most people would agree with Rawls's grand generalization of morality in his seminal paper "Justice as Fairness", wherein he posits that virtue lies in fairness.[2] I will add that we know fairness when we see it. Later on, I will describe what constitutes fairness when it comes to wealth distribution.

I'm not the first person to object to the immorality of modern capitalism, particularly in the US. A number of philosophers and egalitarian economists have voiced such concerns over the years. Such philosophers and egalitarian economists are mainly concerned with justice—in law, economics, and politics—and fall into two groups.

Contractarian or Transcendental Institutionalists

An arrangement-focused group, also called the Contractarians or Transcendental Institutionalists, consisted of people like Thomas Hobbes (1588–1679), the forerunner of the social contract theory and author of *Leviathan*; John Locke (1632–1704), nicknamed the father of liberalism; Jean-Jacques Rousseau (1712–78), a staunch believer in the "goodness of humankind unless rendered corrupt by society", and Immanuel Kant (1724–1804), originator of Transcendental Idealism and a leader of the Enlightenment movement in Europe.

---

2 *Philosophical Review*, 1958, p. 67.

Realization-focused Group

The second one, a realization-focused group, included people like Marquis de Condorcet (1743–94), one of the earliest supporters of equal rights for women and people of all races; Jeremy Bentham, founder of modern utilitarianism; the women's rights advocate Mary Wollstonecraft (1759–97); Karl Marx; and Amartya Sen.

Sen compares the two approaches above to the ancient Indian views of jurisprudence: *niti* and *nyaya*.[3] Niti, the arrangement-focused view of justice, is chiefly concerned with defining what a just social arrangement is, what such an arrangement should look like, and what kind of rules it should dictate. It holds an idealistic view of a just society and maintains that human beings are bound by social compacts to create a just society. Nyaya, the realization-focused view of justice, focuses primarily on "realizable justice". It's concerned with manifest injustices like slavery, homelessness, racial discrimination, famine, and the denial of human rights that can be tackled if given enough attention. If niti is about idealism, nyaya is about pragmatism. The first is about diagnosing all forms of injustice, and the second is about identifying those injustices that can be eliminated. The first is about what *should* be, and the second is about what *can* be. The first is oblivious to political reality, while the second embraces political reality to determine what is achievable.

I'm reminded of a discussion we had once at the Scripps Research Institute. One member of the board, a renowned medical doctor, asked us why we focused on incurable diseases

3 Sen, 2009, pp. 7, 20.

and insisted we develop diagnostic tools only for those diseases that were currently curable. The nyaya group entertains similar thoughts about justice.

We can use boxing lingo to further distinguish between the two groups. The realization-focused group's test for meeting moral requirements only applies to those cases that are candidates for a knockout solution. Most injustices, however, are candidates for a scoring system. In a scoring system, a single event or a single round is not enough to determine a winner or loser. A compilation of scores from different rounds produces a judgement about who won and who lost. Similarly, when we are determining economic immorality, it's difficult to measure an injustice without taking a closer look and analysing it. When we view a forest from a distance, we see only its beauty. To discover the dangers lurking within, we must first enter it. Britain took pride in establishing the rule of law, eliminating superstitions, and bringing modern education to India, the Crown jewel of the empire. But it took insiders like Subhas Chandra Bose and Mahatma Gandhi to discover the injustice within the country and, more importantly, to help India's own people recognize those injustices. Nelson Mandela alerted the world to the injustices in South Africa, the most prosperous African nation. Martin Luther King Jr roused people's indignation towards the injustices of racism in the US. In each case, it took leaders to point out the injustices, articulate them, and make them visible to all.

The injustices within capitalism require a similar examination. Although capitalism appears successful from a distance, a closer look reveals the manifest injustices of an immoral system. These injustices can be traced to several factors, including an overemphasis on capital; the devaluation of human labour, which is treated like an inanimate part of production; a distorted definition of technology; and an unjust distribution of the fruits of the economy. When it comes to international arrangements, meanwhile, US capitalism has become similarly immoral. It will require a scoring system of sorts, not the discovery of a knockout cause, to show that modern capitalism, especially capitalism in the US, has become an immoral arrangement.

Why Has Capitalism Become Immoral?

To answer this question, let's start by taking a look at economic growth models. In the past, when economists talked about growth models, they began with the Harrod–Domar Model, based on Keynesian economics, as the forerunner of other models. The Harrod–Domar Model was independently developed by the English economist Roy F. Harrod and the Polish-born, China-raised, Harvard-educated economist Evsey David Domar (initially Domashevitsky). The essence of their model, when stripped of its mathematical components, is that economic output and economic growth depend on only two factors: quantity capital and labour.[4]

A key implication of the Harrod–Domar Model is that, under inelastic labour conditions, growth depends on policies that increase investments by increasing savings. Put differently, under conditions of full employment, growth or production capacity is proportional to capital stock. Another implication is that in the less developed countries where labour is plentiful, growth suffers due to a shortage of capital.

---

4 Harrod, 1939; Domar, 1946.

The non-Keynesian (neoclassical) economists soon pointed out that the Harrod–Domar Model failed to explain the economic growth in the US during the first half of the twentieth century. Most economists concluded that capital and labour alone couldn't explain growth. Another catch-all term was required: total factor productivity.

The MIT economist Robert Solow was among the first to point out the shortcomings of the Harrod–Domar Model. After studying economic growth in the US from 1909 to 1949, during which the American economy nearly doubled, Solow attributed a whopping 85 per cent of that growth to "technical changes in the broadest sense", a term he used to replace total factor productivity.[5] The remaining 15 per cent of the growth could be jointly attributed to straight capital and straight labour. In his Embodiment Model, Solow changed "technical changes in the broadest sense" to "a common pool of technological progress", a pool of technological innovations that everyone can access, and distinguished it from "new and differentiating technology" that only a few can access. Nations and companies that can quickly invest in the former or both succeed the most. Solow was awarded the Nobel Prize in economics in 1987 for his startling discoveries.

Many other economists have since come to similar conclusions about the relative contributions of capital, labour, and technology. One such view came from Edward Denison, the American economist most regarded for his pioneering work in measuring US GNP. Over a period of fifty-three years—1929 to 1982—Denison attributed a mere 12 per cent of economic growth to capital, 25 per cent to straight labour input, 16 per cent to the increased educational qualifications of the average

5 Solow, 1987.

worker, and the remaining 47 per cent to the total productivity factor, which combined an "improved allocation of resources" (11 per cent) and the "growth of knowledge" or technological progress (36 per cent). The 16 per cent allocation to increased educational qualifications, Solow argued, was included in his "technological change in the *broadest* sense", and if stripped from it, the contribution from "technological progress in the *narrow* sense" would have been 69 per cent—still a big number.[6] Note that capital was never a major contributor to economic growth; its prudent deployment in technological progress was. Solow called this a "commonsense" decision. I called it a "fast follower's strategy" during my talk at Purdue University, and as explored in the introduction to this book, Professor Boehlje decided to teach the subject in his class after hearing my lecture.[7]

Most CEOs and entrepreneurs are alarmingly unaware of economic theories. Of the few that are familiar with them, most either ignore them for their own self-serving purposes or merely pay them lip service. They hear economists in much the same way someone sniffs perfume but never inhales it. Thus economists try to make their voices heard in government, where they can have the biggest impact.

Capitalism's First Sin: Overemphasizing the Role of Capital

Although much has transpired since the Harrod–Domar Model was debunked, its ghost still lingers in the corporate world,

6 Solow, 1987.

7 For more on the fast follower's strategy, see Book 2, *The Makings of PMC Group* (Leadstart Publishing, 2024), Chapter 3.

which means that the owners of large corporations continue to extract undue benefit from capital.

Money was once considered a medium of exchange, but with the passage of time, it has come to mean capital and has assumed the most powerful role in business. In its newly assumed power, it has distanced itself from the so-called physical and intellectual factors of production. The disconnect became complete upon elimination of the convertibility of the dollar to gold in the US in 1971. Money, like the many-headed Hydra, became an all-powerful monster in commerce and business. Its importance far outweighed that of technology and labour. The federal government could print money without accountability as long as its foreign exchange rate didn't plummet. And access to money became an endeavour unto itself. Then another many-headed Hydra—this one called finance—took centre stage. It gave money the power to create more money, and it took the lever of money away from small businesses and gave it to large businesses.

The essence of finance—and a clever use of its power—is leverage. As money was liberated from any connection to physical and intellectual assets, a new connection was established—the connection of money with money. The liberated system allows banks to borrow money from the Federal Reserve at low interest rates and lend it to businesses at higher interest rates. All the bank needs to show the lender (the government) is that it has its own money, which of course comes from the deposits you and I make at the bank. If a bank can show it has five dollars, for example, it can borrow ninety-five dollars from the government at an abnormally low interest rate or even at zero interest or a negative interest rate. The bank can then lend the money to a business at a relatively low rate and still make a profit. This is a bank's profit and the core of its business—the difference between the income it makes from interest from the borrower and the interest it pays to the government. The problem lies in who can borrow money from the bank at a lower interest rate and in large quantities. If a business can borrow a lot of money, it can invest a lot and become rich.

Before we go any further, let's take a moment to introduce a new concept: Earnings Before Interest, Depreciation, Tax, and Amortization (EBIDTA).

A company's EBIDTA indicates its ability to pay its loan. Banks generally lend in multiples, say 2 x EBIDTA, 4 x EBIDTA, or 7 x EBIDTA.[8] To determine how much it will lend, a bank looks at a few factors, the most important among them being how much of their own money (equity) the borrower is willing to co-invest (the assumption here is that by investing their own money as equity, the borrower takes a risk before the bank assumes any risk) and how high the risk is that the business will fail and not be able to pay its debt. Regarding the second criterion, size matters. Recall that the Obama administration rescued Lehman Brothers and several other companies because they were "too big to fail". The argument was that such companies, particularly institutions with few real assets, were so connected with other businesses that their failure would be detrimental to the economy as a whole. So the government came to their rescue, making their loans secure.

While big businesses can get away with a small equity investment and still borrow large sums, small businesses often need to put up a big chunk of equity to borrow less and must pay a much higher interest rate. If you run a small business, this can make a big difference in the return you generate on

8 For a more detailed discussion, see Book 2 of this memoir series.

your equity, which is the ultimate measure of your success. Consider two companies—a big one and a small one—both earning the same EBIDTA margin, say 12 per cent on revenue. The big one is required to put up 10 per cent in equity to borrow 7 x EBIDTA at 3 per cent interest, while the small one is required to put up 50 per cent in equity to borrow 2 x EBIDTA at 5 per cent interest. A little arithmetic shows that the big one will enjoy a 93 per cent EBIDTA return on equity while the small one will achieve only a 19 per cent EBIDTA return on its equity, even though they run the same type of businesses with the same efficiency under the same market conditions to generate the same rate of EBIDTA return on total invested capital (equity plus borrowing). The big company now invests its extra earnings, and the difference between the two companies grows exponentially. This is raw "economic Darwinism" domination—of the weak by the most powerful—and fundamentally unfair. It can't be morally justified. The inevitable result is that wealth becomes concentrated in the hands of a few.

In the US, despite the egalitarian principles of the constitution, the top 1 per cent own 42.5 per cent of national wealth. While I have oversimplified the highly complex field of financing in the above example, the inequity is unmistakable. In fact, the more we probe the complexity of finance, the more unfairness we discover. Business finance was created to serve the interests of the owners of capital at the cost of everyone else.

You can argue that banks aren't supposed to be the guardians of morality. They're not responsible for treating small and big businesses differently in their lending practices. Their job is to reduce the risks associated with lending. There is, however, no reason why lending to small businesses would entail more risk than lending to big businesses. In fact, as I've already shown in the discussion of microfinance in Chapters 1 and 2, the opposite is true. Banks are wise to establish customized lending documents for each type of borrower, but no evidence suggests that small businesses are relatively more risk-prone.

Taxing big businesses more in order to bring parity is only a Band-Aid solution—akin to treating the symptom, not the cause. Some economists argue that the postwar proliferation of the middle class can be traced to high tax rates on corporations and the rich, but the effects were short-lived. Federal tax rates peaked during the Eisenhower administration, and corporations and the wealthy have learned how to shelter their money in tax havens abroad or take advantage of the complex tax code to cheat the system and hide their earnings (see Chapter 7). Meanwhile, the wealth gap persists.

The Immorality of Monopoly

A monopoly is, in my estimation, an immoral economic arrangement. Again, we can trace its roots to the unfair influence of capital. I've explored the definition of immorality in rigorous detail in Book 4. Here I will adopt a non-controversial definition: any action by which any group manipulates an economic arrangement to defraud or unfairly take advantage of others. Below I will explore four companies—Amazon, Facebook, Google, and Apple—that have done a great injustice to small businesses by perpetuating destructive monopolies.

Amazon.com: The Indian epic Mahabharata contains a mythology about the Hindu god of fire (Agni). As the story goes, ascetics perform yagna (sacrificial fire) in the forest using ghee (clarified butter) as sacrificial fuel, and Agni, after eating too much, develops indigestion and a dull appetite as a result. The other gods advise Agni to eat meat to get rid of his indigestion, so Agni seeks the help of the Pandava warriors to make sure that none of the animals can escape as it sets the Dandaka Forest ablaze. After turning the forest and the animals within it to ash, Agni emerges more vigorous than ever before, ready to devour other forests along with their animals.

The Amazon story unfolds in similar fashion. During the COVID-19 pandemic, the federal government put trillions of dollars in relief money into consumers' hands and then shut down brick-and-mortar stores and restaurants. With its home-delivery scheme, Amazon gobbled up the consumers' relief money while the government stood guard and made sure no small or medium-sized retail businesses could open their doors. No one, however, should underestimate the resiliency of the American people. New start-ups will sprout from the ashes of the destroyed businesses, and many of the businesses that barely survived will find a way to return to health. For the moment, however, great damage has been done to local businesses, some of which continue to struggle. Over a period of less than a year, Amazon mopped up an additional $146 billion value and increased its market worth by about $700 billion. With the government as its accomplice, Amazon had built a monopoly with a market cap of $1.6 trillion as of December 2020 and might one day gobble up other big giants like DHL, FedEx, and UPS.

To fund its massive growth, Amazon had no problem borrowing money at low interest rates. The lending institutions were eager to lend any amount Amazon wanted to borrow. It had two things in its favour: phenomenal growth and a too-big-to-fail economic footprint.

In the process of destroying small and medium businesses, Amazon also depleted the world's forests by using unprecedented amounts of cardboard boxes to ship its products. My wife, for example, ordered a two-ounce bottle of something in 2020, and it arrived in a cardboard box ten times its size. Cardboard, of course, is made primarily from wood pulp, and trees are essential for absorbing the greenhouse gas we generate: carbon dioxide. Our government has cast a blind eye towards the wanton destruction of our forests while lecturing us and the rest of the world on the need to cut greenhouse gases.

***Facebook and Google*:** Facebook and Google have amassed an enormous amount of data about people and have used that data to dominate the advertising business. In the process, unbeknown to their users, they have been systematically destroying traditional radio and print industries. Together they now control more than 60 per cent of the advertising market. Their owners want them to maintain their historical growth rate of 10 to 20 per cent or better. Aware that they can't get such growth from the remaining 40 per cent of the market, they have embarked upon creating new markets: fake news and fake products. In the name of freedom of speech, they will advertise anything for a price.

Facebook's 2020 market cap was $0.9 trillion and Google's was $1.5 trillion, which means customers have little power to restrain them. During 2020, several large advertisers like Walmart and Procter & Gamble decided to pull their ads from Facebook in protest against its promotion of hate speech and misinformation. But with more than seven million customers,

Facebook ignored the outrage. In fact, Facebook took revenge by granting market access to counterfeiters that took business away from the former advertisers.[9] Handling Congress and the government was easy. With his billions, Facebook's baby-faced owner, Mark Zuckerberg, wields enormous political power. He can freely enter the offices of the politically powerful in his flip-flops, ensuring that morality takes a back seat to naked capitalism.

***Apple*:** A prime example of price gouging, Apple has created a near monopoly in the cellphone business. Through the clever and skilful bundling of several electronic features in a single product, it has made the iPhone the most profitable manufactured product ever made. While most manufacturing businesses did poorly due to the COVID-19 pandemic, Apple increased its market cap from $1.28 trillion in 2019 to $2.25 trillion in 2020—a whopping 76 per cent increase in just one year. This growth in value was not the result of groundbreaking scientific discoveries; it was a marketing gimmick that incorporated countless electronic features and coproducts—Apple TV, Arcade, Camera, Calculator, Weather Report, *International Times*, News, GPS, iCloud, Apple Music, etc.—into one product that made it convenient to access any and all information from one source. Its success rests on the ashes of countless other businesses, including local journals and newspapers. The younger generation is hooked to these conveniences and in danger of losing an in-depth understanding of issues that require detailed study.

---

9 Galloway, 2020, pp. 78–80.

Anything Scalable Will Not Escape Monopoly

I used the above four cases to exemplify the naked greed of big corporations, which are determined to grow ever more rich by destroying anything that stands in their way. In fact, when it comes to unrestrained capitalism, anything scalable will fall into the hands of the owners of big capital.

Consider the lawn maintenance business in the US. We used to hire local contractors to cut, weed, and fertilize our lawns. These businesses provided livelihoods for thousands of small business owners and employed their family members and individual labourers. Upon discovering that the weed-killing and fertilization part of the lawn care business could be scaled, a leveraged buyout firm started TruGreen and used a massive advertising campaign to steal most of the lawn maintenance businesses from small contractors.

When I drive through the Midwest and the Southeast, I find another ominous development in the US. Wawa and Royal Farms, two giant corporations supported by the awesome financial power of private equity, are building massive gas stations and forcing the individually owned gas stations that have served us since the beginning of the automobile industry to close. Meanwhile, other private-equity-funded monopolies like Pep Boys are gobbling up the car service business formerly run by the individual gas stations. The supporters of these monopolies insist on a fundamental lie—that economies of scale bring lower prices. But once the small businesses have been destroyed, price gouging starts and there is no way to control it.

Am I against capital or capital investment? The answer is a categorical no. I'm against manipulating capital and depriving millions of the fruits of capital formation. But in the current system, a minority of people, operating under the mantra of survival of the fittest, have manipulated capitalism to destroy the interests of the majority.

Capitalism's Second Sin: Devaluing Labour

The most damning indictment of capitalism is the way it treats the working class. Recall that in his subsistence theory of wages, which he called the Iron Law of Wages, David Ricardo proposed that labour's wages should consist only of what will be required "to bring the worker into being as a worker and sustaining him in the job". By labour, he meant all wage earners—the people that make a factory function in return for a salary. To Ricardo, a more important issue was the return on capital to the capitalist that supported the factory. This included not only shares of the "excess value" (profit) but also generous payment for the machines and equipment used in production. With combined returns on capital and equipment, the newly rich in industrial England enjoyed a period of exuberant and ostentatious excess, while the working class was pushed to the lowest rung of the value chain. Treating the working class like inanimate cogs of production without any rights is morally abhorrent and flies in the face of the principles of justice that so many egalitarian economists—among them John Dewey, John Rawls, and Amartya Sen—have defended in their writings.[10]

As explored in the previous chapter, Thomas Robert Malthus and John Stuart Mill, the other two architects of the

10 Dewey, 1989; Kukathas and Pettit, 1990; Sen, 1988, 1992, 2009.

classical economic tradition, degraded the status of labour even further.

And such attitudes remain prevalent in some corners of the world even today. As Yunus observed in Bangladesh, "The trader made certain that he paid Sufiya a price that barely covered the cost of the materials and was just enough to keep her alive."[11] The trader is the bourgeois of the modern era. The evils of capitalism didn't die with Malthus or Mill; they have permeated even the world's poorest economies.

Against mounting criticism, the defenders of the classical tradition took their last line of defence, calling economics a science that need not conform to any moral judgements. Like any other science, they argued, it should be separated from the concerns of justice and injustice, pain and hardship. Instead, its value should be judged in mathematical terms that exclude morality.[12] But unlike physics, chemistry, or biology, economics is not a hard science. If it were, its results should be reproducible over time. If it were, how could Milton Friedman and Robert Solow each win a Nobel Prize while proposing opposing economic policies to address economic downturns? Robert Solow, although speaking humorously, told the truth about economics: "If economics is limited to doctrines that are true forever, then I am afraid there is nothing to economics at all. Economies change over time and work in ways a poor economist cannot understand."[13] Calling economics a mathematical science is even more inaccurate. The use of mathematical and statistical tools in economic analysis says nothing about the quality of data—the raw material

---

11 Yunus, 1999, p. 48.

12 Galbraith, 1987, pp. 124–25.

13 Klamer, 1983, p. 55.

of economics—that these tools are tasked to analyse. When the methods used for the generation of the input data do not satisfy the conditions of scientific rigour, the use of accurate tools of mathematics and statistics does not qualify them as mathematical and statistical science.

Disturbingly, some renowned economists don't even care about using imperfect data. Donald McCloskey, distinguished professor of economic history at the University of Chicago, wrote the following about Nobel laureate Paul Samuelson, one of the most respected scholars of our time: "Samuelson may have sent economics off in the wrong direction by trying to derive quantitative theorems without spending any time with facts."[14] Milton Friedman's disdain for rigorousness of data showed in his comments: "…assumptions do not matter and accepting models that explain is crucial, rather than all the facts."[15] Statements like "assumptions do not matter" warn us of the risks we encounter in taking economists' recommendations at face value. Take the case of financial derivatives. In the name of reducing risk, economists devised complex mathematical models to rationalize the derivatives market that eventually caused the Great Recession of 2008. Several of these economists—Harry Markowitz, Robert Merton, and Myron Scholes—won the Nobel Prize in economics for their mathematical wizardry.[16] The incalculable damage caused by these economists is still fresh in our memory.

By criticizing the way economists have represented their field, I don't mean to degrade the importance of mathematics. To the contrary, I believe mathematics is more fundamental

---

14 McCloskey, 1989, p. 12.

15 Samuelson, 1970, p. 9.

16 Greenspan and Wooldridge, 2018, p. 383.

than any science. It explains phenomena in our universe and beyond in a logical way. It applies to things both real and imaginary and binds them in the same immutable and unfailing algorithms. In this sense, it is higher than material reality. It is also the source of structure in music, poetry, and other artistic expression, endowing our minds with similar structures so that we can enjoy with ecstasy art's hidden algorithms. The algorithms of mathematics are like a black box, but they are of unchangeable logic. They can take us through blind alleys to destinations that are infinitely similar and accurate every time we apply them to the same problem. The algorithms of mathematics are unchangeable and eternal and thus might have existed before the creation of our universe.

When physical scientists apply mathematics to the verified facts of our universe, an unmistakable pattern matches those facts to the minutest of details, and the pattern becomes part of our inventory of facts. If we apply mathematical tools to hypothetical assumptions, they give us a pattern that matches the assumptions, and the same pattern is revealed as long as we use the same assumptions. Economists can use mathematical tools to devise sophisticated patterns of economic arrangements, but these patterns remain hypothetical as long as the mathematical tools are applied to hypothetical assumptions. It is for this reason we see different economic arrangements from different economists. Even though these arrangements are internally consistent, they remain hypothetical and can never be called science.

Defenders of the mistreatment of labour unwittingly fall into the trap of treating morality as if it emanates from the laws of nature. They forget that nature is amoral. Morality is a human construct. But nature *does* provide us with deep-seated patterns that can help us describe the workings of society. When we confuse products (economic arrangements and culture) and process (the method by which we arrive at those products), we are capable of committing crimes against humanity, aided by the false premises propagated by people like Karl Marx, who called for banning religion, and his followers. Bringing back religion and proper spiritual, ethical, and moral reformations could strengthen our humanity and lead to a just world. But in this book I will base my arguments on observable facts and eschew religion and spirituality.

In their approach to improving economic productivity, Ricardo and Malthus degraded labour to the level of other factors of productivity that should be purchased at the minimum possible price. While they reduced the industrial workforce to the status of inanimate cogs, they thought all profits should go to the limited number of factory owners—the capitalists, in modern lingo. A huge divide was thus created between the bourgeoisie and the proletariat, which made the rise of Karl Marx inevitable. The pendulum swung from capitalism to communism, but while the latter turned everything upside down, it produced an even more flawed system.

To redress their maltreatment, workers in the capitalist system formed unions and used their collective bargaining power to regain a place at the table, but unionization degraded the quality of labour input. Our educational institutions, for example, suffer when teachers' unions and the tenure system protect teachers from accountability.

In theory, modern corporations are run by hired employees—from the janitors to the CEOs. A corporation is thus a collection of its workforce. But distribution of wages to employees varies astronomically. CEO remuneration in many American corporations is often a thousand times the remuneration of the lowest-level employee. Is such special treatment of the CEO and a few other top executives justified by their technical or administrative skills? Having once served at the top executive level of one of the largest public companies, I can assure you the answer is no. Such extraordinary remunerations are designed to keep the top management aligned with the ownership's interest. Ownership, although called pubic, consists of only a handful of institutional investors, whose only goal is to increase the return on their equity in the shortest term. But a public corporation has an obligation to enhance the comprehensive interests of all its stakeholders, including employees and the community at large. The lopsided distribution of remuneration flies in the face of John Rawls's concept of justice and inspired me to form what I called a corporation with a soul (described in detail in Book 2 of this memoir).

Capitalism's Third Sin: Wall Street Highjacked the Term *Technology*

Have you heard the term *asset-light strategy*? We've talked already about how big businesses make a profit by leveraging other people's money (borrowed money). With asset-light strategy, they do business with not just other people's money but with other people's physical assets as well. To give their strategy an air of respectability, they call it, with Wall Street's indulgence, technology (tech) business.

What Wall Street really means by tech business is something that deals with software and computers. The new definition excludes the avalanche of new products and advancements that follow inventions in physics, chemistry, and biology. It excludes the genius of theorists like Einstein, whose discoveries paved the way for nuclear power, space exploration, and many modern products and services, including the television. It excludes the invention of drugs that have increased the average life expectancy of a white male in the US by 60 per cent (from forty-nine to seventy-seven years) and a black male by more than 110 per cent (from thirty-four to seventy-two years) in a span of just 110 years. It excludes the skills and techniques used by the labourers, earning meagre wages while they hang from harnesses, who build our houses and offices. It excludes advancements in air conditioning and refrigeration, washing machines and modern plumbing, food production and preservation, hygiene products, landscaping and gardening, swimming pools, steel and plastics, fabrics and clothing, chemical additives, oleochemicals, rubber, and paper printing. The new definition of technology by Wall Street means only information technology. What will such a misguided notion mean for society in the long run? How will it skew our priorities? Few can read the writing on the wall.

When Robert Solow and Edward Denison talked about technology, they talked about any technology that makes a substantive impact on our lives. More than 99 per cent of our workforce is employed in industries like the ones I described above, but together they own less than 45 per cent of our country's wealth.

Unfortunately, "new tech" has infiltrated every product and service mentioned above, presumably to make them more user-friendly. In doing so, it has made our basic technology impotent—as if the tail is now wagging the dog. I took one of my family's cars to the dealership for service recently and found the parking lot empty of any new cars. When I inquired, the manager told me that no car company is shipping new cars—because there is a shortage of microchips. So the metal and plastic that make up the car, the technology and chemicals that go into making the tyres, and the engine block and the engineering that make it function—all are held hostage by a small microchip designed to minimize manual operations and add comfort.

"Can you get me a car that doesn't need a microchip to operate?" I asked, wondering if it was possible to buy a car that operated like cars did thirty years ago.

"No," he said. "The technology is gone. It's been made dependent on the microchip."

In other words, most of what makes a car has become inoperative due to the addition of the microchip. Worse, the microchip shortage has put a major industry—possibly the largest manufacturing industry—at risk, potentially displacing millions of workers, from salespeople to mechanics. It won't end there. Our homes are the tech companies' next target. They want to make our houses "smart", adding some bells and whistles to them so that they can control us at home. Such bells and whistles would have been fine had they not removed my options and then engaged in price gouging. Under the guise of the freedom of capitalism, they steal freedom from millions without remorse or accountability. They already control our power grids, our oil transportation system, and our military operations. One of our nation's gas pipelines was hacked recently, sending gas prices through the roof. Like tremors that presage the coming of a big earthquake, such incidents foreshadow something ominous. The US rid itself of slavery, only to become slaves of information technology, which has no conscience and is controlled by a few immoral capitalists and Wall Streeters.

We spoke of Facebook earlier. Who is rewarded by its shady monopoly of advertisement? Nobody more than Zuckerberg, who is worth $121 billion—about ten times the GDP of Palestine! What does he earn? By some estimates $1.7 million an hour in 2020—the equivalent of 170,000 minimum wage workers' hourly earnings. Now consider Jeff Bezos, Amazon's owner. He increased his wealth by $35 billion in thirty days, easily offsetting the cost of his divorce, the most expensive in history.[17] Did either of these owners give us new technology? No. They gave us zip, nothing. By cleverly exploiting existing technology that Robert Solow called "technological changes in the broadest sense"—technology built largely on the "common pool of technological progress" that belongs to the general public—and by claiming their companies belonged to the tech business, they amassed obscene profits. If this isn't a travesty of economic justice, I don't know what is. When it comes to criminal justice, our system operates from a sense of proportionality. We don't hang a person for stealing an apple. Nor do we give a murderer a mere slap of the wrist and then let them go free. Capitalism, in contrast, lacks any such balance.

As Solow points out, much of the technology that fuels our economy belongs to a common pool that is accessible to all. Such technology must be considered a national asset and should belong equally to everyone. New technology, on the other hand, plays only a limited role in supporting our society. No amount of rationalization—even if it's concocted in the name of capitalism—can justify a small cadre of innovators who know how to manipulate common technology amassing nearly all the benefits of technology.

Am I against information technology? Absolutely not. I'm against granting it the monopolistic power to control

---

17 Galloway, 2020, p. 650.

other technologies and industries. And I'm against the way its purveyors have exploited the system to form all-powerful monopolies that shape society at every turn. As alarming as it might sound, tech businesses' exploitation of modern capitalism makes the case for revolution in the US. Such a development would be unfortunate, for if history has taught us anything, it's that the pendulum always swings the other way eventually, and a revolution could set progress back by several decades.

Capitalism's Immorality on a National Level

The immorality of capitalism can be studied not only on the individual and corporate levels but also on a national scale, particularly in America, where, according to 2019 figures, less than 5 per cent of the world's population owns between 50 and 70 per cent of the world's capital. The numbers might have grown since. Politicians tell us—and many believe them—that we own such a large share of the world's capital because of American exceptionalism.

What is the source of this exceptionalism? Is it the educational genius of our population? Doubtful. According to the Organization of Economic Cooperation and Development (OECD), the top five most-educated countries—those countries whose people have finished two-year or four-year college—are Canada, Japan, Israel, Korea, and the United Kingdom, with Canada being the most educated nation on the planet. The US ranks only sixth. Is it the superior technological knowledge of our educated class? If we analyse Americans educated in science and technology, we find that most are foreign-born first-generation immigrants, with Asian Americans topping the list. Those holding the most advanced science and engineering degrees in the US are from India (25 per cent) and China (10 per cent). In academia, about half (49 per cent) of US-trained postdoctoral research associates were born overseas, according to the National Science Board in 2020. Thus, if American exceptionalism emanates from a superior command of science and technology, credit should go to India and China for exporting so many students to the US. Moreover, if that were the case, India and China, not the US, would dominate the world's economy. But they don't—far from it. Is it America's natural resources? Unlikely, given that the exceptionalism would belong to "the rocks in the sand", namely, to those Arab countries that are awash in oil deposits.

Of course, we could measure a country's greatness not by a single measure but by a cumulative one. Moreover, it could owe its success to its people having the freedom to run their lives and their businesses as they see fit. But American exceptionalism, I would contend, is largely a myth—one that hides the immorality embedded in our economic dominance of the world. The more we study America's success on the world's economic stage, the more we find that it looks like a Ponzi scheme rather than something born from the genius of a nation.

What is a Ponzi scheme? It's an economic scam in which a con artist promises a high return on invested capital by paying the early investors from new investment proceeds. The scheme is named after a 1920s con artist, Charles Ponzi, who extorted huge sums of money from investors with the promise of a 50 per cent return, falsely claiming that he had a lucrative international mail coupon business. A Ponzi scheme's existence depends on the creation of a false sense of security and creditworthiness in the minds of the investors, which is gained through prompt payment of withdrawals. The success of a Ponzi scheme depends on the premise that there will be more new investors than those who want to cash in on their investment. The scheme falls apart when investors discover its fraudulent nature and ask for a refund of their investments en masse. According to estimates, Bernie Madoff, the most celebrated Ponzi scheme artist of modern times, raised more than $50 billion on a Ponzi scheme before his bluff was called and he was given a jail sentence of 150 years. Bernie died in jail on 14 April 2021, after destroying the life savings of many middle-class people who had invested in his scam. The telltale sign of a Ponzi scheme is an ever-increasing rate of borrowing, which is necessary to pay for its current expenses and the demands of earlier investors.

Let's take a look at how America, the wealthiest nation on Earth, props up its economy. When we catch a whiff of America's financial power, it smells a lot like a Ponzi scheme. America's national debt, shown in the following table, tells the story.

It's clear the US has been living on borrowed money for a long time. With the exception of the last three years of Bill Clinton's presidency, every administration since Jimmy Carter's (1977–81) has run a budget deficit. Each presidential candidate talks about balancing the budget but once in office, finds comfort in borrowing. Ronald Reagan campaigned against "out-of-control US debt", which he said was as big as "a stack of one-thousand-dollar bills sixty-seven miles high".[18] But during his eight years in office (1981–89), he increased the national debt from about $1 trillion to $3 trillion. In more recent years,

18 Gross National Debt (https://zfacts.com).

America's Growing National Debt (in Billions of Dollars)

Year	**1980**	**1990**	**2000**	**2005**	**2010**	**2015**	**2016**	**2017**	**2018**	**2019**	**2020**	**2021**
Debt	***907***	***3,233***	***3,569***	***7,913***	***13,551***	***18,138***	***19,560***	***20,233***	***21,506***	***22,711***	***26,938***	***29,000***
Debt as percent of GDP	**33**	**55**	***56***	***62***	***91***	***100***	***105***	***105***	***106***	***107***	***121***	***125***

we have been borrowing and spending like drunken sailors. In just one year, between 2019 and 2020, the US increased its debt by $4.2 trillion. At the time of this writing, the 2022 Congress wants to spend an additional $5 trillion to $7 trillion—again with new borrowings. No wonder US debt as a percentage of GDP is the highest among the advanced economies: US 103 per cent, Eurozone 85 per cent, UK 85 per cent, Russia 18 per cent.[19]

Apologists argue that our debt is spaced over ten years and that the US, with an economy of $22.5 trillion, can afford to borrow $30 trillion or more. They tell us that corporations often borrow at the level of their revenue. What they forget to mention is that before a business can borrow, it must first show that its profit will be sufficient to pay back both interest and principal on time every year. No one will lend a penny to a business that keeps losing money. The US has been running a budget deficit for a long time, and Congress has to raise the debt ceiling every year to keep the country running.

Apologists also tell us that Keynes supported deficit spending. But there is a big difference between habitual deficit spending and what Keynes recommended, which was to use deficit spending in times of economic crisis to speed recovery. Yes, Keynes recommended deficit spending to create consumer demand and stimulate production, but the US government flooded the country with cash in 2020–21 while shutting down restaurants, bars, and retail shops. If borrowing is bad, how come our stock market boomed in early 2022, reaching an all-time record? Recall what the Keynesians said about government overspending. When the government puts excess money in consumers' hands—more than what is needed for expenses and more than what can be spent on goods and services—the

---

19 *Wall Street Journal*, 23 February 2022, p. A8.

surplus goes to the stock market, inflating its value. No wonder the stock market boomed! Too much cash was chasing a fixed number of stocks.

Economists will no doubt debate for many years to come the efficacy of the federal government's response to the COVID-19 pandemic. But my point transcends the current crisis: no Ponzi scheme can go on forever. Sooner or later, it will have come to an end, and when it does, it will be a rude awakening. For the US, it could mean high interest rates and hyperinflation. Our next generations will have to pay for the sins of the present.

As mentioned in Chapter 1, the central bank (the Fed in the US) is charged with managing a country's money supply and thus has nearly unlimited power to create as much money as it wants. Its only constraint is the fear of inflation. Creating too much money can lead to inflation as excess cash chases too few goods and services. However, as pointed out earlier, often a time lag occurs between an increase in the money supply and the onset of inflation. Often the Congress and administration responsible for overspending are replaced by a new Congress and a new administration before inflation arrives. The new administration typically takes the easy way out by borrowing more to pay for the earlier misdeeds.

Why can't other countries create as much money as they want? Because the US dollar is still considered the most stable and thus retains the status of being the world's reserve currency. Such a status gives the US extraordinary spending power, which the US continues to exploit, but that power cannot last forever. To fully appreciate what this means, let's take a step back and look at the history of major currencies, particularly the US dollar, since the beginning of the twentieth century.

On 14 March 1900, the US officially adopted the gold standard, which pegged the value of the dollar to a certain weight of gold, and maintained enough gold reserve to back up its currency. Most of Europe's industrial economies had adopted the gold standard three decades earlier, and the US was forced to follow suit in order to continue conducting international commerce. As the US economy grew, it became the largest in the world, surpassing Britain's. To manage its currency in such a fast-growing economy, the US created the Federal Reserve in 1913. As parts of its framework of operation, the Fed held 40 per cent of the value of the dollar it issued in gold. However, Britain still retained its place as the centre of world commerce, with the majority of international transactions still using the British pound.

All of that changed when war broke out in Europe in 1914. To fund their military expenses, many countries abandoned the gold standard and bought US bonds, which the US was willing to sell in return for their gold reserve. Thus, by the end of World War I, the US owned a vast amount of the world's gold and had enough gold reserve to back all of its issued currency.

Britain, which had never borrowed money before, was also forced to abandon the gold standard in 1919, and the US dollar replaced the British pound as the world's leading currency of commerce. The Great Depression of the 1930s shook people's confidence in bank deposits and led to a march of individuals and firms in the US and overseas to redeem their dollar holdings in gold. To stop this unprecedented flow of gold from the Federal Reserve, President Franklin D. Roosevelt temporarily suspended the gold standard in April 1933, made private ownership of gold illegal, and began buying back at a higher price the gold that had left the Federal Reserve. Later that same year, the US reinstituted the gold standard after devaluing the dollar relative to gold, from $20.67 to $35.00 per ounce. The US also played a clever trick. Although it devalued its own currency, it held other nations to their earlier rate of conversion to gold. Such an arrogant exercise of its financial power was possible because the US held most of world's gold reserve.

As World War II destroyed most of whatever was left of the world economy, forty-four countries from around the world met in the New Hampshire resort town of Bretton Woods in 1944 to agree on an international foreign exchange system. The two orchestrators of the conference—the renowned British economist John Maynard Keynes and the US Treasury Department's Harry Dexter White—clashed over the nature of a reserve currency, with Keynes preferring a new international currency (to be called the bancor) and White preferring to make the US dollar the reserve currency. Ultimately, White's view prevailed, for he had America's financial might behind him. As a result, the US dollar was pegged to gold ($35/oz), and all other currencies were pegged to the US dollar. The Bretton Woods Agreement crowned the US dollar as the official reserve currency of the world, but no one would understand the full implication of the arrangement for decades.

The Nixon administration scrapped the Bretton Woods Agreement in 1971 to cope with the increasing demand of the dollar, thus permanently eliminating the gold standard. The dollar was no longer convertible to gold, its only backing is the sovereign power of the United States of America. But the gold standard's ghost, the US dollar as the world's reserve currency, lingers even today. The dollar's newly anointed status meant that nations had to buy the US dollar and conduct international transactions in dollars, and soon the US became the storehouse of much of the world's capital. Thus the US had the freedom to create as much capital as it wished with few restrictions aside from its fear of inflation.

So let's return to the question asked earlier: Why can't other countries borrow and spend the way the US does? Because their economies are so small in comparison that no one would buy their debt if it became too high. The doctrine of economic Darwinism is embedded in capitalism and ensures that the strong dominate the weak.

During World War II, the US asked its citizens to make sacrifices, and the public responded by buying government bonds. The money so raised provided the funds needed to make munitions and sell them to the Allied forces on credit. By 1944, US national debt had reached a historical high. But the US was forced to act responsibly, thanks to the gold standard, and steadily reduced its debt until 1971, the year it abolished the gold standard. Thereafter, the national debt began to grow once more. Recently, the US realized it could create as much money as it wants by issuing treasury bonds.

The raw power of capitalism gives money the power to create more money in a shameless and irresponsible way. In the name of liberalism, politicians commit the worst crime of capitalism by urging the country to borrow and spend additional trillions of dollars on the welfare system in the US, already the richest country in the world. Some, like Senator Bernie Sanders (Independent, Vermont), want to raise such huge amounts by increasing taxes on US corporations, but such an endeavour would ruin US industries. In any case, every Congress, whether controlled by Democrats or Republicans, has increased national debt to meet increased spending.

Let's look at the sources of these borrowings. About 25 per cent of US national debt is owned by foreign nations, 40 per cent by Americans, and the rest by the federal government's general fund, which includes the Social Security Trust Fund, the Military Retirement Fund, and so on. In any case, the debt is not only unsustainable but unethical. The immorality of the American financial structure can be traced to three deceits:

1. The fund the federal government borrows from isn't supported by any assets. When you borrow money to make a significant purchase, you put your car or your house up as collateral. The US does no such thing.
2. The US knows it doesn't have the ability to pay back the money it has borrowed and still continues to borrow. It has been running a budget deficit for many years, and the size of the deficit is only increasing every year.
3. The US knows it will have to borrow more to retire any of its past debt.

If we take these three factors into consideration, Bernie Madoff's Ponzi scheme pales in comparison. While the gold standard was in place, the US had to restrain its worst impulses. But since 1971, the US has been running a Ponzi scheme, and no Ponzi scheme can last forever. When the shallow funding is exposed, a mass exodus will cause a collapse. When the US finally reaches a tipping point—and that day might be just around the corner—the repercussions will perhaps include high inflation, sky-high interest rates, and possibly high unemployment. China, which owns the lion's share of US bonds, could trigger the collapse. Regardless, if the US, the world's biggest economy, faces trouble, it will drag down the rest of the free world with it. And just as the Soviet economy escaped the wrath of the Great Depression, China might escape the wrath of any such future disaster. In preparation, China is shifting its economy from being export-driven to domestic-consumption-driven.

Am I advocating for the reinstitution of the gold standard or a nationalist economy? Not quite. Gold as a standard had its own problem. But some other standard has to be put into place if we are to avoid another great disaster. I also recommend that we develop a firmer framework of political economy and "guarded free trade" now so that we will be ready to make the changes when the time arrives. By guarded free trade, I mean restricting free trade when it comes to heathcare and defence needs so that we don't put the country at risk if our political relations with our trading partners sour in the future. At the present, we are dangerously dependent on China's manufacturing power for many of our medical and defence needs.

America's Internal Response to Capitalism's Immorality

As we have observed, although capitalism in the US has created enormous wealth, much of it borrowed, it has failed to equitably distribute that wealth among its people. Such a failure amounts to a betrayal of the Declaration of Independence, which stated that all men are created equal. To achieve a more equitable distribution of wealth, the US has gradually introduced various Band-Aid solutions in the form of entitlement or welfare programmes. But such programmess haven't changed the lopsided distribution of wealth. According to a September 2017 study by the Federal Reserve, the top 1 per cent of people in the US owned 38.5 per cent of the country's wealth in 2016—

this despite an increasing number of welfare programmes introduced since the Great Depression. If anything, such welfare programmes made the overall economy worse by lowering economic output at the aggregate level.

America's persistent lopsided distribution of wealth has inspired a political movement in the country that wishes to adopt western Europe's marriage of socialist programmes with a capitalist framework. If we look at Europe's experience, it seems inevitable that better distribution of wealth in the US through further increasing entitlements will come at the cost of significantly lowering GDP. The entitlements will be paid for by higher taxes and borrowing. Perhaps entitlement-based wealth distribution will make the average person more equal, but everyone will be poorer, for by definition, entitlements lower people productivity.

Is Capitalism's Fundamental Formula Wrong?

Some might ask the following: Is the basic macroeconomic formula of capitalism inherently immoral? The formula, as shown below, is a factual representation of the factors involved in determining GNP:

$$GNP = C + I + G + X + Z$$

where

C = consumption; I = investment; G = government expenditure; X = net export; and Z = net income earned by domestic residents from overseas investments minus net income earned by foreign residents from domestic investments.

I find it disturbing that modern capitalism, particularly the type we practise in the US, puts arbitrary relative weights on the three primary contributors of economic growth: capital,[20] labour, and total factor productivity.[21]

Contributors of Economic Growth = Capital + Labour + Total Factor Productivity

I'm less disturbed by capitalism's assertion that, for the economy to work, there has to be an uneven distribution of wealth, with the investor owning more and the labourer less. That said, the *size* of that disparity concerns me. How much economic disparity is morally acceptable? How much is not? I want to determine the minimum degree of disparity needed to produce maximum output. I also want to test the appropriateness of the weight assigned to the different factors of economic growth in our version of capitalism. Are the fruits of economic growth fairly distributed among the various stakeholders? Can we design a better system to treat each contributor—the owners, managers, and labourers—with dignity?

---

20 In the original steady-state growth theories, capital meant savings; it was assumed that only savings could generate deployable capital. In modern capitalism, capital has assumed an independent status because big corporations can increase it by borrowing and the US can increase it by simply printing more money.

21 Total factor productivity is the same as what Robert Solow called "technical progress in the broadest sense", which could be broken into "differentiating technology" and "undifferentiated technology", the former being proprietary to the differentiators and the latter being public property.

The Mixed Arrangements

As mentioned earlier, communism—and by extension, socialism—is impotent in the creation of wealth. Because of that impotency, several communist countries have adopted some of the tools of capitalism within their communist framework. Similarly, many capitalist countries have adopted socialist tools to make them more equitable. Such fusions have created some of the worst economic models possible, with modern China, Russia, and France being three prime examples.

China: An Uneasy Mix of Communism and Capitalism

Modern China represents the worst of both capitalism and communism. As the country adopted Marxist principles beginning with the Chinese Revolution in 1949 under Mao Zedong—wiping out private property and forcibly implementing wealth redistribution—it reduced wealth inequity but at a punishingly high cost. Millions of Chinese died of starvation, and millions more were plunged into extreme poverty as national income sank and China's relative economic position deteriorated in comparison to those of the capitalist countries of the West. It remained so until 1976, when the country's leaders, realizing that their economic system wasn't working, adopted several capitalist tools—private property, market-oriented reforms, entrepreneurship—without giving up autocratic control over the population.

I travelled to China in 2006 to determine if PMC Group should start rubber chemicals operations in China, which was wooing foreign investment in its manufacturing sector. Abject poverty ravaged the countryside. But in the cities, where the number of billionaires was on the rise, I saw countless five-star hotels. Adopting capitalist tools had led to economic growth *and* income inequality.

Now, according to a front-page article in the 5 November 2021 issue of the *Wall Street Journal*, China, the world's second largest economy, boasts "more than 1,000 billionaires, surpassing the US". As of 2020, China's top 1 per cent of income earners own about 30 per cent of the country's wealth (in the US, the top 1 per cent owned 35 per cent of America's wealth in the same year). The disparity will only get worse as capital and the means to gain a higher education becomes possible only for a privileged few, i.e., those that belong to the centres of economic and political power. Like the US, China now also deems some of its companies "too big to fail". Jack Ma, founder of Alibaba Group Holding, is one of the richest persons in the world and Alibaba one of the biggest companies.

Such an explosive mix of the worst aspects of two economic systems could lead to another revolution. It could also lead to a major war. The two world wars taught us that an autocrat will do anything to hang on to power, including shifting the nation's focus towards an outside "enemy". Unfortunately, neither revolution nor war can deliver wealth creation and equitable distribution simultaneously. We will need a new model of political economy to achieve this twin objective.

Russia: A Living Example of a Failed Economic Arrangement

Communism doesn't stop human greed, which merely shifts from the capitalist lords to the handful of elites that control the government. Within its communist structure, it practises what can be called "state capitalism". The system, meanwhile, guarantees that human ingenuity is lost because of a lack of incentive to work and, more importantly, a lack of individual freedom. Russia, the first country to adopt communism, still remains essentially an autocratic communist country under a thin veil of capitalism. It boasts few functioning industries. It derives most of its income from mineral resources—oil, gas, and others—that it sells to the industrially developed world.

Russia makes its common people more equal by making most of them poor. Its ruling elite and the oligarchs that support them squander the country's wealth. Russia's elites, among the richest of the rich, own some of the biggest, most luxurious mansions and yachts in the world. Russian billionaire Gennady Timchenko owns one of the world's largest yachts, a 469-foot vessel with eight decks and several elevators. Russian oligarch Alexey Mordashov owns a 465-foot super-yacht with two helipads and luxury accommodations for thirty-six guests. The list goes on. Their wealth is protected by Vladimir Putin himself, who reportedly owns the biggest mansion on Earth. Communism survives through autocratic control.

Communism, the worst economic arrangement ever created, doesn't create wealth by using human ingenuity. It births super-rich elites and provides equality to the rest of the people in the graveyard of poverty. In 2001, when I was expanding PMC Group's manufacturing presence around the world, I travelled to Russia to see if we should invest in manufacturing facilities there. I returned home convinced that, as long as the ghost of communism persists in Russia, it will provide no opportunity for creative business endeavours. Russia remains a dysfunctional economic arrangement that neither creates wealth nor provides equal opportunity to all.

France: A Swing of the Economic Pendulum to the Left

In France, socialist values have penetrated its capitalist framework so deeply that the country's growth has slowed to a crawl. The balance of power has shifted away from the capitalists towards organized labour. As a result, France's labour productivity has ossified, which has had a devastating effect on its global competitiveness. The same trend is overtaking many other European countries.

Concluding Remarks

Communism and socialism are failed systems, and modern capitalism, although preferable, has degenerated into an immoral system that continues to widen the gap between the haves and the have-nots. Now that we have taken a deep dive into today's economic arrangements and discovered their deficiencies, we are ready to imagine another system that not only generates wealth but distributes it fairly to the people.

5

The Laws of Nature: Thermodynamics

My first day of college was also my first day of formal schooling. During the upheaval of World War II and the communal riots that engulfed India following independence, my family experienced its own share of turmoil as we moved from place to place: first Myanmar, then our ancestral home in a village in East Bengal, then Agartala, and finally Kolkata. Even after arriving in Kolkata, we moved from one apartment to another. Taught at home without formally joining a school, I passed the school final examination as a private student at the age of twelve and entered college at thirteen, enrolling as a science student in what was known as the intermediate course.

Every science lecture room at Surendranath College featured a room-wide lab bench that separated the students' sitting area from the professor, who lectured from the other side of the bench with a huge blackboard behind him. On the morning of the first day in college, I raced to the front of the sitting area of my physics class, eager to soak up everything I had missed while being educated at home.

The professor, in his thirties, stood about five feet and ten inches tall and boasted a medium build and a fair complexion. His name was Kalipada Datta, but we would call him KPD for short. He sported a thick moustache, which, combined with his dark-framed glasses, gave his face a sombre expression. He spoke in a deep voice, measuring his words. When he talked, everyone listened.

"Class," he began, "can you determine the volume of a cube with sides measuring four centimetres?"

We did as we were asked, with everyone offering the same answer: 4cm x 4cm x 4cm = 64 cubic centimetres. Then we completed another rudimentary exercise, determining the volume of a rectangular box 4cm wide, 6cm high, and 8cm long: 192 cubic centimetres.

"Well done," he said. "Now do the same for a sphere with a radius of four centimetres, approximating to the first decimal point."

Everyone wrote down the formula—volume of a sphere = $4/3 \times \Pi \times r^3$—and, using the value of $\Pi=3.1416$ and radius=4cm, calculated the volume at 268.1 cubic centimetres. Next, we correctly determined the volume of a cylinder with a radius of 4cm and a length of 4cm (201.1 cubic centimetres), using the formula $\Pi \times r^2 \times l$ (r = radius, l = length).

"Wonderful!" our professor said with a pleased smile. "It's clear you are all prepared for this class. You know your geometry well. Can you calculate the volume of a cylinder with a radius of four centimetres and a length of six centimetres?"

No such thing as a hand calculator existed back then, so once again, most of the students bent their heads and began working the equation—$3.1416 \times 4^2 \times 6$—by hand. Most of them would need a couple of minutes to determine the answer.

But I needed only a second and announced, "Three hundred and one point six cubic centimetres."

My classmates looked up from their work, barely begun. I could feel their eyes on me as they stared at me in awe.

"Is he some kind of genius?" a student behind me whispered.

"He must be a spy of the professor," another whispered as others murmured in disbelief.

"Yes," another student agreed. "Here to embarrass the rest of us."

After everyone had worked through the problem, KPD addressed me directly. "How were you able to solve the problem so promptly while the others took so long?"

"I broke the cylinder into two pieces," I said, "one of which we'd already determined the volume for and the other of which was half its size. Then I multiplied the first answer by one point five."

I wasn't a genius. Or a spy. I had merely found an easier—and quicker—way to solve the problem.

"Congratulations!" KPD said and then turned to the rest of the students. "It often helps to break a problem into known pieces to easily come up with a solution." He paused a moment. "Now, I want you to imagine that the cylinder is made of clay. Turn it into a perfect sphere and then tell me what the volume of the sphere is."

Most of my classmates shook their heads in protest, informing the professor that, without measuring the radius of the sphere, they couldn't calculate its volume.

"It's the same as that of the cylinder," I said.

"Yes," KPD responded. "When you don't change the material, the volume will remain the same, no matter what shape it takes. What I'm going to do now is present a more difficult problem, for which you will not be able to use any known formula to solve." He gave each of us a xeroxed copy of a picture of a pig with measurements of the various parts of its anatomy written on them. "Compare the various parts of this pig to the closest structure for which you have a formula—like a cylinder, a rectangular box, or a sphere—and then use the formulae to come up with an approximate volume."

Only later in my life would I come across John Harte's book *Consider a Spherical Cow* (1988), which taught the technique of approximation required to reach an answer when the problem is complex. But I had no such book to guide me at the time. Each of us grappled with the approximation, and during class the next day, we wrote our answers on the blackboard. Every answer was different but close—within about 10 per cent of each other.

"Did anyone know how to determine the exact volume of the pig?" KPD asked.

We shook our heads.

KPD had already arranged five 1-litre measuring cylinders on the lab bench. Each cylinder was half-filled with water. He took a metal cube, a rectangular metal box, a metal sphere, and a metal cylinder whose volumes the students had already calculated and put one in each of the four measuring cylinders. He then invited a couple of students to come up to the bench, measure how many millilitres the water had risen in each cylinder, and then write the numbers on the blackboard. "Now compare the volume you calculated to the numbers on the blackboard," he said.

They were the same.

KPD then lowered a miniature metal pig into the fifth cylinder. "The volume of the pig," he said matter-of-factly, "is the volume of water it displaces in the cylinder." He stepped back from the bench. "Have you heard of Archimedes? He was a Greek mathematician who lived from 287 to 212 BCE. He discovered the principle of displacement, in which the amount of liquid displaced by an object determines its volume. He made his discovery when he lowered himself into a bathtub full of water and the water overflowed. By measuring the volume of the water that overflowed, he determined the volume of his body. Using the Archimedes' Principle, we can determine the volume of any object irrespective of its shape, and there's no need for complicated maths to impress people." KPD turned to me. "If the volume of the clay cylinder is the same as that of the sphere made from the cylinder, will the surface area of the two be the same?"

"Yes," I answered.

"No," KPD countered. "The surface area is the smallest when an object takes a spherical shape." He addressed the rest of the class. "Do you know why raindrops are spherical?"

Once again, we shook our heads.

"Nature conforms the raindrops to the smallest possible surface area," he explained, "so that they experience the least possible drag as they fall through the atmosphere." He smiled. "The main purpose of the past two days of lessons wasn't to teach you how to determine the volume of different shapes of objects, although that was one of my purposes. It was to teach you the importance of the scientific process. The scientific process must be consistent and reproducible. Determining the volume of the pig by approximating it to known shapes was not science, although each of you used the precise tools of mathematics to calculate the volume. The inconsistency came from your individual assumptions about what those shapes would be. Applying good maths to bad data does not make it a science."

I remembered KPD's lesson later in life, when I objected to various economic theories, which, although derived using maths, had been based on poor data.

KPD imparted another lifelong lesson to us that day: always be observant of nature. Science, he told us, is about observing nature and finding the hidden patterns behind it. When we learn the laws of science, we can consider their broader applications. Doing so is the only way to invent new things.

During my second year of college, KPD left for Germany to pursue higher studies. I was among some of his favourite students who went to his home to bid him farewell.

As we were leaving, he took me aside. "I was impressed with your answers on your first day of class," he said. "I want you to study hard so that you can become a good scientist someday."

I never saw KPD again, but I never forgot his advice.

*

Communism and socialism, as we've already proven, have failed. We've also explored why capitalism, while a better system, has devolved into an immoral framework. Most economic arrangements fail because they were built on an economist's ideas about human nature and human needs. Such ideas are never linked to or derived from immutable principles that are independent of the economist's personal beliefs and biases, which vary from person to person, era to era, region to region, and so on. Thus the systems we have inherited today diverge widely, from communism on one end of the spectrum to capitalism on the other, with hybrids and various variations existing between the two extremes.

But what if we could design a better economic framework—one that could curb the excesses of capitalism to make a wealthier, more just society? What if we could build a framework from proven scientific processes and then apply ethical constraints to make it a positive moral force? The framework I'm about to propose, which provides maximum economic output while maintaining a fair distribution of wealth, is based on the following scientific principles:

- The laws of thermodynamics
- The Boltzmann law of distribution and energy
- Darwin's law of evolution

Why Seek Guidance from Science?

Our universe was born thirteen billion years ago and has been expanding ever since. It's ruled by the immutable laws of physics and probably will continue to be ruled by them for another thirteen billion years or longer. Of particular interest to us are the laws of thermodynamics. Entropy, a concept that provides a capsular description of the second law of thermodynamics and that we will explore in more detail later, essentially means "state of disorder". It tells us that the universe has been moving unidirectionally towards increasing disorder since its inception. Our planet's birth—about 4.5 billion years ago—represents a fleeting moment in time compared to the age of the universe, and yet its physics follows the same laws that guide the universe.

Approximately half a billion years after Earth was formed, however, a strange phenomenon occurred on the planet:

the appearance of life. In contrast to what was happening everywhere else in the universe, life created order out of disorder. And it gave rise to an organic world distinguishable from the rest of the universe, which was inorganic. As life evolved, single-celled algae, microscopic and macroscopic plants, single-celled amoebas, microscopic bacteria and viruses, large animals, and finally, a mere 300,000 years ago, Homo sapiens appeared. The organic world followed a special law: evolution. Discovered by Charles Darwin, the law of evolution is based on natural selection and the principle of "survival of the fittest". According to this principle, which, as far as we know, exists nowhere else in the inorganic world of the ever-expanding universe, an organic species genetically evolves by adapting to its environment. Typically this means the strong survive while the weak perish.

Humans are unique—even in the organic world. We possess emotions, free will, and the ability to contemplate and ask questions about the purpose of life. The culmination of the organic world, it seems, is the human mind, which can explore the magnificence of the universe and much more. Our body is made of matter, but we are more than our material construct. The power of the human imagination has enabled us to perceive a higher purpose. To carry out this purpose, we must survive as a race, not just as individuals. While evolution has ensured that we adapt to the environment around us, we have found the inorganic world hostile to our survival and thus have tried to make it more livable. We have improved our living conditions by discovering the laws of nature and using them to build cities and travel by land, sea, and air. We have become scientists. We have learned biology and anatomy to develop medicines that help us live longer. We have learned to preserve our body of knowledge so that we might pass it on to each successive generation. And to survive, we have developed a sense of morality—inborn like free will—that protects the weak and that gives us a sense of pleasure as we sacrifice self-interest. The philosophers among us have constructed elaborate moral laws just as the scientists among us have built formulae to express the laws of natural science.

The science that has helped us flourish also has the potential to destroy us if we fail to subordinate it to morality. Nuclear power, for example, can meet our energy needs or annihilate the planet. A combination of scientific and moral laws helped build civilization and gave us power over the wanton forces of nature. Economics, as a product of social arrangement, should be no exception. It should be built using scientific processes, and the arrangement we devise must also comply with the laws of morality. If we use only science, the arrangement will become amoral. If we use only moral laws, the arrangement will become non-functional. We need both. Scientific processes must guide how we develop our economy, and our sense of morality can help us judge whether any such arrangement is just.

What scientific principles can we use to develop a just economic arrangement? The laws of thermodynamics. Amazing parallels exist between the processes that apply to thermodynamics and those that apply to economics. Such parallels don't imply sameness, but they can serve as a better guide than pure speculation. Thermodynamics and economics are statistical in manifestation, which means the processes are true for a majority of cases but not in each minute detail. Meanwhile, the Boltzmann law of distribution, which nature uses to distribute energy among molecules, can provide a basic model for reducing—not eliminating—the wealth gap. Here we will seek guidance from our moral laws.

Our new economic framework might not give us much guidance on what to do if a corporation becomes unable to create economic value—a clear possibility for something that depends on statistical laws. Statistical laws are about probability. They don't represent one value but rather a *range* of values that reflect what we call "the most probable value". The values that veer farthest from the most probable value are possible but of low probability. Thus, it's possible that a company will become sick once in a while. In such a case, we will rely on evolution to guide us and let the sick die. Those companies that die will make room for stronger, more adaptable ones to flourish.

I'm not the first person to suggest using thermodynamics to build an economic framework, but such work has been sporadic and isolated. The obvious reason is that scientists are not economists, and economists are not scientists. In any case, the dearth of such research has inspired me to marry the two—economics and thermodynamics. Towards that end, I have told the story of economics and have suggested why the laws of thermodynamics can provide the best template for developing a functionally sound and comprehensive framework for economic arrangements. We will be exploring this framework over the course of this chapter and the two that follow.

Mainstream economists discourage outsiders from intruding on their field. But although I'm not an economist by training, I've made it my business to understand the origins and the basic concepts of the prevailing economic theories. And in doing so, I've discovered that the theories aren't based on any fundamental scientific principles. They and their champions are largely products of their time. In any case, I'm not the only amateur to venture this way. Perhaps John Maynard Keynes's greatest asset was that he wasn't a trained economist.

Since my goal is to develop a basic framework and not the detailed formulations of various aspects of a new economic arrangement, I decided not to include many mathematical equations. The equations that have been developed in thermodynamics over the course of more than two centuries can be applied with minimal modification to economics once we establish an equivalence between economic and thermodynamic terms. I will leave the rest to aspiring scientist-economists. Speaking of which, it will perhaps take a scientist—either a chemist or a physicist—to develop my theories further. Most economists don't have enough of a scientific background to boast a keen understanding of thermodynamics.

With all of this in mind, before we build our new economic framework, let's take a moment to explore the basic tenets of the laws of thermodynamics.

The First Law of Thermodynamics

The first law of thermodynamics, which concerns conservation of mass and energy, has evolved over the centuries. Let's look at the way it has changed since it was first introduced in the eighteenth century.

Conservation of Mass

Scientists originally presented the first law of thermodynamics as a law of conservation of mass. In 1789, the French chemist Antoine Lavoisier formulated the law of conservation of mass, which stated that matter cannot be created or destroyed. A physical process or a chemical reaction can change the nature of matter, but the aggregate amount of matter remains constant before, throughout, and after the changes.

When you boil water, it changes from a liquid to steam. It might appear as if the water has disappeared because the steam is less visible, but if you capture and condense the steam, the amount of liquid will remain unchanged. The conversion of water to steam and back to water is called a "physical change", as is the conversion of water to ice. The mass of a substance doesn't change during a physical change.

Wood contains cellulose, which is a compound made of carbon, hydrogen, and oxygen. When you burn wood in air, it consumes additional oxygen from the air and changes into carbon dioxide and water. The weight of carbon dioxide and water formed from burning wood is equal to the weight of carbon, hydrogen, and oxygen present in the wood, plus the additional oxygen consumed from the air during burning. Nothing is lost. The matter has merely changed form. But in this case, you can't simply cool the products of combustion to reconstruct the wood. It has undergone a more deep-seated change. This type of change is called a "chemical change". Chemical changes, like physical changes, don't change the aggregate amount of mass.

Conservation of Energy

Between 1824 and 1860, physicists and chemists found that a similar law of conservation also applies to energy. They found that all forms of energy are interconvertible and that, in a closed system, conversion of one form of energy into another doesn't change the total amount of energy. Thus the first law of thermodynamics came to reflect the law of conservation of energy.

The most common expression of the first law of thermodynamics is as follows: energy can't be created or destroyed, and the total amount of energy within a closed system remains constant. Energy can exist in various forms. The most commonly encountered forms are the following:

- Mechanical energy is the energy of movement, such as the energy involved in moving matter from one place to another.
- Thermal energy is the energy required to heat something from a lower temperature to a higher temperature, expand a gas at a constant temperature, or change the physical form of matter, such as converting ice into water or water into steam.
- Electrical energy is the energy in our powerlines. It powers our electrical equipment and lights our homes. It also causes lightning.
- Electromagnetic energy, or radiation energy, is the energy found in sunlight, ultraviolet light, and infrared light. It can also be found in the radio waves that transmit radio signals.
- Chemical energy is the energy involved in chemical changes. For example, it's the energy stored in oil or wood. Part of this energy is released as heat when something is burned.

We can also classify energy as "potential energy" and "kinetic energy." Potential energy is stored energy or energy in reserve. Kinetic energy is energy in use, including energy being used to perform work.

The many forms of energy discussed above are interconvertible. The law of conservation of energy states that they can be changed from one form to another and that nothing will be lost; the sum total will always remain unchanged.

Let's use an example to illustrate the energy-based definition of the first law of thermodynamics. When you pick up a book from the floor and place it on a bookshelf, you use the chemical energy stored in the food you've eaten. This energy is converted and stored in the book on the shelf as potential energy. The chemical energy spent is equal to the potential energy created. Nothing has been lost. The conservation of energy is maintained throughout the process.

Conservation of Mass and Energy

In the early twentieth century, Albert Einstein took the conservation law one step further, combining the two earlier conservation laws to include changes of mass in the release of energy in nuclear reactions. His was a grand conservation law: the law of conservation of mass and energy. He connected the two earlier conservation laws in his famous formula:

> $E = mc^2$
> Where E stands for energy, m for mass, and c for the speed of light.

The unifying law of mass and energy states that in rare events mass can be converted to energy and vice versa, but when this happens, the total amount of mass and energy is always conserved. Einstein's equation explains the change of mass into energy in nuclear reactors and in the atomic bomb: a minute amount of matter is converted to produce an enormous amount of energy.

The conversion of mass into energy is often called nuclear energy. The energy stored as condensed mass within the atomic nuclei can be released by nuclear reactions like fission and fusion. Fission of uranium and plutonium in nuclear reactors provides vast amounts of energy, which we use to generate electricity. It's the same type of energy that was released when the US dropped two atomic bombs on Japan during World War II. Fusion energy, meanwhile, is the energy released when hydrogen atoms fuse to form helium; it's the energy that fuels the sun.

On the ordinary level of everyday experiences, the individual laws of conservation of mass and conservation of energy serve us well. The latter will inform the development of our economic framework.

The Second Law of Thermodynamics

While the first law of thermodynamics is about conservation of energy and equivalence and the interconvertibility of different types of energy, it says nothing about the process itself. Enter the second law of thermodynamics, which defines the process. We will describe it in two ways: first, in terms of the concentration or intensity of matter or energy, and second, in terms of entropy.

The second law of thermodynamics, according to the first definition, states that matter and energy flow spontaneously from an area of higher concentration or intensity to an area of lower concentration or intensity. Thus, wind blows from higher pressure to lower pressure until the pressures of both sides become equal. When saline water and soft water come into contact through a semipermeable membrane, pure water spontaneously moves from the soft water, which has a higher concentration of water, to the saline water, which has a lower concentration of water, until salt concentration becomes equal on both sides of the membrane. Similarly, when hot water and cold water are separated by a semipermeable membrane or just brought in direct contact with one another, the hot water flows spontaneously towards the cold water until the temperature on both sides becomes equal. More generally, heat flows from higher temperature to lower temperature, electricity flows from higher voltage to lower voltage, sound moves from its origin towards sound-free areas, and so on.

The second law of thermodynamics, according to the second definition, states that spontaneous changes always favour maximum dispersal of energy or matter. This is based on a central concept in thermodynamics: entropy. Entropy in its simplest terms is a state of disorder in a system. The higher the disorder, the higher the entropy. Entropy has a directional arrow, and the arrow in any spontaneous process is directed towards higher entropy, which means higher disorder. Thus, when you drop a glass plate on a cement floor, the plate shatters into pieces, but the pieces never spontaneously come together to reconstruct the plate.

Fundamentally, there's no difference between the two statements above. We simply have two different ways of describing the same law. Thus, when we talk about air moving spontaneously from higher pressure to lower pressure, the net effect is an increase in randomness or entropy of the aggregate air molecules.

The importance of the second law of thermodynamics lies in the generation of work from energy flow. We will discuss the relation between work and energy in more details later and establish how we can take advantage of these two important thermodynamic functions to develop a rational theory of economics.

The Third Law of Thermodynamics

The third law of thermodynamics is an extension of the second law and states that at the temperature of absolute zero, the entropy (*S*) of a system is also zero. It follows from the fact that at absolute zero, all molecules or atoms are motionless, as if fixed in a perfect crystal, and in such a state possess zero entropy.[1] We can write the third law mathematically as follows:

$S = 0$, at $T = 0$

Where S stands for entropy and T for temperature in absolute scale.

Definition of Key Thermodynamic Terms

Let's define a few important thermodynamic terms, which we will pair with economic terms later in order to apply the well-proven equations of thermodynamics to parallel equations of economics.

1 Atkins et al., 2018, p. 94.

Temperature

In thermodynamics, as the name of the field implies, energy is typically expressed as "heat energy". The importance of heat as the currency of energy has made temperature, which expresses the presence and concentration (i.e., intensity) of heat energy in matter, one of the most fundamental functions of thermodynamics. The difference in temperature between two objects determines the direction of spontaneous flow of heat energy when the objects are in contact. As mentioned above, this flow takes place from the hotter object to the cooler one.

According to the kinetic molecular theory, the temperature of a substance represents the average kinetic energy of the atoms or molecules contained within it. The lowest theoretical temperature is absolute zero, which is defined as a temperature with zero thermal energy and no kinetic energy left to be associated with the atoms and molecules of the system. As is the case with all extremities, absolute zero can be approached but never reached.

The most commonly used temperature scale is the Celsius scale, also known as the centigrade scale. In this empirical scale, the difference between the temperature of the freezing point of water and its boiling point, with both at sea-level pressure, is divided into one hundred equal divisions, with each division being called a degree. The freezing point of water is assigned a value of 0°C and the boiling point a value of 100°C. The temperature scale that is used in thermodynamic equations and calculations, however, is the Kelvin scale, represented as K. In the Kelvin scale, the size of the one-degree interval is the same as it is in the centigrade scale, but the lowest temperature, 0K, is absolute zero, which is –273°C. In thermodynamic calculations, when the temperature is provided in Celsius, it first must be converted to Kelvin by adding 273 to the centigrade numbers. We will use a thermodynamic equation later to show why monopoly is bad for an economy. In any case, one advantage of the Kelvin scale is that temperatures are expressed as positive numbers, since there is no temperature below 0K.

Entropy

Like temperature, entropy is a central concept in thermodynamics. The second and third laws of thermodynamics have been enriched by expressing them in terms of entropy. Entropy is also valuable in considering chemical reactions and changes in energies during such reactions, as we will observe later.

The most rigorous definition of entropy comes from statistical mechanics. A subject that is beyond the scope of this deliberation is the derivation of an equation from Boltzmann's distribution theory (to be discussed later). This equation, known as the Boltzmann formula for the second law of thermodynamics, is based on statistical analysis and relates entropy to the number of allowable "energy distribution states" of the system. The Boltzmann formula can be represented mathematically as follows:

$S = k \, lnW$ (see footnote[2])

2 Ibid., p. 81.

Where *k* is the Boltzmann Constant ($k = 1.381 \times 10^{-23}$ JK^{-1}), *ln* is the natural logarithm, and *W* is the number of microstates (the number of ways in which the molecules of a system can be distributed over the energy states for a specified total energy). At absolute zero, the molecules are fixed in a single configuration as if confined motionless in one perfect arrangement in an ideal crystal, where *W* becomes equal to 1 ($W = 1$). Since $\ln 1 = 0$, it follows that *at* $T = 0$, $S = 0$, as shown above.

As with most thermodynamic functions, the absolute definition of the function is less important than its change (Δ) as it changes from one thermodynamic state to another. In this sense, a change in entropy (ΔS) is defined by its relationship with heat transfer (ΔQ) and temperature (*T*). The common equations are as follows:

$$\Delta S = \Delta Q/T \text{ or}$$
$$\Delta Q = T\Delta S$$

Entropy is best defined as the state of disorder in a system. Entropy of a system increases when the disorder or state of chaos in the system increases. The second law of thermodynamics, as described above, is a statement about the direction of change in entropy. This direction, also called "the arrow of entropy", points towards its increase over time. An increase of entropy—a movement from order to disorder—is a fundamental law of nature and has been ruling the universe since its birth.

The arrow of entropy is a statistical concept. It cannot be violated only when considered in macroscopic quantities and in a closed system (see below). As we will explore later, the arrow points towards order in the living world, but when the organic world is considered in combination with its inorganic surroundings, the arrow towards disorder becomes the overriding rule. Of course, "the pockets of order within the broader disorder" have been more important to humanity, and civilization is based on our ability to create these pockets of order in the ocean of disorder.

Closed, Isolated, and Open Systems

A strong parallelism exists between economic and thermodynamic systems when we consider whether a system is closed, isolated, or open. Before we can apply thermodynamic principles to economics, we must understand how these terms are defined in thermodynamics.

Matter cannot escape or enter a closed system, but energy can. The example used earlier of lifting a book and placing it on the shelf demonstrates a closed system. No matter escaped from the book when it was lifted. Energy, however, transferred from your body to the book as you lifted it and placed it on the shelf.

In an isolated system, meanwhile, neither matter nor energy can enter or leave. If you pour hot coffee into a closed thermos with perfect insulation and tighten the cap, you have trapped it in an isolated system. No heat or water can enter or leave the thermos. But what if you poured coffee into a coffee cup? The coffee will lose heat to the atmosphere, and it will lose water in the form of steam, which will evaporate in the air. Now the coffee is in an open system. The first law of thermodynamics applies to the coffee in the thermos but not to the coffee in the cup.

Spontaneous and Non-spontaneous Processes

As we have observed, the second law of thermodynamics applies only to spontaneous processes. A spontaneous process is one that works naturally—with no interference from an external agent. A rock rolling downhill on its own, water flowing downhill, a radioactive element decaying and emitting radiation at a constant rate—these are examples of spontaneous processes. Spontaneous processes occur when a polarity or a gradient is created from uneven distribution of matter or energy. The natural flow of matter or energy in such cases is always from the higher concentration to the lower or from lower to higher entropy.

When an external agent interferes with the natural process, the process becomes non-spontaneous. An external agent can cause a non-spontaneous process by blocking the path of its flow or applying an opposing force to the natural flow. In the example of the coffee cup, the flow of heat from the hot coffee to the cold atmosphere and the escape of steam from the top of the hot coffee to the atmosphere, which has lower water vapour, are spontaneous processes. If we, as an agent, place the coffee in a microwave to reheat it, we create a non-spontaneous process. When water flows from a water reservoir to our houses, it is a spontaneous process, but when we pump water to the reservoir, we use a non-spontaneous process. As we will soon see, when a barrier (a machine) is placed in the path of the flow of energy, directing a source of higher concentration to a sink of lower concentration, we get work. The same principle also applies to economics.

Concluding Remarks

Energy, mass, and entropy each play a role in thermodynamics, as do the systems they occupy and the processes they utilize. Now that we have a basic understanding of the laws of thermodynamics, let's take a closer look at the way energy works.

6

Work and Energy: Where Thermodynamics and Economics Meet

When I was a child, our family owned a grandfather clock. It was a pendulum, one of the oldest forms of timekeeping devices. We saw similar clocks in churches and large buildings. I was fascinated by the pendulum's back-and-forth movement and wondered if an invisible person sat inside the clock to move the bob. Later, I learned that the invisible person was the restoring force of gravity, which could make the bob swing forever if it was suspended by a cord from a frictionless pivot.

When I studied physics in college, I learned about the equations that explain the mechanical energy of the moving pendulum. And I learned about the play between kinetic and potential energy created by the pendulum's repetitive, spontaneous back-and-forth movement. But perhaps Einstein saw more in those equations. Perhaps his observations of the motion of a pendulum led to the discovery of the most profound equation in Einsteinian physics: $E = mc^2$. The science behind the pendulum has advanced no further than where it was more than a hundred years ago, but Einstein's equation revolutionized physics.

To be sure, Einstein never explicitly told us that the pendulum inspired his famous equation. And nothing in the literature pinpoints his moment of inspiration. All we have is speculation. Was he divinely inspired? Did he stumble upon the equation in a fit of genius? Was he simply ruminating about the nature of energy and matter? People have wondered why he didn't postulate $E = mc$ or $E= mc^3$ or some other form of relations. When Einstein discovered his equation in 1905, no proof existed to support it, and no theoretical ground suggested it was true. Such proof would come later. But at the time, he needed a mass–energy equivalence equation for his theories of relativity.

I don't believe that anyone—genius or not—can invent something without first recognizing an existing pattern in nature or without the advantage of some prior knowledge. Hence my pendulum theory. Most inventions start with intuitive speculation and become science when the intuition is later proven correct by evidence. What experience inspired Einstein's intuition? I wondered about this for a long time and then made a connection after I read "$E = mc^2$: The Most Urgent Problem of Our Time", an essay Einstein wrote for *Science Illustrated* in 1946, long after the validity of his equation had been established.

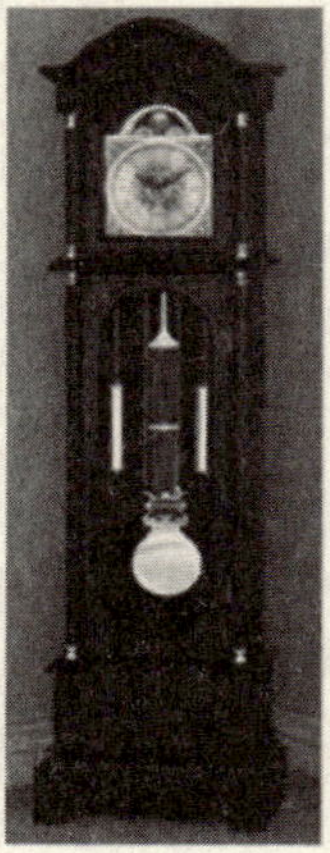

The Grandfather's Clock

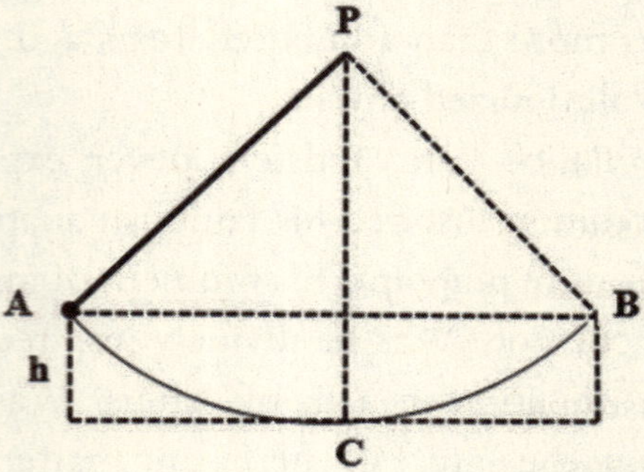

Drawing of the pendulum from Einstein's Essay

In the article, Einstein starts with the pendulum.[1] The mass of the pendulum swings from one extreme (height A) to another extreme (height B). In doing so, it passes through the lowest point (C), which can be expressed as h = 0. At A and B, the pendulum's mass has no velocity. The energy of the pendulum's mass at these two points is entirely potential energy (energy of position) and is equal to *mgh* (*m* is mass, *g* is the acceleration due to gravity, and *h* is height). At point C, the mass achieves maximum velocity, and its energy is entirely kinetic energy (energy of motion), which is equal to $\frac{1}{2}mv^2$ (*v* is velocity). While referring to the kinetic energy at C, Einstein wrote, "It is as though the lifting height could be converted entirely into velocity", and "vice versa [at A and B]". He then observed that the law of conservation of energy (the first law of thermodynamics) states that at any point along the path of

1 Gardner, 1997, p. 414.

the pendulum the total energy (potential plus kinetic) should remain constant:

$$E = mgh + \frac{1}{2}mv^2 = \text{constant}$$

The observation contained nothing new. It belonged to classical physics. My classmates and I studied the very same equations in physics class in our first year of college.

In the second part of the article, Einstein wrote, "It is customary to express the equivalence of mass and energy (though somewhat inexactly) by the formula $E = mc^2$, in which c represents the velocity of light, about 186,000 miles per second." He doesn't say when it became customary. What inspired the equation when he discovered it in 1905?

In the third part of the article, Einstein used the example of atomic fission, which had been demonstrated by America's use of the atomic bomb during World War II, to explain $E = mc^2$. "What takes place," he wrote, "can be illustrated with the help of our rich man. The atom M is a rich miser, who during his life, gives away no money (energy). But in his will he bequeaths his fortune to his sons MÅå and MÅç, on condition that they give to the community a small amount, less than one thousandth of the whole estate (energy or mass). The sons together have somewhat less than the father had (the mass sum MÅå + MÅç is somewhat smaller than the mass M of the radioactive atom). But the part given to the community, though relatively small, is still so enormously large (considered as kinetic energy) that it brings with it a great threat of evil. Averting that threat has become the most urgent problem of our time."

Let's explore what might have been in Einstein's mind. We will start by assuming that the mass of the pendulum he described in the first part of the article is slightly—*very* slightly—bigger than 2m'. The kinetic energy at the point C would be:

$$E = [2 \times \tfrac{1}{2} \times m'v^2] = m'v^2$$

Now consider we have to find a value of *v* where it's a constant. This must be the speed of light *c*. Wouldn't the above equation look like Einstein's equivalence equation? Einstein knew that to make his relativity theory stick he had to produce a mass–energy equivalence equation. What else could provide a better intuitive equation? Of course, his equation had to be proven correct. Most pivots start with an intuitive speculation. Some people admit what inspired them. Others tell us the whole story.

At an awards banquet held in his honour in London in 1890, Dr Friedrich August Kekulé described having a daydream years earlier while an organic chemistry professor at the University of Ghent. During a moment of reverie, he imagined a snake seizing its own tail, and the visualization inspired him to discover the structure of benzene, which until then had been a mystery. In benzene, the two end-carbons of the unsaturated structure, $CH_2=CH–CH=CH–CH=CH_2$, are linked together to make a six-member ring, thus eliminating two hydrogen atoms. Kekulé's eureka moment, although simple on its face, sowed the seeds for explosive growth in aromatic organic chemistry.

The branch of chemistry known as organic chemistry, alternatively called chemistry of carbon compounds, was already known at the time. In fact, Kekulé had already determined that carbon has four valences—four arms it can use to link to other elements and other carbon atoms. In comparison, the hydrogen atom and the chlorine atom have only a single valence each.

The ability to self-link gives carbon a singular position in chemistry. For instance, carbon and hydrogen can lead to the formation of compounds like $CH_3–CH_3$; $CH_3–CH_2–CH_3$; $CH_3–CH_2–CH_2–CH_3$; $CH_3–CH_2–CH_2–CH_2–CH_2–CH_3$; etc. of the general formula C_nH_{2n+2}. These compounds are called saturated hydrocarbons, in which the successive carbons are linked to one another by single bonds. In other compounds, two or more carbons are linked to one another (not the successive ones) by double bonds, such as in $CH_2=CH_2$; $CH_2=CH–CH=CH_2$; $CH_2=CH–CH=CH–CH=CH_2$, etc. These are called unsaturated hydrocarbons.

Since only alternative carbons can be linked to one another by a double bond, the general formula of the unsaturated hydrocarbons is either C_nH_{2n} or $C_nH_{2n-2x+2}$, where x is the number of double bonds. According to this scheme, the minimum number of hydrogen atoms required to make a six-carbon-chain compound with the highest number of unsaturation is eight—the formula C_6H_8. One distinguishing feature of the unsaturated hydrocarbons is that they can add more atoms like hydrogen or chlorine to form saturated compounds in which the carbons are linked only by single bonds. For instance, when the six-carbon unsaturated compound C_6H_8 is hydrogenated, it is converted to the saturated six-carbon compound C_6H_{14}, with the addition of two hydrogen atoms per double bond.

Back to Kekulé's discovery. At the time, a new group of organic compounds had been discovered. They produced a sweet aroma, and their destructive distillation resulted in benzene, which was shown to have the composition C_6H_6. No one knew how to write benzene's structure, which was two hydrogens short of the least number of hydrogens required to form a six-carbon unsaturated structure. No one, that is, until Kekulé was inspired by his daydream to reimagine benzene's structure. His discovery would shape the development of organic chemistry and permanently secure his name in the annals of history.

Such experiences are quite common in scientific discoveries. For my part, most of my memorable inventions were likewise inspired by a common experience. While I worked for PPG Industries, our marketing people told us that in order to create a viable transition lens, the colour needed to change from colourless to grey. But all the photochromic dyes known in those days changed from one primary colour to another. If we could mix red, blue, and yellow paint to make grey paint, I mused, why not try to include the features of red, blue, and yellow photochromic dye in the same molecule? It took ten scientists and several years to bring the concept to fruition, but eventually the Transition[R] lens—a global business—was born.[2] When such an intellectual pivot is tested and proven true, it generates a cascade of results that goes far beyond the stimulus that inspired it.

The Gas Laws: Boyle's and Charles's Laws

Two laws describing the behaviour of gases—the first formulated by the Anglo-Irish scientist Robert Boyle in 1662 and the second by the French scientist Jacques Charles more than a century later in 1787—presaged the development of a great body of physical chemistry, particularly the evolution of the second law of thermodynamics, the exploration of work as an important thermodynamic quantity, and the development

2 Little, 1994, pp. 8–9.

of the heat engine. Given that they form the key concepts behind the new economic framework I plan to propose, let's take a moment to examine them.

Robert Boyle (1627–91) showed in his experiments that when a fixed amount of gas is confined in a closed cylinder with a moveable piston at a constant temperature, its volume will vary inversely with changes in pressure. Put a different way, the product of volume (V) and pressure (P) of a fixed amount of gas at a constant temperature (T) will be constant. This can be expressed mathematically as follows:

$$PV = \text{Constant, at constant } T$$

Jacques Charles (1746–1823) formulated the second gas law, also based on empirical evidence, which states that the "volume of a given amount of gas varies proportionately with changes in temperature at constant pressure" and that "pressure of a given amount of gas varies proportionately with temperature at constant volume". The equation is as follows:

$$V/T = \text{Constant at constant } P$$

$$P/T = \text{Constant at constant } V$$

where P and V are pressure and volume of the gas, and T is temperature expressed in Kelvin scale.

Boyle's law and Charles's law were later combined in what is known as the combined gas law. It states that the product of multiplication of the volume and pressure of an ideal gas is directly proportional to the amount of gas and its temperature. The combined law can be expressed by the following equation:

$$PV = nRT$$

where *n* represents the quantity of gas (number of moles) and R is called the universal molar gas constant. Its value is as follows:

$$R = 8.31446 \text{ joules per kelvin per mole, i.e., } JK^{-1}mole^{-1}$$

where joule (J) is a unit of energy, K is the unit of temperature in the Kelvin scale.

R is the molar equivalent of the Boltzmann constant, expressed in units of energy per temperature increment per mole. The value of the Boltzmann constant is 1.38065×10^{-23} joule per kelvin (JK^{-1}). The value of R is obtained by multiplying the value of the Boltzmann constant with Avogadro's number (the number of molecules in a mole), which is 6.02214×10^{23} molecules per mole ($mole^{-1}$).

The gas laws are limiting laws. As such, they are valid for ideal gases and are only approximately true for real gases. An ideal gas, like idealism, is never achievable. It's a target and a guide that helps us to deal with events and phenomenon in a logical and mathematical manner. Even the closest expression of ideal behaviour is an approximation. The deviations from the ideal can also be logically explained based on limitations of actual systems. The best definition of an ideal gas is one that obeys the perfect gas laws, i.e., Boyle's law and Charles's law.

Work

- The fundamental link between thermodynamics and economics is work, and in thermodynamics, the currency of work is energy. Different types of energy can be converted into one another. They can also be used to perform work. Energy and work are equivalent. They share the same units of measurement—erg in the CGS unit or joule in the SI unit (1 joule = 10.7 erg). We will discuss work in more detail as we go.

Pressure–Volume Work

Like the gas laws, pressure–volume work (PV work) took a central role in the development of the laws of thermodynamics. PV work is the work done by a gas when its volume increases against a constant pressure. Imagine a fixed amount of gas in a cylinder fitted with a frictionless piston under an external pressure (P). In order to expand this gas, say from volume V_1 to volume V_2, we must add external heat to it. If we want the work to be done by the expansion only, we must keep the temperature constant (P = Constant; T = Constant). This will be difficult to accomplish by heating the gas quickly. If we add considerable heat to the gas, its temperature will suddenly increase, which will increase the internal pressure well beyond the external pressure. We can't assume constant temperature or constant pressure any more. The objective can be achieved, however, by adding an *insignificant* amount of heat to the gas so that the temperature of the gas increases insignificantly. The temperature will return to its original value after the added heat has increased the pressure infinitesimally, and the change in pressure will match the external pressure. We can write the following equation to represent the tiny amount of work (δW) done by the system:

$$(\delta W) = (P + \delta P) \times \delta V = P \times \delta V + \delta P \times \delta V$$

In this equation, δ represents an insignificant yet finite change. If we replace δ with *d*, where *d* stands for an infinitely small change, the second term will disappear. By integrating these infinitesimal steps between two volumes—V_1 and V_2—we should be able to get the amount of PV work done, and it should be equal to the heat added to the system:

$$-W = \int_{V1}^{V2} PdV$$

The negative sign before work (W) indicates that the work is done by the system. The above derivation is for an isothermal expansion (an expansion with no change in temperature) in a closed system, where transfer of heat—but not matter—between the system and its environment is allowed. Such a system is called a reversible system because the process can be reversed by infinitesimally reducing the pressure and removing an infinitesimal amount of heat from the system every time.

PV work can also be done by a gas in an adiabatic system (an isolated system where no exchange of heat is allowed between the system and its environment). In such a case, expansion will lead to a decrease in temperature and the work done by the system will be equal to the reduction in internal energy due to the adiabatic cooling.

A Commentary on Work

Since we will soon argue that work links thermodynamics and economics, let's establish what work is. Is it energy? If so, shouldn't the law of conservation of energy be called the law of conversation of energy and work? Many textbooks state that performance of work is caused by loss of energy. An accurate understanding isn't necessary to solve thermodynamic problems, but it's crucial if we are to relate thermodynamics to economics.

The first law of thermodynamics can't be violated. Nor can its definition be expanded. Work is not energy. It's not generated at the expense of energy. It results from the transfer of energy from one system to another and through the transformation of one form to another. Work performed is equivalent to the energy transferred and transformed. Equivalence, however, does not mean sameness. My twin brother looks like me. He weighs the same, talks the same, and can even proxy for me without being caught. He could drive a car using my driver's licence, and if I were to die, he could pretend that I'm still alive and occupy my home. Despite all these things, he can never be me. Similarly, although work might look like energy, although many problems of thermodynamics can be solved by assuming that work is energy, work is *not* energy. Think of it instead as a ghost of energy. Adam Smith used the metaphor of the invisible hand. Work is like an invisible *substance* that behaves like energy. But it's not energy.

Let's return to our example from earlier and assume that we use Q_1 amount of heat energy to generate W_1 amount of work. What happens to the heat (Q_1) during the process? Q_1 sits comfortably in a heat-reservoir as potential energy (energy of position) until it's called into action. As soon as it's called into action, it moves to the gas in the cylinder. During this movement, it becomes kinetic energy (energy of motion). This kinetic energy lifts the piston—this is work—acting as mechanical energy, and when the movement is complete, the gas changes from its original state of PV_1 to a new state of PV_2. The kinetic energy that caused this change of state becomes potential energy, its amount equal to the difference between the potential energies of PV_2 and PV_1. No energy is lost. The sum total of potential and kinetic energy at every point of the changes remains constant. The energy involved in the process of transformation of the gas from PV_1 to PV_2 never ceases to remain energy.

If we reverse the process, i.e., compress the gas from the state of PV_2 to bring it back to PV_1, the excess potential energy in PV_2 returns to the heat reservoir in exactly the same amount of heat (Q_1) and rests there in its potential form. Such subtleties might not change the calculations that students are asked to perform in their thermodynamic classes, but the fact remains that we're talking about different substances in energy and work. And such a distinction is important, for we can't use thermodynamics as a template for our new economics model without a clear understanding of each thermodynamic term. For example, we can't call work of labour money even though work performed by a labourer can be paid with money.

Machine and Agent

Generating work by movement of energy requires a machine. The efficiency of the machine is important, since it dictates what fraction of the energy moved can generate work. But machines don't function on their own; they need agents to operate them. Since agents aren't energy, they don't factor into thermodynamic equations. But that doesn't mean they're unimportant; they are a crucial part of the chain that generates work. Adam Smith's invisible hand was more important in his theory than his "visible hands" of capital and labour, which are impotent without the invisible hand working in the background. Similarly, work and agents that aren't energy are crucial in the functioning of the principles of thermodynamics for human benefit.

The Heat Engine: The Carnot Cycle

Every invention boasts a history that goes beyond the mere facts of the invention. And that history makes it come alive as we view it in relation to other events of the era—events that connect it to and those that separate it from the circumstances that birthed it. The period between 1760 and 1840, when production in Europe and the United States transitioned en masse to the use of machines, is often called the Industrial Revolution, which featured the introduction of steam engines as a primary part of machinery. Although the power of steam pressure to cause mechanical movement was known as early as the first century, nothing operational was available until an Englishman named Thomas Newcomen introduced the commercial steam engine in 1712. The Newcomen engine, which consisted of a cylinder and a piston, used steam very inefficiently. Later, James Watt, who worked as a repairman at the Glasgow University, determined the sources of some of the steam wastage. Watt, in collaboration with Matthew Boulton, developed an improved version of the Newcomen design and introduced it commercially in 1776. The Watt steam engine fuelled the explosive growth in the use of machines during the Industrial Revolution.

While Watt was developing his steam engine at Glasgow, Adam Smith was putting the finishing touches on his masterpiece, *The Wealth of Nations*, in another building at the same university. Smith's work, which offered capitalism as an alternative to mercantilism, became an instant sensation because it provided the economic framework for the Industrial Revolution. These two developments—the steam engine and capitalism—ushered in a new era.

Great inventions often come from the most unexpected sources. The most often cited is Einstein, who, when he was merely a patent clerk and only twenty-one years old, changed the course of physics forever. But much earlier, twenty-five-year-old Sadi Carnot, working in Napoleon's Army Corps of Engineers, changed the course of the gas engine while pushing the boundaries of its performance. Although the Watt steam engine was an improvement over the Newcomen engine, its fuel efficiency was still meagre—stuck at around 10.6 per cent, compared to 6.4 per cent or lower for the Newcomen design. For the next half-century, scientists struggled to determine how efficient a steam engine could be. Then came Sadi Carnot with an answer to the question.

While Carnot worked on the problem, the only thermodynamic principles known were Boyle's law of ideal gases and the first law of thermodynamics. The second law of thermodynamics had yet to be formally introduced, although scientists intuited that heat flows spontaneously from a high to a low temperature. Scientists also understood that converting heat into work requires a machine, and the machine needs a fluid or a gas to convey heat.

Carnot approached the problem from a theoretical perspective. His theoretical engine was a cylinder with a frictionless piston, and it contained an ideal gas as its fluid. The machine operated between two heat reservoirs: one kept at a high temperature to act as a source of heat, the other kept at a lower temperature to act as a sink. To determine efficiency, Carnot broke the machine's operation into cycles, each cycle comprising the following four stages.

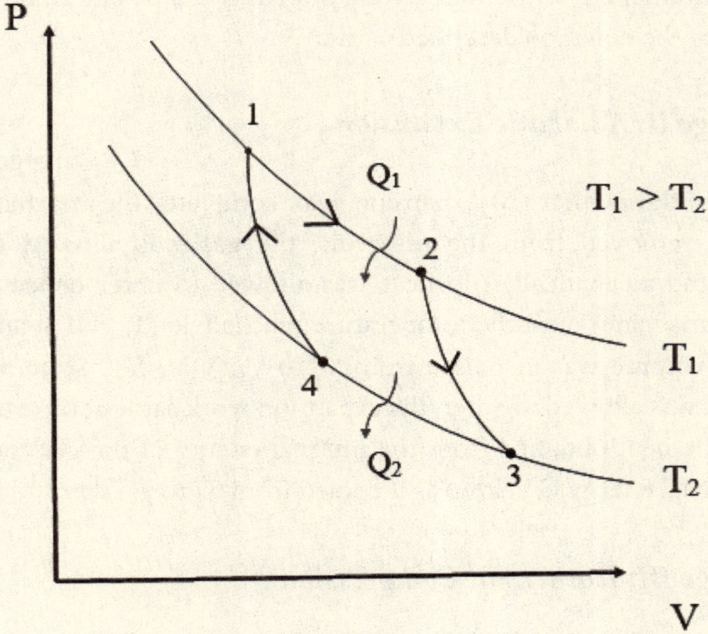

The four stages of the Carnot cycle. Positions 1, 2, 3, and 4 correspond to P_1V_1, P_2V_2, P_3V_3, and P_4V_4 respectively. Stage I: Isothermal Expansion from 1 to 2; Stage II: Adiabatic Expansion from 2 to 3; Stage III: Isothermal Compression from 3 to 4; Stage IV: Adiabatic Compression from 4 to 1.

Stage I: Isothermal Expansion

The engine was placed in the hot reservoir at T_1 and allowed to expand isothermally (at the same temperature—in this case at T_1) from volume V_1 to V_2. During the process, the piston had to lift, working against the external pressure. For the expansion to occur, heat had to be added to the machine from the hotter reservoir. The work done by the system was equal to Q_1, the heat absorbed in the process, and was equal to the PV work, where P was the external pressure on the piston. The isothermal PV work done by the system could be determined using the equation described earlier.

Stage II: Adiabatic Expansion

After the isothermal expansion was complete, the machine was removed from the reservoir, the gas was allowed to expand adiabatically (no heat was allowed to enter or leave the machine) until the temperature reached T_2 ($T_1 > T_2$), and the volume was increased from V_2 to V_3 ($V_3 > V_2$). Since no heat was allowed to enter, the expansion work came at the cost of the heat obtained from the internal energy of the gas (see internal energy U below) as it cooled from T_1 to T_2.

Stage III: Isothermal Compression

Next the engine was placed in the cold reservoir at T_2, and the gas was compressed by applying external pressure to the piston until the volume decreased from V_3 to V_4 so that $V_3 - V_4$ equalled $V_2 - V_1$. During the process, the piston had to drop, this time working against the *internal* pressure. For the contraction to occur, heat had to be transferred from the machine to the cold reservoir at T_2. The work done on the system was equal to Q_2, the heat removed from the gas and transferred to the cold reservoir, and to the PV work so that it remained thermodynamically reversible.

Stage IV: Adiabatic Compression

After the isothermal compression was complete, the machine was removed from the cold reservoir, and the gas was compressed adiabatically until the volume reached V_1, the original volume ($V_4 > V_1$), and the temperature increased from T_2 to T_1. Since no heat was allowed to leave, the compression (work done on the system) increased the temperature of the system. The system thus returned to its original state at $P_1V_1T_1$.

Since during the four-stage cycle the only heat transfers were removed from the hot reservoir and added to the cold reservoir, the theoretical efficiency was $(Q_1 - Q_2)/Q_1$, which was shown to be equal to $(T_1-T_2)/T_1$. The last expression can be written as follows:

> Maximum Efficiency of a Heat Engine = $(T_1-T_2)/T_1$ = 1 – T2/T1

The mathematical deduction of these equations is beyond the scope of this discussion, but it can be found in any thermodynamics textbook.[3] The results, however, are critical to developing a new economic framework. What the efficiency equation tells us is that the Carnot engine is the most heat-efficient engine possible. It sets the theoretical limits of efficiency, since ideal conditions are met, and no leak of energy is allowed in the assumptions.

Carnot shared his findings in 1824 in the only book he ever published: *Reflections on the Motive Power of Fire*. He was only twenty-seven years old. The book didn't receive much attention at the time, and few had heard of Carnot when he

---

3 Atkins et al., 2018, pp. 82–84.

died of cholera eight years later. But he eventually became known as the father of thermodynamics due to the importance of his discovery. Every chemist, physicist, and engineer in the world today has studied the Carnot cycle.

Before we discuss our new economic framework, we must define several additional thermodynamic terms. As we explore them, we will connect them to important economic concepts, but we will make these connections more forcefully in the next chapter.

Chemical Energy

Like heat, chemical energy has played an important role in the evolution and application of thermodynamics. Chemical energy, the energy stored in chemical bonds that link atoms in a molecule, is released to or absorbed from the environment during the breaking or formation of chemical bonds. The energy involved in chemical bond breakage or formation can be thermal, electrical, or radiative. See the following examples:

Combustion: C (carbon) + O_2 (oxygen) = CO_2 (carbon dioxide) + heat

Electrolysis: H_2O (water) + electrical energy = H_2 (hydrogen) + O (oxygen)

Photochemical reaction: AgCl (silver chloride) + UV radiation = Ag (silver) + Cl (chlorine)

Chemical energy, among the least available of all forms of energy, is stored in various materials, including food, batteries, coal, gasoline, and the energetic materials in ammunition.

Although chemical reactions can be initiated by different types of energy (if and when released), they almost always appear in the form of heat.

Chemical thermodynamics have introduced several new concepts: internal energy (U), enthalpy (H), and Gibbs free energy (G). We will take a quick look at each of these terms shortly and their economic counterparts later. But first, we need to discuss another important concept: energy of activation.

Activation Energy

As mentioned above, chemical energy is among the least easily available forms of energies. In order to release such energy, the chemical's molecules must be raised to what is called a transition state, at which point they can undergo a chemical reaction. The chemical reaction between a fuel (wood, coal, oil) and oxygen produces combustion. The combined chemical energy of fuel and oxygen is higher than that of the products of combustion (carbon dioxide and water), but for combustion to occur, the fuel molecules and the oxygen molecules must be heated to bring them to a transition state. The energy required to bring the reactants to the transition state is called the activation energy.

In the above example, as soon as the transition state is reached, combustion begins. The energy released is significantly higher than the activation energy and is enough to bring more fuel and oxygen to transition states, continuing the process of combustion. Thus only a spark is often enough to start a forest fire. The energy barrier—the activation energy—keeps chemicals safe and stable. Otherwise, fuel and oxygen couldn't coexist without everything going up in flames. The same is true of every other material or chemical that undergoes a chemical reaction.

In economics and finance, many challenging but potentially lucrative business opportunities won't go anywhere without the seed investments that generate interest from big investors. Such seed money is the counterpart of activation energy.

Internal Energy (U)

In thermodynamics, the total energy of a system is called its internal energy and is represented by the symbol U. Internal energy is the total kinetic and potential energy of the constituents of the system, namely, of its atoms, ions, and molecules. In the special case of an ideal gas, that energy consists of the translational, rotational, and vibrational energies of its molecular, atomic, and subatomic particles.[4] Internal energy does *not* include potential or kinetic energies associated with the position or the translational state of the system as a whole. Such energies that are the result of the influence of external forces on the system don't affect the internal composition of the system, and since they are not internal, they are not included in the definition of internal energy.

Analysing how the internal energy of gas in the four stages of the Carnot cycle changes will give us a better understanding of internal energy. Since no chemical change is involved in the Carnot engine, the molecules and/or atoms remain the same throughout the process. This means that the rotational and

4 Ibid., 2018, p. 37.

vibrational energies of the molecular, atomic, and subatomic particles in the gas remain unchanged. The only change we are concerned with occurs in the translational energies of the particles, and these energies depend only on temperature.

In stage I of the Carnot cycle, no change occurs in internal energy because no change occurs in temperature. In stage II, the temperature decreases from T_1 to T_2 ($T_1 > T_2$). The internal energy decreases because the temperature decreases. The change involves PV work done by the system, and the energy involved in the PV work has to come from the internal energy of the system. Stages III and IV are the reverse of stages II and I, respectively. So what happens to the heat added to the system from the outside reservoir source in stage I and the heat removed from the system and dumped into the reservoir sink in stage III? They either increase the potential energy of the system as a whole through work done *by* the system or decrease it by work done *on* the system. Stages I and III are connected to the outside environment through heat exchanges. In the case of the adiabatic changes, where no heat exchange occurs with the outside environment, work done *by* the system or *on* the system is accounted for by a reduction or increase in internal energy.

In economics, the counterpart of internal energy is the reserve potential of human creativity combined with the resources of the surrounding environment that remain dormant until exploited.

Enthalpy (H)

When a system undergoes chemical change, the products no longer have the same internal energy that the reactant molecules have. As a result, some amount of internal energy is either released to the environment (*exothermic* reactions) or absorbed from the environment (*endothermic* reactions). To account for the interaction with the environment, a new thermodynamic term is needed: enthalpy (represented by the symbol H). The concept of enthalpy, although initially introduced to describe energy changes in chemical reactions, has become a fundamental concept in thermodynamics that also applies to physical changes.

Enthalpy, defined as the total heat content of a system, is equal to the internal energy of the system plus the product of pressure and volume:[5]

$$H = U + PV$$
$$\Delta H = \Delta U + PV \text{ work}$$

Such a scientific definition can leave us with an empty feeling. Although we have explored how PV or PV work relate to energy and chemical change, we need a more intuitive understanding of the process involved, particularly if we want to apply it to a new economic model. To understand enthalpy intuitively, we can start by noting the following difference between internal energy and enthalpy: while internal energy is unaffected by its surroundings, enthalpy *is* affected by the environment. Enthalpy is internal energy plus the energy required to maintain the volume of the system at constant pressure. This means open communication with the environment. In other words, enthalpy is the energy associated with a closed system—one that can exchange energy but not matter with the outside. Internal energy, on the other hand,

5 Ibid., p. 46.

is energy associated with an isolated system—one that can't exchange energy *or* matter with the outside.

A student named Aravind Nair provided a creative description of the relationship between internal energy and enthalpy several years ago. I found it online while using Google to search for an easy visualization of the relationship. Nair quoted Daniel V. Schroeder's *An Introduction to Thermal Physics*: "Enthalpy is the total energy you would have to come up with to create the system out of nothing and put it into its environment." Nair further explained the equation $H = U + PV$ by writing the following: "To create a rabbit out of nothing and place it on the table, the magician must summon up not only the energy U of the rabbit but also some additional energy, equal to PV, to push the atmosphere out of the way to make room." Such an intuitive explanation nicely explains enthalpy's relationship with its external environment and internal energy's lack of a relationship with its surroundings.

As mentioned earlier, thermodynamic operations are more concerned with changes in thermodynamic functions than with the absolute values of the functions. To understand "change in enthalpy", let's take a look at how heat is dissipated to the environment in an exothermic reaction:

$$[A + B] = [C + D] + q$$

where q is the heat evolved.

Let's assume that the internal energy of [A + B] is U_1, and the internal energy of [C + D] is U_2. If we consider only the energy of the reaction above, we get the following:

$$U_1 = U_2 + q$$

But since in a chemical reaction we are in communication with the environment, we would be better off using enthalpy—rather than internal energy—in our calculation. After adding the term PV to both sides, our calculation looks like this:

$$H_1 = H_2 + q$$
or
$$\Delta H = -q$$
Where ΔH represents change in enthalpy, $[H_2 - H_1]$.

Note that in an exothermic reaction, ΔH is considered negative. We can now write the initial exothermic reaction as follows:

$$[A + B] = [C + D] - \Delta H$$

If the reaction was endothermic, we'd write the following:

$$[A + B] = [C + D] + \Delta H$$

In economics, the counterpart to a closed system is a closed economy, i.e., an economy that doesn't allow trade but *does* allow an exchange of currency. And the counterpart to an isolated system is an isolated economy: an economy that allows neither trade nor the exchange of currency.

Gibbs Free Energy (G)

In 1873, Josiah Willard Gibbs coined the term "available energy" (later called "Gibbs free energy") while exploring the necessary conditions for a chemical reaction. Gibbs took into consideration the role of non-PV work, such as electrical work, while determining whether conditions are favourable for a chemical reaction. The change in Gibbs free energy, ΔG, is defined in terms of changes in enthalpy and entropy (in reversible reaction conditions) and can be expressed in the following equation, which is measured in joules:

$$\Delta G = (\Delta H + T\Delta S)$$

If we were to create a chemical reaction in a closed system (when we aren't considering PV work), ΔG would represent the maximum amount of work that can be extracted from the system as a result of the reaction. A positive ΔG would mean that conditions are favourable for chemical reaction. Thus we can consider ΔG the amount of "free" or "useful" energy—specifically, non-PV-work-related energy—available to do work.

We don't have an economic counterpart to Gibbs free energy, but the concept can help us develop economic equations based on detailed economic data (an idea we will revisit later).

Boltzmann Law of Distribution

The Boltzmann law of distribution of energy, like temperature, is fundamental to thermodynamic function. Earlier, while describing the ideal gas laws, we established the following equation to express the combined gas laws:

$$PV = nRT$$

Where P, V, and T represent pressure, volume, and temperature in absolute scale of the gas, respectively; *n* represents the total number of moles present in the gas; and R is a constant (the molar gas constant). A mole is equal to the molecular weight of the molecules in the gas. This relationship was established by experimental measurements.

The Boltzmann constant *k*, as defined, can be called the molecular gas constant, which means that *k* is a constant, equal to the average value of R for each molecule in the gas. As we have observed, the relationship between R and *k* is obtained by dividing R with Avogadro's number, which is the number of molecules (6.02214×10^{23}) in a mole of a chemical.

$$k = R/(6.02214 \times 10^{23})$$

The values of R and *k* are experimental values. Their measurements have undergone many revisions as experimental techniques continued to improve. The latest values of R and *k* are as follows:

R = 8.31446 joules per kelvin per mole
$k = 1.3806 \times 10^{-23}$ joules per kelvin per molecule

The kinetic energy of every molecule in a gas is dependent on its absolute temperature. The temperature, in turn, determines the average value of the energies of the individual molecules. The energies of the individual molecules, however, vary within a range. This is where the Boltzmann law of distribution applies, and the Boltzmann constant *k* enters the distribution equation. The Boltzmann law of distribution gives the population N_i of any energy state in terms of energy of the state, ε_i, and absolute temperature T, according to the following equation:

$$Ni = e^{-\varepsilon i/kT}$$ (see footnote[6])

This equation has also acquired a theoretical basis, having been established by the rigorous techniques of statistical thermodynamics, a subject that is beyond the scope of this book.[7]

A basic principle of quantum mechanics is that the energy of any particle—atom or molecule—is quantized. Thus, a molecule can only occupy certain energy states and not all. The Boltzmann law of distribution tells us that at lower temperatures (in a system using an ideal gas) the total energy is distributed predominantly among the populations of molecules that belong to the lowest available energy levels. As the temperature increases, more molecules occupy higher energy levels and the population of energy-rich molecules increases at an escalating rate.[8]

Although the relative populations of various energy levels remain constant at any particular temperature, no particular molecule retains its acquired energy level for too long. A high-energy molecule soon collides with a low-energy molecule, thus transferring its energy to the low-energy molecule and itself falling back to a lower-energy state.

The Boltzmann law of distribution applies only to ideal gases. The behaviour of real gases will deviate from the

6 Ibid., p. 1.

7 Ibid., pp. 531–37.

8 Ibid., p. 1.

theoretical predictions, and the deviation will depend on how far the real system deviates from the "ideal conditions of molecular non-interaction". The more condensed the system, the more it deviates from the ideal conditions.[9]

The Boltzmann law of distribution will have an immense implication when we consider the equitable distribution of wealth in society. It tells us that something like the equality principle, which many egalitarian economists support on moral grounds, is embedded in the laws of the amoral inorganic world. Thus, even though a particular molecule in an energy-rich system might acquire excess energy, and even though the distribution law allows such excess, it can't retain this excess energy for too long and must pass on the excess to another molecule so that every molecule has an equal chance to receive the excess energy.

Darwin's Theory of Evolution

Darwin presented his theory of evolution in 1859 in *On the Origin of Species*, which explains how different species have evolved to populate the world at any time. Evolution sparked an intellectual revolution and is now considered one of the most vetted theories in history, its validity having been confirmed by a great body of irrefutable evidence. The underlying principle of evolution is natural selection, a concept often equated with "survival of the fittest". Two important tenets of the theory are as follows: 1) phenotypic variation exists among individuals, and the variation is heritable; 2) those individuals

9 Ibid., pp. 1, 531–37.

with heritable traits better suited to the environment will survive. Put differently, nature produces many progenies (genetic variations) in any population it produces. Among these progenies, those individuals with the genetic fitness most suited to the environment will produce offspring that can more successfully compete and survive.

A resounding confirmation of this theory has recently been observed in the laboratory in directed evolution experiments using microscopic forms of genetic material (DNA). DNA can be used in micro-organisms to produce biological catalysts called enzymes. Many enzymes are valuable to industry because they can perform the unit chemical reactions necessary to make valuable drugs and chemicals. Those enzymes that are produced naturally are optimally designed to conduct reactions in natural environments. But for industrial use, we often prefer controlled environments. These controlled environments can include the reaction medium and the substrate upon which the specific reaction is to be performed.

In directed evolution, the DNA, which is responsible for making the enzyme for a particular type of chemical reaction in a natural environment on a natural substrate, is made to undergo mutations (changes) at different locations using techniques known in molecular biology. The library of mutants thus produced is then used to make a library of enzymes with artificial variations. We select those variations that best perform chemical reactions in our artificial (industrial) system, and the process of mutation and selection is repeated over several cycles. The process has developed enzymes that are a thousand times more active and efficient for industrial reactions. Such experiments prove that evolution optimizes suitability of a system not only for a given environment but also for a new environment when the environment is changed.

Evolution is not among the general laws that rule the vast physical universe. In geological time, it arose on our planet only a fleeting moment ago—as if an afterthought of an invisible power that created the universe. The human race is the pinnacle achievement of the laws of evolution. The purpose of evolution, assuming it has one, remains beyond our comprehension. One thing is clear, however: if we're to survive as a species, much less understand the purpose of existence (a subject of the last chapter of Book 4, *The Highest Reality* (Prabhat Prakashan, 2024), we must create our own laws—moral laws—that protect not only the fit but the weak and the unfortunate.

We will argue later while connecting economics to thermodynamics that social Darwinism—a politically cut-throat interpretation of natural selection popularized by economists and sociologists in the nineteenth century—is fully applicable to business entities that are arbitrarily given the status of a person.

Concluding Remarks

When stripped of its ornaments, economics at its core is about production, distribution, and consumption of goods and services. Thermodynamics, meanwhile, is about work—or more accurately, work's transformation of matter and energy into products and services. As we have observed, the two disciplines have progressed in tandem—thermodynamics with the development of the heat engine and economics with the development of industry. Both are concerned with production—thermodynamics with the work needed for production and economics with the means necessary for production.

Without energy, there could be no generation of products and services, and without products and services, there could be no consumption and distribution. What brings the two branches of knowledge together is work—one devoted to mechanics and the other to human benefit. Work is where most thermodynamic functions merge, and it's also the source of all economic value and productivity. The goals of thermodynamics and economics—to create work through energy and to value products through money—are intertwined, and work is the linchpin that connects them.

Economics and thermodynamics require human intervention and action. Both need an agent. Both serve humanity, enhance the social compact, and allow us to flourish individually and collectively. So far, the two disciplines have progressed by following two sets of laws: one the objective laws of physics and the other the subjective laws of social science. It's time for economics to learn from thermodynamics so that it might rest on a similarly solid foundation. It's time to apply the laws of thermodynamics to economics. Our purpose here is to provide a broad framework and leave full development of the field to others. Our hope is that the new framework will render economics a well-orchestrated arrangement for wealth creation and a moral force that enhances the welfare of all members of society, irrespective of one's social, cultural, or ethnic identity.

7

The Framework of a New Economic Order

"Please, sir, this is the boy's first offence," the elderly Black woman said. "We don't have the money. Isn't there something you can do?"

The officer frowned sadly. "It's not within my power to pardon or excuse the fine. If the boy can't pay the hundred-and-sixty-dollar fine, he will be sent to the juvenile detention centre for a week or more."

The year was 1996, and my wife and I had just taken a fresh college graduate to Philadelphia's municipal building for the Medical College Admission Test (MCAT). We lived nearby in Cherry Hill, New Jersey, twenty minutes away, and had recently purchased a house there after moving from Pittsburgh. The MCAT was being administered on the second floor, and we were waiting in a long corridor outside a courtroom on the main floor. We had been watching an officer administer fines to several dozen defendants, who had already been found guilty of minor crimes by a judge. Many of those waiting to have their names called sat nearby in the corridor and would approach the officer when called. In each case, the officer would levy a fine, and if the defendant couldn't pay the fine, he or she would be given a prison sentence ranging from a few days to a few weeks.

The current case involved a young Black teenager who had approached the officer with his grandmother. From what we could make out, the boy had been found guilty of shoplifting a pair of shorts from a clothing store. The grandmother was begging the officer to wave the sentence, but the officer insisted he had no choice but to administer the fine or, if the boy couldn't pay it, impose a prison sentence.

As I watched the back-and-forth discussion, I couldn't help feeling sorry for the boy and his grandmother. It seemed the boy had been unable to resist the temptation of stealing a fancy pair of shorts, which no doubt he'd hoped to show off to his friends.

"I've already given him a good scolding," the grandmother told the officer. "I promise he will never do it again. He is under my care. We rely on food stamps and don't have the money to pay the fine. Can't you show mercy?"

"I'm sorry, ma'am," the officer said. "If I had the power, I would have pardoned him."

When it became clear the boy was going to be sent to the juvenile detention centre, I decided to approach the officer. "Sir," I said, "I will pay the fine on behalf of the grandmother. Please release the child."

The officer studied me for a moment, his face softening. "That's very kind of you. You don't have to pay the entire amount. I will pay the other half myself."

"Excuse me." Another Good Samaritan approached the officer. "I can pay a share of the fine too."

We talked over the matter and agreed to a compromise. I paid eighty dollars, the officer paid forty dollars, and the other man paid forty dollars. With that, the boy was set free.

Afterwards, the grandmother walked towards me with the boy at her side. She turned to her grandson. "You need to thank this gentleman for paying your fine."

"Your grandson has an innocent look," I said. "Given proper guidance, he might one day become a successful man."

The boy started to thank me.

"Son," I said, interrupting him before he could finish, "I don't want you to thank me. But I want you to make a promise to me. You must promise that you won't shoplift again. If you ever feel like having something, please call me, and I will buy it for you." I gave him and his grandmother my name and my phone number.

Everyone in the corridor, including the petty criminals awaiting sentencing, stood up and applauded. My wife and I felt embarrassed but joyful.

"I don't know how many youngsters we push into a life of crime by not showing compassion towards them," I said for everyone, including the officer, to hear.

The officer nodded in agreement.

I thanked him and the Good Samaritan, and we shook hands.

As my wife and I turned to leave, I addressed the crowd. "Remember that kindness can be contagious. The generosity of the officer and this man was much more praiseworthy than mine. I hope everyone can take a lesson from what was witnessed today. Everyone should extend a helping hand to the best of their abilities whenever an opportunity to help arises."

We earned another standing ovation, and we returned to our seats in the corridor feeling a renewed confidence in the goodness of people. The officer and the Good Samaritan were White. My wife and I were Brown. And the boy and his grandmother were Black. Two Whites, two Browns, two Blacks. A whole racial spectrum had come together to make a statement of unity, of caring and love for one another.

On that day, I didn't see racism in America, and I hoped I would never see it again. But there was no denying the extreme economic disparity that existed among my fellow citizens. I couldn't ignore that I lived in a country of haves and have-nots. It was a sobering experience. Despite the goodwill of the people, America's moral failure was evident for all to see. Unfettered capitalism was undermining the country's egalitarian principles. Why did the boy have to shoplift a pair of shorts? Why hadn't he been in school studying to become an engineer or a teacher or a doctor? Why did his grandmother depend on food stamps to feed him? Why did they have to depend on the mercy of the government and people like me? Didn't they have a right to their share of the national wealth? I couldn't help thinking about the need to create wealth—and to provide a means of sharing it equitably. Capitalism provided a partial answer to the first challenge but failed to address the second. The problem lingered in my mind, but I had no answers. I had yet to conceive an economic framework that could address both wealth creation and America's inequity.

The boy never called me or asked for my help. I hoped he would turn out to be the next Nelson Mandela someday. Even if he achieved the tiniest fraction of what Mandela had, I told myself, the eighty dollars was one of the best investments I would ever make. Moreover, it had inspired two other people—the officer and the Good Samaritan—to make a similar investment in our children's future. Maybe, just maybe, the people on hand that day would commit similar acts of compassion, creating a chain reaction, however brief. Better still, I thought, maybe we would create an economic arrangement one day that would eliminate such problems.

Corresponding Terms and Concepts

Having described the various thermodynamic functions and related scientific principles, we are ready to establish parallels between them and their economic counterparts. Then we will be able to use a process to build an economic framework based on the immutable laws of nature.

The Economic Equivalent of Temperature

Temperature in very simple terms helps us differentiate hot from cold. It measures the level of heat energy present in a system. Just like the level of water in a tank doesn't represent the quantity of water in it and the level of water in the ocean or in a pond doesn't tell us about the quantity of water in the ocean or pond, temperature doesn't tell us about the quantity of heat energy in a system—just its level.

A corresponding economic term to temperature would be something that differentiates rich from poor. It would tell us about the wealth gap. On a national level, it's per capita GDP. On a community level, it's household income or net worth per family. Any term that represents wealth disparity can replace temperature when we apply thermodynamic equations to economics.

The Economic Equivalent of Energy

To a chemist or engineer, the purpose of energy—the various manifestations of which are the subject of the first law of thermodynamics—is work. Scientists are interested in energy—chemical, mechanical, electrical, etc.—because they can use it to do different types of work. The interconvertibility of one form of energy into another and the principle of conservation (the first law) makes energy the prime substance in thermodynamics. In fact, it's not an exaggeration to say that energy is the currency of thermodynamics and that the generation of work using energy is its main business.

In a similar manner, the purpose of money, as originally conceived, is to represent values of different commodities: land, crops, livestock, labour, manufactured products, and all other things that are of use to humans. It's used as an exchange for commodities and to pay for the work involved in the production of goods and services. Since the primary natural resources—labour, land, minerals, water, etc.—are limited, conservation is also embedded in the basic concept of money.

Energy can't exist on its own. We can't create heat without hot matter. We can't create electricity without electrical wires for current flow or batteries for storage. We can't create light without glowing matter. We can't create chemical energy without a chemical reaction between different types of matter. In short, energy is always associated with matter. Likewise, money, as originally conceived, was also to be associated with physical things—to represent value of commodities of different kinds.

Based on these similarities, the laws that define the treatment of energy and the interconvertibility of different forms of energy are perfectly suited to determine the interrelationship of values of different types of commodities. In other words, in economics, money should be treated the same way energy is treated in thermodynamics using similar equations. Such a system's legitimacy will come from the rigour of the scientific process, not the arbitrary whims of people in positions of power.

Internal Energy and Enthalpy and their Economic Counterparts

Internal energy (U or ΔU) can be compared to the GNP of an isolated economy, i.e., countries like the pre-Depression-era Soviet Union, which didn't have trade or business relations with other countries. Internal energy, understood properly, can also mean the reserve potential of human creativity that, when combined with natural resources, can create an unlimited amount of wealth. Communist countries don't qualify since they fail to meet another necessary condition of wealth creation: an inequitable distribution of wealth.

Enthalpy (H or ΔH), meanwhile, can be compared to the GNP of countries whose economy is open, i.e., countries that interact and actively promote trade with other countries.

Gibbs Free Energy and Its Economic Counterpart

No economic term directly correlates to Gibbs free energy or to changes in Gibbs free energy (ΔG and ΔΔG). However, Gibbs free energy has assumed such a prominent role in thermodynamics that it should be possible to derive some highly predictive subset of economic formulae when the subtle and not-so-subtle commonalities between other economic and thermodynamic terms have been firmly established. For example, scientists have used ΔΔG calculations to predict if a minor modification in the structure of a complex chemical structure will lead to stabilization (a reduction in entropy) or destabilization (an increase in entropy) of the parent molecule.[1] Once the main framework of an economic arrangement has been established using the principles of thermodynamics, it would be helpful to be able to test whether incorporating minor changes leads to an improvement in the framework or pushes it along nature's eternal march towards entropy's graveyard.

Economic Equivalent of the First Law of Thermodynamics

Money is the currency of wealth creation. Money and wealth are equivalent and thus share the same value, which is measured in a nation's currency, whether the dollar, euro, rupee, etc. Such currencies are convertible from one to the other using the prevailing foreign exchange rates.

Money from different currencies is interconvertible into wealth, but in the aggregate, currencies remain constant in a closed system. A closed system in economics is bounded both by region and time. The additional parameter, time, is included because an economy is an expanding system, and its size depends on when we observe it. Thus, when applying the principles of the first law of thermodynamics to economics, time must be taken into consideration.

1 Ondracek et al., 2017. "Mutations that allow S1R2 orthologs to function in a NAD+-dependent environment". Cell Reports, Vol. 18, pp. 2310–19. Rodrigues et al., 2018. "Dynamut: predicting the impact of mutations on protein conformation, flexibility, and stability." Nucleic Acids Research, Web Server Issue, Vol. 46, pp. W350–W355.

Economic Equivalent of the Second Law of Thermodynamics / Carnot Cycle

A necessary condition for thermodynamic work is the movement of energy. In economics, a necessary condition for wealth creation is the movement of money. An unequal distribution of money must exist for movement to take place. It must move from the investor, who has more money, to the worker, who has less. No inequality, no movement. No movement, no creation of wealth. Equality of wealth kills wealth creation.

We can examine this concept further by comparing money movement in an economy to energy movement in the Carnot cycle. The Carnot heat engine confirms the thermodynamic principle that polarity in distribution of energy is an essential condition for the generation of work. The Carnot cycle must operate between two different temperatures—a hotter source and a colder sink—in order to use heat to generate work.

Without the movement involved in the heat engine's energy flow, we wouldn't have kinetic energy, and without kinetic energy, we wouldn't have work. Equality of energy distribution is not a recipe for work. In economics, no individual will work without a financial incentive, which requires someone (a person or organization) with more wealth from whom wealth can flow to someone with less. Uneven wealth distribution is thus an essential condition for a society to generate products and services. This doesn't yet tell us anything about how uneven the distribution must be to produce maximum work. We will discuss efficiency vis-à-vis inequality later.

Although a flow of energy from a source of higher intensity to a sink of lower intensity is fundamental for generating work, such an inequality alone doesn't suffice. If we simply connect the source and sink, energy will flow spontaneously from the source to the sink, and such spontaneous flow doesn't generate work. Consider a cylinder that contains high-pressure steam. If we open the valve in the cylinder, steam will spontaneously flow from the cylinder (the source) to the atmosphere (the sink) without accomplishing any useful work. The kinetic energy from the movement of the steam will dissipate into the atmosphere, and we will complain that some stupid operator has wasted our steam.

Work can be defined as force multiplied by displacement. Work = Force x Displacement. To produce useful work, a force must be applied to a subject placed on the path of energy flow. This requires a machine. The Carnot cycle provides a model of an ideal machine. It can also provide a template of an ideal economic output.

Polarity vs Efficiency: Nature Doesn't Give Any Advantage to Monopoly

In our critique of monopoly, we showed that it invariably leads to immoral outcomes, with large corporations thriving at the expense of smaller ones. But does nature support monopoly's advantage? More specifically, do the laws of thermodynamics provide an advantage to monopoly? Let's take another look at Carnot's engine and see if its efficiency can be improved by the horizontal integration of several such engines.

As we observed earlier, the fraction of kinetic energy that can be converted into work—i.e., the efficiency of an ideal heat engine—is determined by the polarity or the difference in concentration of energy (temperature) at the source and the sink. The relation is expressed by the following equation:

> Efficiency = $1 - (T_{sink}/T_{source})$
> where T_{source} = Temperature of the Source and T_{sink} = Temperature of the Sink, both expressed in absolute scale.[2]

As can be seen from this equation, the efficiency of a mechanical engine depends on the ratio of the temperature of the source and that of the sink. Since temperature represents concentration of heat energy and not its quantity, the efficiency doesn't depend on the engine's size. In economics, we can consider a corporation an economic engine. The efficiency of a corporation doesn't depend on how big it is; the efficiency depends on the capital employed, capital being the difference between the money owned by the owners of the corporation and that owned by its employees. Thus, monopoly doesn't improve efficiency. As long as we can provide funding at the same cost to a large or small corporation, efficiency will be the same.

Polarity vs Efficiency: Nature Provides an Advantage to Forward or Backward Integration

Although efficiency doesn't depend on multiplying the energy levels at the source and the sink, breaking the temperature

2 See also Atkins et al., 2018, p. 84.

gradient into two or more parts will increase efficiency. Consider the following two-stage process and compare it with a single-stage process. The single-stage operates between two temperatures: 573K (= 300°C, where K represents the absolute scale of temperature and C the centigrade scale) for the source and 293K (= 20°C) for the sink. The efficiency of this single-stage machine is reflected in the following equation:

$$\text{Efficiency}_{\text{single-stage}} = (1 - 293/573) = 0.4887$$

Now let's break this machine into two single-stage processes, the first operating between 573K (source) and 400K (sink) and the second between 400K (source) and 293K (sink) so that the total gradient is the same as that of the single-stage process (573K to 293K). The efficiencies of the first and second stage and their combination can be expressed as follows:

$$\text{Efficiency}_{\text{first-stage}} = (1 - 400/573) = 0.3019$$
$$\text{Efficiency}_{\text{second-stage}} = (1 - 293/400) = 0.2675$$
$$\text{Efficiency}_{\text{stage-1 + stage-2}} = 0.3019 + 0.2675 = 0.5694$$

A two-stage machine operating between two temperatures is more efficient than a single-stage machine that operates between the same temperatures (0.5694 vs 0.4887 in the current example).

In economics, a company that can be broken up vertically—so that one of its operations makes the parts of an auto, for instance, and another assembles them—will be more efficient than a vertically non-integrated company. Moreover, when we compare the capital intensity of two companies, the lower the difference, the higher the efficiency. Both factors speak against monopoly and in favour of multiple small companies, with an advantage only to forward and backward integrations.

If we break up the same temperature gradient among many stages, efficiency increases further. Maximum efficiency occurs when the machine is a multistage machine operating between the same two temperatures, but the gradient in each stage is infinitesimally small. However, to run such a multistage machine is practically impossible.

Would choosing the same gradient (573K–293K = 280K) at a different temperature spectrum make any difference? Let's consider the source at 673K and the sink at 393K, which will give the same gradient (280K). The machine's efficiency will be as follows:

$$\text{Efficiency}_{\text{single-stage}/673\text{–}393} = (1 - 393/673) = 0.4160$$

Thus, it appears that not only the temperature range but also where the range is chosen makes a difference. The higher up the scale, the lower the efficiency. When applied to economics, such a phenomenon has moral implications, which we will discuss shortly.

Polarity vs Efficiency: Does Scale Matter?

As we have seen, thermodynamics doesn't support horizontal integration (monopoly) but *does* support vertical integration (vertically integrated companies). This brings us to our next question: Does thermodynamics provide any guidance about economy of scale for vertically integrated companies? Or does scale matter while considering polarity vs efficiency? The question is pertinent, considering we argued against too-big-to-fail policies on moral grounds. The answer is that thermodynamics is silent in this respect, but our intuition tells us that scale matters under certain conditions.

Consider several creeks that merge into a river, with each creek boasting the same flow rate as the river itself. If we were to place micro-generators in each creek in place of a large generator in the river, the amount of work obtained from the sum total of the generators in the creeks would be the same as that obtained from the large generator in the river based on the principle we have already introduced. However, we won't be able to run a big machine via the small generators placed in the creeks. We will need to put a large enough generator in the river to run a big machine. In this sense, the size of the company indeed matters and will depend on our requirements. This doesn't promote unrestrained increase in size. Once a company—even one that is vertically integrated—reaches a size that is so big that the advantage of vertical integration no longer yields additional benefit, it should be broken into smaller companies.

In economic terms, although small businesses with the same capital intensity can achieve the same efficiency, we can't run an automotive assembly line using a combination of small businesses. One will need a minimum infrastructure to support automotive assembly. Size also matters in another sense: when a company runs a complex business that requires employment of an array of technologies, it will need an organization that is equipped with different skill sets. Although the thermodynamic principles applied to economics might not eliminate too-big-to-fail corporations, a morality that guides us towards equality would limit size even in complex organizations like an automotive assembly business.

Efficiency vs Wages of the Labourer: The Moral Conundrum

Let's look again at the efficiency equation of the Carnot engine:

$$\text{Efficiency} = 1 - (T_{sink}/T_{source}) = (T_{source} - T_{sink})/T_{source}$$

This equation tells us that with the same difference in temperature between the source and the sink ($T_{source} - T_{sink}$), the Carnot cycle's efficiency will increase as the temperature of the sink (T_{sink}) decreases and will reach the theoretical maximum of 1 when T_{sink} hits absolute zero. When applied to economics, it means that the efficiency (return on capital employed) of a factory for the same amount of capital and the same number of labour will rise in tandem with the poverty of the labour class. David Ricardo, remember, recommended in *On Principles of Political Economy and Taxation* that we pay labour minimum possible wages "to bring the worker into being a worker and sustaining him in the job". Although Ricardo's goal was to increase profit by reducing the cost of labour, it seemed to produce an additional benefit of higher efficiency when labour cost was reduced to the absolute minimum. When the West moved much of its manufacturing industry to China, where labour was cheap, the benefit to the capitalists was not only lower labour cost but also more efficiency of each dollar spent on labour. Although capitalists celebrated this gain, the practice turned capitalism into an immoral force—something we will explore later in greater detail.

Morality requires us to reduce the wealth disparity between the capitalist and labourer, but a sound economic policy calls for higher productivity from the factory. This creates a conundrum: How do we support an economic arrangement based on thermodynamic principles if adopting such a framework increases the disparity between capital and labour? The answer lies in technology, which is a common link between Carnot's heat engine (the origin of thermodynamics) and Robert Solow's growth theory of economics (the first treatise to draw attention to technology's oversized contribution to economic growth).

We may recall that at the time, Carnot was working on a model for the maximum theoretical efficiency of a steam engine. Watt's engine was the only commercially available steam engine, and its efficiency was stuck at a dismal 10.6 per cent. Although it applied only to theoretical limits, Carnot's work showed scientists and engineers that the steam engine's efficiency could still be greatly improved. With improvement still going on, modern steam engines operate at or slightly above 70 per cent of theory—a giant improvement over Watt's design. Technology helped make that improvement.

When Ricardo degraded labour to the lowest rank in the economic value chain, the role of technology on economic growth was barely understood. As we recall, even in the early versions of economic growth theories, the impact of technology on growth was still poorly understood and the emphasis was placed on capital and labour as the major contributors to economic growth. Total factor productivity, a catch-all term, was added to the growth equation to include other factors not covered by capital and labour. Robert Solow first showed that total factor productivity was indeed "technology" and contributed a whopping 85 per cent to economic growth, far outpacing labour and capital.

An important objective of a moral economy is to improve everyone's economic fortunes, not just those of a few—and certainly not just those of a few that control capital. Towards that end, technology can play the role of the great equalizer between advanced economies that have less labour and developing countries that have more. Through the aggressive application of technology, the advanced economies should try to absorb higher labour costs in order to close the gap between the haves and the have-nots rather than move their industries to countries with lower labour costs. An economic framework based on thermodynamic principles can help calculate how much productivity-gap technology is required to largely offset the rising cost of labour. Allowing labour costs to rise in advanced economies is a moral requirement, and the new framework I'm proposing can make that happen.

The Economic Equivalent of Entropy and the Energy Barrier: Further Confirmation of the Overriding Principle of Morality

As already discussed, entropy's directional arrow points from order to disorder, from confinement to liberty, from control to freedom, from calm to unrest, from a city to its ruins, from an intact coffee cup to its shattered pieces, from crystalline matter to amorphous matter—each seeking release from confinement. For the spontaneous process to take hold, however, there may exist an energy barrier that must be overcome. We have described it in chemical reactions as the energy of activation.

What is the economic implication of entropy? It can mean increasing the liquidity of the money supply, converting savings into consumption, and even breaking down the socio-economic order. In each case, a barrier must be overcome before the spontaneous process can take hold. The Fed increases liquidity when demand falls below a certain level, people start spending their savings when the economy falters, and a socio-economic revolution ignites when wealth disparity reaches a tipping point. We can use the second law of thermodynamics to maximize wealth creation while building enough safety measures (the economic counterparts to the activation energy of thermodynamics) to reduce, if not eliminate, the need for "activating" disruptive measures. Such safety measures will become clear when we discuss the common ownership of a great segment of technology that facilitates a nation's production and services.

As we discuss economics, we must remember that the living world, particularly the world humans inhabit, is an infinitesimally small pocket within the vast universe, a pocket where the directional sign of entropy is reversed. Within this pocket, order emerges from disorder. Products and services are about making order out of disorder, even though in the long run and within the broader context, the entropy of the inorganic world will win. Perhaps the reversal of entropy in our small pocket explains why we've evolved to embrace morality—something wholly absent in the inorganic universe. Our rules and laws often run counter to the process of natural selection that led to our existence in the first place. In order to survive and prosper as a race, we've found it necessary to cultivate morality, which also means protecting the weakest among us.

Our sense of morality—and purpose in life—makes us unique as a species. We don't expect our economic order to contradict our moral laws or be subservient to the laws of evolution. Nor do we want the laws of physics to override our moral laws. When and where morality conflicts with the laws of physics, we invariably side with the former. It follows that no evil force exists that would destroy us. Instead, we battle only those forces of nature that are amoral and that might contradict our moral laws. Most humans believe that the world belongs to each of us, but we recognize that we must seek guidance from nature while continuing to build civilization.

The Distribution of Wealth: Common Property and the Distribution of Excess According to the Laws of Physics

An economic arrangement must establish how the fruits of the economy will be distributed among the citizens. So far, the existing models have produced lopsided results. As discussed earlier, in the US, the top 1 per cent of the population owns 42.5 per cent of the wealth. In communist countries, the distribution might be more even-handed, but not enough wealth is generated. Supporters of the US system argue that it's better because even those belonging to the lowest economic rung do better than the average citizen in a communist country. But such an argument avoids the tough question of justice in distribution. Justice, of course, is not egalitarianism. If we were to adopt egalitarian principles of distribution like those recommended by ethicist John Rawls, we would turn the economy into a socialist one that lacks a mechanism for wealth creation.

The prevailing economic arrangements have focused on wealth creation or wealth distribution, never trying to reconcile the two. Each system tries to address its weaknesses by borrowing some of the tools used by other systems to generate more wealth or to achieve better distribution, with communism borrowing from capitalism and capitalism borrowing from socialism. The result has been a hotchpotch of systems without consistency or continuity. If we want to model an economic arrangement after the laws of thermodynamics, we can also establish a model of distribution in the same branch of science.

Unfortunately, as we have already learned, the maximum efficiency of a heat engine occurs when the sink has the lowest possible temperature. In economics, that means paying labour the minimum wage—something David Ricardo, Robert Malthus, and John Stuart Mill proposed in their treatment of labour under the classical economic order. This approach, of course, has helped turn capitalism into an immoral force. Karl Marx, meanwhile, proposed resolving inequality by granting ownership to labour, which robbed the economy of its wealth-producing power.

Such principles, upon which the current economic orders rest, are based on personal opinions and have become pure dogma. No scientific laws support them. We must find a way of defining common property if we are to avoid the immorality trap of capitalism and the impotency of socialism. If we can establish a certain segment of economic output that doesn't belong to capitalists or to labour, that amount should legitimately belong to everyone equally; the rest can be distributed for maximizing economic output according to nature's law of distribution of energy among molecules (Boltzmann distribution). Distributing the commonly held wealth will establish a floor for personal wealth, and it will be of sufficient size to eliminate poverty in rich nations and create equity in not-so-rich nations. Let's explore what that common property might look like.

Common Property: Undifferentiated Technology

As we have already established, the three factors of economic growth are capital, labour, and technology. To recap, the last one was originally called "total factor productivity", which economist Robert Solow later called "technological changes in the broadest sense" and divided into "the common pool of technological progress" and "new and differentiating technology". The common pool of technology comprises what can be learned in school and in any professional field, i.e., the knowledge that is freely available to anyone who knows how to mine it. Differentiating technology, on the other hand, comprises newly invented knowledge and newly created combinations of existing knowledge. The common pool of technology should rightfully belong to all members of society because it was created not by the users but by social funding in the past. It turns out, depending on whose analysis we use, it accounts for between 52 per cent (Edward Denison) and 69 per cent (Robert Solow) of the US's GDP. Common ownership means that it must belong equally to every citizen regardless of wealth status.

Of course, not all such common economic output can be distributed to citizens. Our new economic framework, after providing citizens with common services, will distribute the rest of the common economic output in cash. The common services, meanwhile, will include the following:

Education

The sources of common technology are twofold: creating an educated workforce and developing technology through publicly funded higher education and research. Accordingly, the first allocation of the collected common revenue will fund education at all levels. Education from kindergarten to higher secondary level must also include healthy meals for students. The US, the wealthiest nation in the world, has one of the highest children's poverty rates in the developed world, and malnourished children face a significant disadvantage.

In a companion volume of this book—Book 4, *The Highest Reality* (of my memoir series)—I have shown with a preponderance of evidence that reality appears in nature as pairs of opposites from neutral positions or nothingness. All products and services that form the basis of national wealth belong to these pairs of opposites. Since nothingness is unlimited, so too is the opportunity to create pairs of opposites, and as such, wealth. The only factors that determine the production of wealth are knowledge, freedom to conduct experiments, and a level playing field. Knowledge, the most critical aspect, helps us start a new business. It helps us build a new motor. It helps us develop energy: fossil, nuclear, hydroelectric, geothermal, solar, and so on. It helps us construct wonderful cities and marvelous buildings. It helps us get rid of diseases and prolong life. It helps us stop famines and produce copious amounts of food. It helps us protect our environment. It helps us build culture and civilization. And it will help us escape doomsday scenarios that many predict while showing us the dawn of new opportunities and a more meaningful life.

Knowledge means understanding the way nature works—both scientifically and spiritually. The source of all knowledge, of course, is education. Thus, we must support education and make it freely accessible to all. Of course, the value of knowledge will become apparent only when we're using our acquired knowledge to solve practical problems. Since we can never achieve perfect knowledge, we must apply everything we know to solve the problems at hand, to see what works and what doesn't. Many of our efforts will fail, but the power of knowledge ensures that we will succeed in more cases than we fail. The freedom to try is also a part of education. To make the most of education, we must provide every educated person an equal playing field to apply their knowledge to create new value. Free education, then, isn't just a question of morality but also the key to human survival and prosperity.

Infrastructure

The next allocation of the common pool from collected revenue will go to building and maintaining physical infrastructure. Roads, bridges, waterways, and so on are critical for wealth creation.

Defence

The next allocation will go towards maintaining a strong defence. Strong defence does not mean that military might is to be used for offence or revenge. Military power is only to be used for defensive purposes and against those who want to subvert the freedom of nations.

Environment

Protecting the environment is of common interest and will be funded at the federal level from the common fund.

Emergency healthcare

This is discussed in detail in Chapter 8.

Contraception

To be provided free of cost to all women of childbearing age. This is discussed in detail in Chapter 8.

Time-limited abortion

This is discussed in detail in Chapter 8.

Other services

The final allocation will go to other services that can't be controlled by individuals on their own but are of vital interest to every citizen.

*

After we have paid for the common services mentioned above, the remaining output that belongs to common technology will be distributed equally to every citizen. I'm unable at this moment to define what that amount will be, but it will be substantial. Moreover, it will establish a poverty floor by eliminating abject poverty. And it will make the economy more robust and the future more promising by supporting education.

No Welfare Programme

Welfare, a demeaning term, robs people of their self-respect. It comes across as patronizing as the haves allocate fee aid to the have-nots. After providing common services, the distribution of common property in cash, as an inherent right, will eliminate the need for social welfare programmes and the stigma associated with them.

Philanthropy, voluntary contributions by those who want to share their wealth with others and donate to worthy causes, will remain an important mechanism to connect people at individual, group, and societal levels. But it won't be monopolized by the rich. Everyone in society will be able to find something of their own to share.

Revenue Collection (No Income Tax or Internal Revenue Service [IRS])

The capitalist economy raises funds for common services through various taxes on income and consumption. The biggest source, of course, is income tax imposed by the federal government. In the US, the agency charged with collecting these revenues is the IRS.

As part of our proposed new framework, we must replace the current system of levying an income tax to raise funds for common services and common distribution. The capitalist mode of imposing an income tax, having evolved from a flawed capitalist economic arrangement, favours the owners of capital. To make it politically acceptable, the system creates a facade of fairness to hide a grossly unfair system. Although the federal government keeps tax rates high for most people and companies, it provides an overly complex system of tax breaks to the wealthy. Such tax rates are illogical and depend on who is in control of the presidency and which party controls the legislature. Let's consider the following examples:

- From 2008 to 2015, the official corporate income tax rate in the US was 35 per cent. But during that same period, 258 Fortune 500 companies paid rates of only 21.2 per cent because of various tax breaks.
- During the Trump Administration (2017–21), the passage of the Tax Cuts and Jobs Act (TCJA) reduced the official corporate tax rate from 35 per cent to 21 per cent. Many of the tax loopholes remained, however. In 2018, eighteen Fortune 500 companies paid no taxes on their income. In 2019, the top 379 Fortune 500 companies averaged a rate of only 11 per cent.
- Corporate tax loopholes, which include foreign subsidies, tax havens, and accelerated depreciation, amounted to more than $73 billion in corporate subsidies in 2019.
- Fortune 500 companies transfer corporate wealth to a limited number of executives by offering stock options and stock appreciation rights. Such practices encourage short-term measures at the cost of ordinary employees' job security and the long-term health of corporations.
- President Trump never disclosed his tax returns. The obvious implication is that Trump, who publicly claimed to have a net worth of more than $10 billion, paid no

income tax during the years preceding his presidency and will probably pay no income tax for several years to come.

- According to multiple news reports, billionaire Warren Buffett, one of the wealthiest people on earth, pays an annual income tax of 12 to 17 per cent—about half the rate of an average wage earner. He has openly criticized the system, pointing out that his tax rate is less than that of his secretary. However, his criticism of the system doesn't stop him from taking full advantage of tax loopholes. He claims only $100,000 in salary, which is taxed at a high rate, and categorizes the rest of his income as distribution, which is taxed at half the rate of ordinary income. Should we blame him for what most rich people do? Probably not. At the individual level he is taking advantage of the existing system. Adam Smith, remember, helped to replace the mercantile economics with capitalism but took a well-paying job in the mercantile administration.
- The Biden administration is replacing the tax policy of the Trump administration with a new policy of much higher taxes while continuing to borrow money irresponsibly. The next administration will perhaps change the tax policy again, and based on history, none of these policy swings will have much effect on wealth distribution in the US.

Under the circumstances, the prudent and fair thing to do is to abolish federal income tax, which in turn will eliminate the need for the IRS. The IRS has been accused of partisan biases in its auditing practices. Furthermore, because it audits less than 1 per cent of tax returns annually, it no longer serves as a deterrent to tax cheating. Eliminating the IRS will save the treasury an estimated $13 billion annually.

Our new framework will replace the federal income tax with a consumption tax on products and services. Meanwhile, turning a large portion of the national income into common property will allow us to tax products and services based on the amount of public technology they use in generating their revenue. An independent team of experts will determine the contribution of common technology to a company's product. Thus, products and services of the so-called tech industries, which depend heavily on university- and government-generated public technology, will be taxed at a much higher level than products and services of, say, a building product or a food distributor. To eliminate undue advantages gained by importing products from countries with cheap labour, appropriate tariffs will be levied to ensure an even playing field for domestic industries.

In our new arrangement, the basis for imposing tax will move *away* from political whims and *towards* people's legitimate rights, which, as I have already discussed, come from a company's use of public property to generate income through products and services. Moreover, consumption taxes will eliminate corruption and favouritism.

Some might counter that a consumption tax is inherently regressive, since much of the poor's income is spent on basic necessities like food, gas, and phone services. But in our new framework, no one will be poor, for everyone will receive an equal distribution of a significant portion of GDP and thus have their basic needs met.

Distribution of Excess Output

As mentioned earlier, excess economic output—after deducting common property—should be distributed to create optimal polarity for maximum wealth creation. Since we've already equated money with energy, the place to look for such a model is the Boltzmann law of distribution of energy among molecules. The beauty of such a system is that energy distribution depends only on the temperature of the system. If we were to use a similar system in wealth distribution, it would depend only on per capita GDP.

A statistical derivation of the Boltzmann equation starts with the assumption that at low temperatures energy will be distributed primarily to the lowest energy levels and that every molecule in an ideal gas will have equal probability of occupying any of the lowest allowed energy levels—as if following an ideal egalitarian principle. Such analysis also tells us that in the Boltzmann distribution the relative population of energy-rich molecules will increase with an increase in temperature. The law gives us the precise distribution of the different energy-state populations based on the immutable first principles of statistical thermodynamics.[3]

Statistical thermodynamics also predicts that, although the relative ratios of a population of molecules occupying different energy levels remains fixed at any fixed temperature, no individual molecule can retain its energy level for long. In economic terms, this means that no individual has the right or opportunity to hold on to their wealth forever and that every member of society has an equal right to climb to a higher rung of wealth whether or not they are born rich—the ideal goal of a just society. Nature achieves this arrangement not through some external force distributing the energy equitably but rather through the internal properties of the thermodynamic system itself. A distribution framework based on the principles

3 See also Atkins et al., 2018, pp. 531–35.

of thermodynamics would create very little need for the government to interfere in our life or raise excessive taxes to redistribute wealth. Wealth would no longer accumulate in a few privileged hands. And government's role would be confined to overseeing a few items of common benefit.

Private Property: No Inheritance Tax

The right to private property forms the sharpest dividing line between communism and capitalism. Karl Marx considered private property the root of all evil and called for its elimination in *The Communist Manifesto*. Capitalism, on the other hand, is built on the premise of private property. Without private property, capitalism contends, there's no incentive to create wealth. Private property is embedded in the very core of capitalism's mantra of self-interest. If we adopt Boltzmann's law as a model of wealth distribution, its statistical interpretation tells us that private property will create multiple pockets of polarity in wealth concentration.

If we include private property in our model, we must know how long it can remain in one person's possession. In our framework, it won't be long. Allocating significant economic output (as common property) equally to every member of society will reduce the pool of excess wealth in the hands of a few. The extent of this concentration will be further reduced by eliminating monopolies and by limiting the size of any enterprise. Inheritance, which in most cases involves more than one heir, will further dilute individual ownership. Using Boltzmann's distribution law as our model will necessitate the transfer of wealth from one hand to another. An increase in education and entrepreneurial spirit that comes with it will not only increase wealth but also competition for wealth. This competition will favour the transfer of wealth from lazy to active individuals. Awakening religious sentiments and encouraging philanthropy—a topic I discuss at length in Book 4, *The Highest Reality* (Prabhat Prakashan, 2024), of this memoir—will further reduce the permanent concentration of wealth in the hands of a few. The right to transfer one's hard-earned wealth to the heirs of one's choice is a strong incentive to create wealth. Any tax on inheritance would only encourage cheating (as is done now) or discourage wealth creation. On a more fundamental level, a tax on inheritance denies the right to private property. Given these factors, we won't need to impose inheritance taxes. The new framework, if properly implemented, will reduce the need for government interference in our lives.

Wealth Distribution and Equal Right to Be Rich

Since equal rights are a fundamental principle of a moral society, distribution of excess wealth needs further consideration. As the Boltzmann distribution law has already shown us, no individual molecule can retain its high energy for long and must pass on the excess or more to another molecule due to constant molecular collisions. Put in egalitarian terms, the thermodynamic system provides an "equal right to high energy to every molecule".

Some people in any generation are by nature lazy, and others are entrepreneurial. The lazy live on their inheritance, while the entrepreneurs work hard to grow theirs. This increases the lopsided concentration of wealth in the hands of entrepreneurs. However, as we pass from one generation to the next, some rich parents will raise lazy children, and some lazy parents will raise entrepreneurial children. Recall that the new framework calls for free education, which will not only increase the average number of educated people in society but make education available to rich and poor alike. Education, of course, is synonymous with technological growth. When education is equally distributed in society and the population of lazy and entrepreneurial people is being constantly reshuffled, kids of yesterday's rich may not remain rich for long. Wealth will move to a new generation of entrepreneurs, and the principle of equal right to new wealth will be maintained even though the lopsidedness of wealth concentration will increase with increasing wealth creation. This naturally increased lopsidedness will accelerate wealth creation, and every member of society will benefit.

A Clearing Mechanism for Sick Companies

We have established the immorality of treating labour like an inanimate cog of production. We've also discussed our moral duty to protect the weak among us. But what about weak or sick companies? Do we have a moral obligation to protect them? In 2010, the Supreme Court ruled that companies have the same legal status as a person.[4] By definition, a sick company is unable to generate a profit. How should our new framework deal with such companies?

Communist and socialist countries have nurtured sick companies on the grounds that they employ people. Capitalist countries, in contrast, have allowed them to fail. In our framework, we will side with capitalism's approach and let them face the survival-of-the-fittest test. The laws of morality arose in us through our consciousness, but they should not

---

4 See *Citizens United v. Federal Election Commission*.

apply to anything that lacks consciousness. Such entities should answer to the laws of physics or the laws of evolution. In our framework, since every member of society will be entitled to a basic payment, no one will have to worry about people plunging into poverty due to temporary unemployment. Employment will be for those who are best suited for a job.

One of the two pillars of our economic model is that it must generate optimal national wealth. Sick companies drain national wealth. Letting them die will improve the financial conditions of everyone, including those employed by sick companies, since a part of an improved economy will also flow to the unemployed. In our model, we will allow the bankruptcy process to clear the way for new companies. A robust economy will provide ample employment opportunities to those who are willing to work. Substantial additional benefits to the employed will create incentives for the unemployed to seek work. As already shown, economic polarities are a necessary conditions of wealth creation in our model. So not everyone will live at the same economic level.

Minimal Government

Our new framework will require minimal intervention from the government, just as the laws of thermodynamics work without supervision. In fact, most problems of the current economic arrangements are caused by the government's excessive control of the economy. Governments are often corrupt—and run by people who answer first to self-interest. When we look at communist governments, we see that the people at the top become filthy rich at the expense of the public while ostensibly working on their behalf. And when we look at the personal wealth of even the most liberal politicians in capitalist governments, we see that they accumulate enormous fortunes while in office. Why do the super-rich support politicians by funding them during elections? And why do Russian oligarchs support the autocratic government in their country? Because each will benefit from financial favours granted them by those in government. The framers of the US Constitution knew as much, which is why they wanted to curtail federal power. With the passage of time, our legislators have changed the constitution or manipulated it to give the government an increased role in our lives. Our new framework will place ironclad restrictions on government's role. The government's role will be limited to maintaining law and order, ensuring our national defence, building and maintaining our infrastructure, and protecting the environment.

When our economic framework is converted into a fully structured economic arrangement, the governmental organization necessary to deliver the requirements of this new arrangement will become apparent. Rather than trying to reform existing departments and institutions, we will build from the bottom up new ones that are consistent with the new economic arrangement and the new role of government.

Banking Reform

Leveraged financing is an essential part of modern businesses. However, today's lending practices favour big corporations. Government can help level the playing field by requiring banks to provide loans to all businesses, large and small, at the same interest rate. Banks can decide which enterprises to lend to in each bracket based on creditworthiness, but they won't be allowed to require different equity/loan rates. Banks also must meet certain ratios to ensure that enough small businesses are financed.

Inheritance and Private Property Have Parallels in Nature

Our main criticism of the existing economic frameworks is that they're based on a few people's opinions on what should constitute a proper framework. All other aspects—including data analysis and the sophisticated mathematical equations that follow—have been about constructing the complex body of modern economics atop those existing foundations. The focus of any legitimate economic framework should be twofold: the creation of wealth and its equitable distribution. These two foci have never been properly integrated into a single economic arrangement, which has created tension and social unrest in countries that have adopted either of the two options.

Our framework is an integrated one that encompasses both wealth creation *and* its equitable distribution. We have used the natural laws of thermodynamics as a template to create wealth. For distribution, we have divided our national economy into two parts: (i) equal distribution of a significant part of GDP to all members of society as their inheritance right and (ii) distribution of the rest unequally to entrepreneurs based on their individual contribution to wealth creation. By entrepreneurs, we mean anyone who makes a positive contribution towards creation of wealth. Here again we have used the principles of Boltzmann's law as a guide to determine the nature of the distribution.

Regarding the distribution of that part of the economy inherited by all, we used the doctrine of inheritance right: the equal inheritance right of all members of a generation to that part of the economy that depends on common technology or what Robert Solow called the "common pool of technological progress". Inheritance also involves a right to private property as absolute and the unobstructed right of individuals to transfer their private property to their designated heirs.

So far, we have supported the inheritance right on the basis of moral arguments. But inheritance also has a sound scientific parallel and useful template in genetic heredity, which means that we inherit our genetic composition from our parents. Our parents are the exclusive source of our genetic composition, and we are the exclusive heirs to our parents' genetic information. While discussing Darwin's theory of evolution in an earlier chapter, we noted the theory's two basic tenets: (i) phenotypic variation exists among individuals, and the variation is *inheritable*, and (ii) those individuals with heritable traits better suited to the environment will survive.

At the time Darwin described his theory of evolution (1859), the molecular basis of genetics and inheritable traits wasn't known. Later work on molecular biology provided a sound and experimentally verifiable basis of genetic inheritance. The principles of equality (equal right and equal obligation) and diversity (needed for resiliency) are each enshrined in genetic inheritance.

Briefly, the blueprint of our phenotype is contained in our genome (genotype), which is comprised of the chromosomes in our cell. The blueprint is our DNA in the chromosomes. The cells of our body contain two sets of chromosomes. We inherit one member of each pair of chromosomes (and the corresponding DNA) from our father and another from our mother. This inheritance is guided without exception by the principle of equality. No cells have more DNA from the father than from the mother. Each of our cells contain exactly twenty-three pairs of chromosomes—no more, no less. All the cells will have the same numbers of the same DNA, the composition of which, of course, will be different in different people (see below).[5]

Phenotype describes our physical traits: the colour of our eyes, skin, and hair; our behaviour and our ability to acquire knowledge; our body size, morphology, physical strength, and biological orientation; and all other bodily traits. These are our inherited traits (properties) through natural law.

The equality principle in the transfer of genetic information is enshrined in a process, called mitosis, by which our body cells divide to generate new cells to help us grow or to repair damage to our body parts, such as when we sustain a cut. Mitosis also helps to replenish those cells that routinely die to keep us rejuvenated and healthy; this includes the routine and frequent replenishment of our blood cells and skin cells. In mitotic cell division, the chromosomes faithfully reproduce themselves by self-replication. The new cells produced by mitosis are the same as those from which they are generated so that the equality principle remains intact.

Although equality is enshrined in all autosomal cell divisions by the egalitarian principle that underlies mitosis, diversification is the purpose of the other type of cell division called meiosis,

---

5 The twenty-three chromosome pairs consist of twenty-two pairs of non-sex (autosomal) chromosomes and one pair of sex chromosomes. In the case of males, the sex chromosome is XY. In females, it's XX. Although all twenty-two autosomal pairs differ from one another in terms of size, the two chromosomes in each pair share the same size. In sex chromosomes, the X is significantly larger that the Y.

which is responsible for procreation (reproduction). This process can occur only to produce sperm in men's testes and eggs in women's ovaries. In meiosis, the male-derived and female-derived DNA can exchange their genes (genes are segments within a DNA) by "crossing over", so that when the sperm and egg combine to make a zygote (the cells that further divide by mitosis to generate the embryo), each sibling born is different from the other (even though they possess equal shares of their parental DNA). For that matter, every person born on earth is different from every other. This diversity gives any living species resiliency without compromising the principle of equality in inheritance. Without this resiliency, a single calamity could wipe out an entire race.

While we are given an equal right and obligation to our genetic inheritance, it's up to us as individuals to acquire additional traits on our own—tangible things like wealth and worldly possessions that we acquire through hard work, and intangible things like morality, respect for others, compassion, religion, education, knowledge, and other traits that are acquired, not inherited. These are our own property, individually acquired, just like the economic status acquired by an entrepreneur through their own effort.

We all love our children. This is an instinct—nature's gift to us. Because we love our children, we try to teach them important values that we ourselves learned from our parents and through our own endeavours. We want to give them the best education—even better than what we received. The more benevolent among us try to do similar things for others in society. This love for others—our instinct to give our best to others—is what virtue is all about.

At the root of all progress lies the freedom to acquire virtue and pass it on to others. Our virtues are uniquely ours.

It's our right and absolute freedom to become virtuous and pass on our virtues to anyone we feel is a proper recipient. Nobody, particularly not our government, should interfere with our fundamental right to acquire virtue and pass it on to the next generation. Entrepreneurship, under our framework, is like virtue. It involves acquiring material, educational, and spiritual assets by inheritance or through our own endeavours. Accordingly, our natural laws tell us we should be free to pass on the fruits of our entrepreneurship to our children and the next generation without hindrance or interference from others.

Our acquired traits make us unequal, and this inequality makes society grow and flourish. It also makes us unique among all living things. If we are to grow as a society, we must promote acquired traits, and this promotion must include the absolute right to distribute these personal acquirements to our heirs, without interference. The origin of the right to private property lies in this freedom to acquire, accumulate, and distribute both material and moral/spiritual wealth to our heirs without external interference. And this principle, as just shown, is grounded in the laws of nature.

In fact, we pass along to our children not only material wealth but virtues. When we are benevolent, our children become benevolent. We can teach our children to be kind and respectful towards others when we ourselves practise the same behaviour. Such virtues are based on the doctrine of sacrifice. In essence, we teach our children to practise sacrifice. When we become a benevolent society, a society that values sacrifice, we help the next generation become richer—materially and morally.

Cell division, as mentioned above, is responsible for the growth of our body. But this growth is controlled by a restraining factor so that our organs, rather than growing disproportionately, stop growing when they reach optimal size. At this point, an equilibrium is established; what is lost is only replenished. If we use natural laws as our guide—via the equal distribution of a large part of the GDP to all members of society and the unequal distribution of acquisitions through entrepreneurship (and the inheritance thereof) as proposed in our framework—an equilibrium will soon be reached in which the overall distribution resembles Boltzmann's law of distribution. Such a system, just like our body, will be self-regulated with a minimum need for government oversight. Less government means less corruption. Less corruption means more entrepreneurs. More entrepreneurs means more GDP. And more GDP means a bigger pool for equal distribution. It's a win-win situation for everyone.

The Missing Link: An Anchor for Reserve Currency

To make our new framework applicable globally, we will need a concrete formula to convert one currency to another. Thermodynamics is based on a concept of conservation of energy that implies an immutable formula of conversion of one energy form to another. When it comes to currencies, the last solid connectivity among different currencies was severed in 1971, when the US eliminated the gold standard and failed to replace it with another solid link.

The elimination of the gold standard allowed different nations to create as much of their own currencies as they wanted, the only restraining factor being the concern about inflation and the effect on their free-floating exchange rates.

These two factors, economists thought, would stop countries from doing things that would hurt their currency's standing international trade. The re-establishment of exchange rate equilibrium after a country changes its money supply has never been instantaneous. The time lag has hurt the smaller economies more than the larger ones. This has led to large-scale manipulation of currencies by bigger countries and bigger businesses. As already discussed, the size and power of the US dollar as the reserve currency gave the US an ability to print almost unlimited money without feeling the effect—yet. This arrangement can't continue forever. The time gap needed to re-establish equilibrium will end soon, at which time the country will face high interest rates, large-scale currency devaluation, and high inflation.

China has taken advantage by hoarding enormous amounts of US dollars and now has the power to manipulate its own currency to steal manufacturing businesses from other countries, particularly Western ones. China has become the world's manufacturing hub and won't hesitate to use its position to blackmail the West at any time of its choosing.

Robert Zoellick, president of the World Bank and former US Treasury secretary, called for reinstituting the gold standard in 2010. In an op-ed in the *Financial Times*, he wrote, "The system should also consider employing gold as an international reference point of market expectations about inflation, deflation, and future currency values ... Although textbooks may view gold as the old money, markets are using gold as an alternative monetary asset today." Indeed, as mentioned earlier, countries are hoarding gold. Zoellick suggested that the new system of pegging currencies to gold could start with at least five of the world's largest currencies: the dollar, the euro, the yen, the pound, and the renminbi.

I'm not convinced gold should once again become the reference point for establishing convertibility of different currencies, but it could be better than giving that role to the US dollar. Gold has its own problems, the most critical of which are its origin in mining and the leakage of its supply to jewellery. The lure of gold as a reserve currency lies in its rareness and not in its constancy. The gold standard would allow unfair advantage to countries that possess gold mines and would distort the monetary system as gold is funnelled to luxury items.

What should be the nature of a new anchor? If currencies need to be converted to a reserve currency for international trade—either by law or by necessity—fairness dictates that the reserve currency should be linked to a solid anchor. To be legitimate, that anchor must be transparent and must not favour one region or nation over another. Gold can't be that anchor for the two reasons mentioned above. Moreover, because the supply of gold is mostly fixed, it provides no opportunity for economic growth, which, as you might recall, is one of the reasons why the gold standard was abolished. A fixed exchange rate with gold can't support the kind of growth of the money supply needed to support an expanding economy. If we vary the exchange rate with gold to accommodate growth—seemingly a reasonable proposition—the issue becomes who will decide when the exchange rate should be escalated. To maintain transparency, the reserve currency holder can't unilaterally make such a decision. The G20 countries could determine the escalation rate, but achieving a consensus would be impossible without strong guiding principles.

What then is the answer? We could tie the value of the reserve currency to the products and services whose value it's supposed to represent. If two nations make the same product, its value should be the same, without tariffs and trade restrictions. Tying the reserve currency to products and services will eliminate the barrier to growth, since growth means growth of products and services.

Since there are so many products and services and because different nations use different ones, trying to include every variation will become an impossible task. But perhaps we can use a basket of products and services that represent a fair distribution among most nations. Wall Street uses a similar model: the Dow Jones Industrial Average. The Dow tracks thirty large, publicly owned blue-chip companies trading on the New York Stock Exchange. Although limited to thirty companies, the Dow represents the pulse of all industries, and it does so quite successfully. In like manner, nations could agree on a limited number of commodities (major products and services) to represent an index linked to the value of the reserve currency. In addition, rather than allowing a particular nation's currency to become a reserve currency, the world should revisit Maynard Keynes's suggestion at the Bretton Woods Conference: the reserve currency should be a new international currency called the bancor. If it were accepted as the reserve currency, the bancor would be indexed to a basket of commodities, and all other currencies would be indexed to the bancor.

Details Count, and They Are Limitless

At this stage, trying to add details to our proposed framework can come at the cost of losing its elegance. And doing so can reduce the framework's range of applications. Such a framework should always be kept simple and anchored to a few fundamental rules. That doesn't mean that details are unimportant. Details give a theory its practical utility.

Consider Einstein's one line equation, $E = mc^2$, one of the most elegant theories ever formulated. It fuelled the Manhattan Project, which led to the development of the first atomic bomb. And since then, thousands of nuclear scientists all around the world have added countless details to the equation to help produce an abundance of nuclear energy.

Consider another similarly powerful equation in physics: Schrodinger's equation. Though more complex (and therefore not shown here), it's still a one-line equation. An entire field of quantum control is being developed as a result of the equation, and thousands of research papers are being published to add details. In fact, theories that look simple but boast immense applications have driven the physical sciences since the beginning and will continue to do so.

Back to economics. Poor people, as we've shown, are no less trustworthy than rich people. When Dr Muhammad Yunus established the Grameen Bank to provide credit to the poor, the bank's employees explored countless details while determining how to operate the bank. How, for example, should they define poverty? Yunus, noting that we lack a concrete definition of poverty and that people use their own understanding of poverty to define it, wrote, "Such conceptual vagueness greatly damaged our efforts to alleviate poverty … In my work, I found it useful to use three broad definitions of poor to describe the situation in Bangladesh. P1 (bottom 20%—the hardcore or absolute poor); P2 (bottom 35% of the population); and P3 (bottom 50% of the population) … Within each category of poor, I often create subclassifications on the basis of region, occupation, religion, ethnic background, sex, age, and so on. Occupational or regional categories may not be quantifiable as income-asset criteria, but they help us to create a multidimensional poverty matrix."[6]

These definitions helped Yunus develop specific targets for Grameen Bank's financing. To make our new economic framework apply to specific cases, we will need details. For instance, one of the objectives of the new framework is to establish equal treatment of people of different classes. Suppose we want to apply our framework to the treatment of women in the workplace. Men and women belong to various subcategories—Black, White, Hispanic, etc.—and among each class are subclasses based on religion or regional origin. We can prepare a multidimensional female matrix as Yunus did with poverty and apply it to the framework to determine a detailed action plan.

Since details can be endless, they can only limit the utility of our framework if we try to add more at this stage.

A Movement: Not a Revolution or an Evolution

"Virtue lies in the middle."

—Aristotle, *Nicomachean Ethics* (325 BCE)

Not a lake or a flood can run a generator
You need a steady flow of water
Lakes sleep, rivers make, floods shatter

6 Yunus, 1999, p. 41.

The calm air does not make the turbine turn
Only blowing wind makes the turbine run
A violent hurricane makes the turbine burn
—The Author (2022)

Our new framework must take hold in the form of a movement and through a democratic process—not too slowly, nor too violently. My reasoning is reflected in natural and social processes, as discussed below.

Changes in Natural Processes: Scientific Observations

The universe is in a state of constant change. All phenomena are moving towards so-called "attractors", but they do so at different speeds.

Consider the example of wood and oxygen, which we explored in connection with activation energy. The combination of wood and oxygen is thermodynamically unstable because the products of combustion (carbon dioxide and water) possess less energy than the contents of wood (carbohydrates, which are comprised of carbon and hydrogen, and oxygen). Here the great attractor is the energy gradient. According to the second law of thermodynamics, wood and air should change to carbon dioxide and water and release heat to the environment. The process can occur (i) very slowly, maybe over tens or hundreds of years, (ii) very explosively within seconds or minutes, or (iii) in a controlled manner at a speed of our choosing. As already discussed, for this change to occur, we need to provide activation energy. Let's look at how the three processes work:

The Slow Process

If we let the wood rot in the soil, bacteria in the soil will decompose it by taking oxygen from the air and converting it in stages to carbon dioxide and water. The heat from decomposition will be released to nature. The process occurs slowly, and the activation energy is provided in tiny amounts by enzymes at every stage of the rotting process. Such a process provides the energy necessary for the growth of flora and fauna. But if we want to use the released heat for domestic or industrial purposes, the process is useless.

The Explosive Process

Consider a forest fire. Some miscreant lights a match and tosses it into dry leaves in a forest. The match provides a tiny amount of activation energy to start a small fire in the leaves. The burning leaves provide more activation energy, and more leaves catch fire, starting a bigger fire. The fire spreads to nearby trees, a chain reaction begins, and soon the forest is ablaze. The process occurs at exponential speed, destroying every house and burnable substances in its path. Such an explosive process is destructive to our interests.

The Controlled Process

Now consider a fireplace. We put a few logs and kindling in our fireplace and ignite the kindling, which ignites the logs. As the logs burn, we add more logs to keep the fire going. The heat released provides comfort to us and our family. The same phenomenon occurs when we burn natural gas to fire the furnace that heats our house in the winter. Such a controlled burning of a fuel is directly helpful to our interest, and we control its speed as we see fit.

The energetics of the above reaction—the conversion of carbon, hydrogen, and oxygen to carbon dioxide and water with a release of energy—are the same in the three processes, but the second one (the explosive one) is detrimental to our interests. The first is of ultimate benefit to us, and the third one is both beneficial to us and occurs at a speed that we control to suit our purposes. Put in social terms, the first process occurs at very slow "evolutionary" speed, the second at a destructive "revolutionary" speed, and the third at a controlled "movement" speed.

Now consider a nuclear reaction. When you bombard a uranium isotope of atomic mass 235 with a neutron, it undergoes thermal fission, splitting it into two or more lighter atoms and emitting three neutrons.[7] In the process, a tiny amount of mass (*m*) is converted into a large amount of energy (*E*) as heat. The amount of heat released can be calculated using Einstein's famous equation, $E = mc^2$, where *c* is the speed of light. Because three neutrons are generated from bombardment by a single neutron, the reaction can readily lead to a chain reaction. When the chain reaction is carried out in a configuration that occurs as an uncontrollable chain, we get the destructive atomic bomb. But when the same reaction is carried out in a controlled mode in a nuclear reactor, we get the same energy in a usable form.

---

7 The isotope of uranium with atomic mass of 235 is written as ${}_{92}U^{235}$. The subscript on the left indicates the element's atomic number, which identifies the atom as uranium with 92 protons in its nucleus, and the superscript on the right indicates its atomic mass.

Nuclear energy provides 20 per cent of America's electricity. In France, it provides 70 per cent.

Finally, consider the difference between natural evolution and directed evolution. We have seen that changes by natural evolution generally occur over millions of years, but they can also take place at explosive speed. The mutation of the COVID-19 virus into the more virulent delta variety or the more transmissible omicron variety, for example, occurred in a matter of months, wreaking havoc on human health worldwide. But when we control evolution in the laboratory in directed evolution, we can produce desirable changes in enzymes with medical and industrial uses. We carry out directed evolution at a controllable speed of hours or days. The slow process is of unknown consequences to us, the explosive is harmful, and the controlled is beneficial.

Changes in Political Economy: Social Changes

Social changes, particularly in political economy, mimic scientific processes. Consider the major divide in political economy—capitalism on one side and communism on the other. Capitalism replaced mercantilism and evolved via small changes that entailed democratic back-and-forth movements. Communism, on the other hand, has largely evolved through revolution and under autocratic control. Although neither system has produced optimal results, the process by which the systems were implemented has favoured the former (democratic capitalism) over the latter (autocratic communism). Thus, our experience tells us that a democratic movement is far preferable to a violent revolution.

Concluding Remarks

In every phenomenon, things change rapidly and often at an exponential rate at the beginning and end. The gestation period, the time during which the phenomenon develops and matures, takes the longest. During the first few seconds of the Big Bang, things proceeded at infinite speed. Then billions of years passed. Scientists predict that when the Big Crunch comes, the universe will end in a few seconds. Similarly, a newly formed human embryo develops rapidly at an exponential rate during the first few weeks. The foetus then enters a period of growth and maturation. When it's time for delivery, the process progresses again at rapid speed.

Political and economic arrangements are intertwined, and it seems clear that ours have entered a phase dangerously close to the end. The world is becoming almost equally divided between two ends of the political and economic spectra: democracy vs autocracy; capitalism vs socialism. When the population is sharply divided between socialism and capitalism or between liberalism and conservatism, the message is as unmistakable as it is urgent: unless we can solve the underlying causes of such polarization, the clash between the two systems will only intensify until it leads to the breakdown of both in a revolution.

George W. Bush won the US presidency in 2000 by only 393 votes. Most of the presidential elections since then have been narrowly won in the electoral college. Such a close division makes claiming a mandate from the people impossible, not to mention illogical.

Opinion writers like Paul Krugman of the *New York Times* and Eugene Robinson of the *Washington Post* blame the polarization on deniers. Election deniers, economy deniers, climate deniers, science deniers—anyone who doesn't fit their definition of the truth is a denier. They forget that their political opponents consider *them* to be deniers of the opposing views. Philosophy professor Crispin Sartwell of Dickinson College of Pennsylvania argued as much recently in the *Wall Street Journal*.[8]

Blaming events like the riots and the assault on the US Capitol on 6 January 2021, the January 2023 assault by the supporters of the narrowly defeated Brazilian president Jair Bolsonaro on the presidential palace, or the violent protests by the leftist supporters of the ousted Peruvian president Pedro Castillo on election deniers comes at the cost of peaceful coexistence. Similarly, dismissing those who don't support the sudden elimination of fossil fuels as "climate deniers" or "science deniers" might be politically convenient but constitutes dangerously flawed thinking. In such cases, we need to recognize that when differences of opinion become so extreme, both opinions are flawed. When such controversies arise, the truth typically lies somewhere in between. What we need in such cases is a heathy debate. When the "politically correct" try to stigmatize others in order to shut down opposing views, it deadens the spirit of innovation. We need to find a system that addresses the concerns of both sides rather than dismissing one in favour of the other.

Most political clashes can be traced to economic issues. The first communist revolution that overthrew the tsar of Russia in 1917 wasn't just a political revolution; it was the victory of one economic arrangement over another. Our current economic systems, as I have indicated, have become defunct. Capitalism has led to indefensible economic disparity, and in trying to

---

8 12 January 2023, p. A13.

support our capitalist economic order, we have incurred more national debt—$31.4 trillion at last count—than we will ever be able to pay. According to a recent article by Vince Kolber, when all types of debt are considered, Washington actually owes $100 trillion.[9] The escalating rate at which our national debt has been increasing indicates that a catastrophic end is near.

The UK's economy, meanwhile, is in shambles, and the country has had three prime ministers in three years! The political upheaval is the direct result of economic problems. The majority of the common people are suffering, while the rich remain unscathed. France and Germany, the two biggest European economies, are also facing economic distress and internal turmoil. The communist countries are facing even more discontent.

History tells us—and Russia's recent invasion of Ukraine confirms it—that when a country faces economic distress, it resorts to war in a bid to deflect the public's attention. Wars, of course, make matters worse.

It's time we replace the existing economic systems with the framework I propose. It's my hope that, in response to my clarion call, the independent voices of the world will carefully read my proposal and begin the process of making a sustainable change to the new economic arrangements. A failure to do so will only worsen the state of chaos, which will require a costly and time-consuming recovery.

Clearly, we would be wise to implement our new economic framework through a movement rather than a revolution or slow evolutionary process. But the strongest reason to implement our system through a movement is that our new framework is perfectly structured for just such a process.

---

9 *Wall Street Journal*, 21 December 2022, p. A17.

Our new framework is not a compromise between capitalism and communism and / or socialism. It's a new system built on nature's laws and subordinate to morality. Yet a critical analysis of our system suggests that many of its policies—including distribution of a part of national income that is common property to every individual and a drastic reduction of the role and size of government—can be implemented gradually as amendments to the capitalist model. Hence, I propose a movement approach—neither a violent revolution nor a slow evolution—to implement our new framework. Revolutionary changes are destructive and short-lived, and evolutionary changes are too slow to produce an effect within the foreseeable future. A movement—a steady and well-conceived process—mirrors the activation energy needed for chemical reactions to occur in nature.

Our movement must, however, be started now in Western democracies before capitalism's excesses swing the political pendulum too far to the left and destroy the productive capacities of the world economy. This book is not written to gain instant popularity but to provide the initial activation energy needed to inspire a controlled chain reaction, with various individuals fleshing out the details without changing the spirit of the framework.

How could such a controlled chain reaction begin? Perhaps a few learned and rational-minded people from capitalist and communist countries can gather to declare that both economic systems have failed us. Mixing two toxic systems will only produce another toxic brew and won't solve the problem. It's time to give up age-old dogma, start anew, and implement a radically different approach. Our new economic framework provides just the right place to begin such a dialogue.

8

Healthcare and the New Economic Framework

On a beautiful winter day in January 2012, I visited Kolkata for my annual review of PMC Rubber Chemicals India Private Limited—the name I had given to the chemical plant in Rishra, West Bengal, that I had purchased from ICI seven years earlier. As part of my review, I would study next year's budget, and since the fiscal year began in April, I typically visited in early winter.

Like always, Akhtar, my driver, would be chauffeuring me from one appointment to the next. We were scheduled for a visit to the Indian Association for the Cultivation of Science (IACS), a premier research university in the affluent locality of Jadavpur, about six miles from Kolkata's city centre. Dr C.V. Raman, a Nobel Prize winner in physics in 1930, pioneered the famous Raman spectrum, an indispensable analytical tool used globally for research and medicine, while at IACS. I was excited for my upcoming visit and hoped to discuss a potential research collaboration between PMC Group and the IACS faculty.

At about one o'clock in the afternoon, Akhtar picked me up at the Oberoi Grand Hotel on Jawaharlal Nehru Road, formerly Chowringhee, Kolkata's busy city centre. As we passed through Gol Park, I remembered with pride delivering the prestigious annual Surendra Paul Lecture the previous winter at the Ramakrishna Mission Institute of Culture. Continuing south, we joined Raja S.C. Mullick Road, the main avenue in Jadavpur that would take us to our destination. A narrow strip of greenery and flowering plants divided the beautiful avenue, separating the traffic. The neighbourhoods around us were home to some of India's most storied educational and research institutes, including Jadavpur University, the Central Glass and Ceramic Research Institute (CGCRI), and, of course, IACS. I had done my doctoral research at Calcutta University and had often visited the institutions here to consult their extensive libraries. A nostalgic mood swept over me as we drove past them.

"An old abandoned public hospital used to be there." Akhtar pointed to a new sprawling private hospital, jolting me from my memories. "A few weeks ago, there was an accident at this intersection. A labourer was crossing the road when a car hit him. The labourer was bleeding profusely, and the crowd that gathered around him took him to the new hospital. The hospital demanded a deposit of something like one hundred thousand rupees before it would admit him."

I sat back in amazement. No one, let alone a labourer, carried one hundred thousand rupees in cash with them. Indeed, it would take a labourer five years to earn such a sum.

"Why didn't they take him to a public hospital?" I asked.

Akhtar glanced at me in the rear-view mirror as he drove. "Because public hospitals in Kolkata are miserable. There's always a big queue of sick people, and many critical patients die waiting before a doctor can see them. Besides, the nearest public hospital is much too far away. The man wouldn't have survived the trip."

"What happened to him?"

"There was a Good Samaritan doctor in the crowd. He took the man to his car and tended to his wounds. The man survived. Had it not been for that kind-hearted doctor, the man would have died."

We arrived a few minutes later at IACS, where several professors were waiting for me in a conference room. As they described their individual research, I struggled to focus on their presentations. Akhtar's story reminded me of something that had occurred while I was working on my research project at the University College of Science in Kolkata in the early 1960s. While performing a vacuum distillation, I cut my left middle finger after it got caught between the belt and the metal disk of a vacuum pump. The cut was so deep that the top quarter of the finger practically hung from the rest of the finger. I wrapped the finger with a towel and held it together as I took a rickshaw to the Calcutta Medical College Hospital, a public hospital, where the Emergency Room (ER) doctor promptly stitched the finger back together. If I'd been required to deposit money before receiving treatment, I would have lost the finger. Back then, no private hospitals had existed, and public hospitals had been well funded.

My mind wandered to the US. What would have happened had a similar accident occurred in an American intersection? Most hospitals in the US are for-profit businesses and run as such but are required to accept patients in the ER, regardless of their ability to pay. After treating a patient, they ask for billing information and typically collect payment from the patient's health insurance provider. If the patient has no insurance, the hospital will bill the patient directly. If the patient can't or won't pay, the hospital typically eats the costs, thereby passing them on to other patients in the form of higher charges. According to one of my doctor friends, approximately 6 per cent of all hospital bills in the US remain unpaid, which might be one reason why US healthcare costs are so high. In any case, denying emergency care to a patient would cause far greater misery.

When the professors at IACS finished their presentations, I asked them to give me the copies of the slides they had used and promised to get back to them after I got a chance to determine what synergies might exist between their research and ours. I thanked them for taking the time to talk to me and left, still distracted by Akhtar's story.

*

Ten years later, I returned from an overseas business trip. April was about to give way to May, and as I drifted off to sleep for a much-needed nap on a Thursday afternoon, I felt a twinge of pain in one of my upper right molars. Fearing that the pain might worsen over the weekend, I paid a visit to my dentist in Cherry Hill. I hadn't seen him in two years, thanks to COVID-19.

After I arrived at his office, his clerk handed me an eight-page questionnaire and consent form to fill out and sign. The consent form essentially stripped me of my legal right to sue for any unnecessary procedures performed. I was surprised to have to sign such an elaborate legal document before my dentist would see me. When I was finished, the clerk checked to make sure I had signed everywhere required and then filed the documents away. To my surprise, my dentist didn't bother to check the paperwork I had just meticulously completed, which meant he knew nothing of the changes in medication and health conditions I had just documented, considering that some of the changes in my file might have a direct bearing on my treatment. He didn't bother, I could only assume, because I had just signed away all my rights.

I exchanged pleasantries with a nurse I knew from previous visits, and she told me that my dentist wanted her to X-ray the area of my mouth that was in pain. A few minutes after she had finished, my dentist came to see me.

"Because of COVID," he complained, "I don't have as many patients as I used to—even though I spent forty-five thousand dollars on air purifiers for all nine rooms here." He studied the X-ray of my molar and then showed me a dark spot at the root, which had required a root canal treatment and crown several years earlier. "Looks like you need a fresh root canal treatment."

"Fine," I said, eager to address the problem. "Please go ahead."

He frowned. "I'd like to have an endodontic specialist evaluate your tooth first. His practice is just a couple of blocks away."

Strange, I thought. I'd been seeing my dentist for more than twenty years, and he'd performed several root canal treatments for me and my wife. Never before had he suggested we see an endodontic specialist for an evaluation.

He told the nurse to prescribe for me the standard medications and then set up a referral with the endodontic dentist nearby.

The nurse produced two preprinted and pre-signed prescriptions: one for twenty-eight capsules of Clindamycin HCl, an antibiotic, to be taken every six hours until finished, and one for extra-strength Motrin for pain.

"My nephrologist has advised me not to take Motrin because of my impaired kidney function," I said as I stared at the prescription, which was four times the strength of a standard Motrin tablet. "I specifically mentioned this in my questionnaire."

"Oh," she said. "Well, just take whatever painkiller you think you can tolerate."

I took the antibiotics as prescribed, but on Saturday, the pain intensified. When I called my dentist's emergency number, nobody answered. I left a message for my dentist to call me, and a couple of hours later, someone with a female voice returned my call. My dentist didn't want to be disturbed on weekends, apparently, because he spent that time with his grandchildren.

"You should call nine-one-one," the woman suggested, "and go to the nearest hospital by ambulance."

I shook my head in disbelief. If I went to the hospital, I'd have to fill out more paperwork and wait five to six hours in the ER lobby—only for an intern to prescribe for me an opioid painkiller while advising me to see my dentist on Monday. For my troubles, I would receive in the mail one or more big bills.

I opted to call the endodontist's office instead. A female assistant answered and assured me the doctor would call me back. And he did.

He instructed me to call his office at eight-fifteen Monday morning and make an appointment to see him that day. In the meantime, he said, I had no choice but to tolerate the pain. "Applying a heating pad or hot compress might help," he added.

I did as instructed and got in to see him early Monday afternoon. By then, the pain had subsided. Neither the endodontic specialist nor my regular dentist had informed me that the antibiotic would need forty-eight to seventy-two hours to kick in and begin curing the infection and related pain.

I filled out the same questionnaire and the same consent forms at the endodontist's office. A nurse took another X-ray. And after a short wait, the doctor found time for me between visits to other patients.

"Looks like you need a fresh root canal treatment," he said.

"That's fine," I said.

He nodded. "Before I can schedule you for a root canal treatment, I have to evaluate the tooth using a scan. But since your insurance company won't cover it, you will have to pay for it in cash."

The nurse took me to a tiny room and scanned my teeth with what looked like a miniature CT scan. It took ten seconds and cost $381. My insurance company, I was told, would be billed for the visit, and I'd have to cover whatever the insurance company wouldn't. I was given an appointment for 1 June—a month away.

By the time I visited the endodontist on 1 June, my insurance company and I had already spent thousands of dollars. The insurance company removed the bloodthirsty endodontist from its network, which meant if I had to use his services, I would have to pay him in cash.

I returned to my original dentist to see if he would be able to perform the root canal treatment. He could not. After I made a couple of visits, he put a crown on the tooth, which he could have done during my first visit, thereby sparing me from spending thousands of unnecessary dollars. The pain never returned.

*

No discussion of a new economic framework can be considered complete without establishing how we plan to provide and pay for healthcare, which consumes a large part of per capita GDP—somewhere between 2 per cent and 17.4 per cent, depending on the country.

The two episodes mentioned above took place a full decade and half-a-world apart, but each reveals a challenge in providing healthcare to the masses. The first anecdote reminds us why emergency healthcare must come from the common fund in our new framework: because in a just society, everyone should have access to emergency care, regardless of income or means. The second anecdote, meanwhile, shows how a byzantine system can result in runaway costs and poorly managed care. In a just society, healthcare costs should be reasonable and transparent, and no one should be funnelled from one provider to the next or forced to fill out countless forms, give away their rights, or pay for redundant services.

In our new system, the cost of emergency care will be reimbursed from a fund created from the common pool. For our purposes, emergency care must be narrowly defined as healthcare that requires immediate medical intervention. All other health expenses—except for birth control and limited abortion services, which we will discuss later—should be handled by individuals according to their own judgement. Everyone will be required to maintain minimal insurance coverage so that no one becomes a public liability. Medicare, Medicaid, the Affordable Care Act, and other government-run healthcare programmes will become unnecessary.

Comparing Healthcare Costs of Different Countries

In the following table, we list thirty countries and divide them into three groups of ten based on life expectancy: eighty-one to eighty-five years, seventy-one to eighty years, and sixty-one to seventy years. Not included are those impoverished countries whose life expectancies have sunk below sixty years. An assumption at the root of our analysis is that better healthcare provides longer life expectancy. The countries listed in the table have been chosen randomly, but if every country within each group were listed, our conclusions would remain the same.

Table Showing Healthcare Expense vis-à-vis Life Expectancy

Country	Life Expectancy[1] (Years)	Per Capita GDP 2019–2020[2]	Per Capita Healthcare Expense 2019[3]	Per Capita Health Care Expense as Percentage of Per Capita GDP
Japan	84.4	34,366	4,823	14.0
Switzerland	83.6	86,602	7,732	8.5
Spain	83.4	27,057	3,616	13.3
Australia	83.2	51,812	5,187	10.0

Sweden	82.6	51,926	5,982	11.5
France	82.5	38,625	5,376	13.9
Canada	82.2	43,242	5,418	12.5
Norway	82.2	67,294	6,647	9.9
Germany	81.1	45,724	6,646	14.5
UK	81.1	40,285	4,653	11.6
Average of Ten Countries	**Range 81–85 Average 82.6**	**48,093**	**5,608**	**11.5**
Qatar	80.0	50,805	1,870	3.7
United States	78.8	63,544	11,072	17.4
Poland	78.5	15,656	1,104	6.5
Turkey	77.3	23,880	396	1.7
Columbia	77.0	5,333	113	2.1
Hungary	76.6	15,899	1,062	6.7
Brazil	75.6	6,797	853	12.5
Mexico	75.0	8,326	540	6.4
Russian Federation	72.3	10,127	653	5.9
Philippines	71.0	3,300	142	4.3
Average of Ten Countries	**Range 71–80 Average 76.2**	**20,367**	**1,781**	8.7
Nepal	70.3	1,155	53	4.6
India	69.3	2,000	64	3.2
Botswana	69.1	1,901	481	25.3
Pakistan	67.0	1,194	40	2.6
Kenya	66.2	1,838	83	3.4
South Africa	63.6	5,094	547	10.7
Zambia	63.3	985	69	7.0
Uganda	62.8	817	32	3.9
Niger	61.8	2,097	31	1.5
Burundi	61.0	274	21	7.7
Average of Ten Countries	**Range 61–70 Average 65.4**	**1,736**	**142**	**8.2**

[1]At birth 2015–20.

[2]World Bank Estimate.
[3]World Health Organization Global Health Care Database.
Source: UN World Population Prospects, 23 July 2019.

What does this table tell us?

- Countries with the highest life expectancy (81–85 years) on average spend $5,608 per capita—that is, 11.5 per cent of their average per capita GDP.
- Countries with medium life expectancy (71–80 years) on average spend $1,781 per capita—that is, 8.7 per cent of their average per capita GDP.
- Countries with low life expectancy (61–70 years) on average spend $142 per capita—that is, 8.2 per cent of their average per capita GDP.
- The US spends on an absolute basis twice as much (~191%) as the highest life expectancy group and yet achieves 4.9 per cent lower life expectancy (78.8 years vs 82.6 years).
- The US spends on an absolute basis 6.2 times as much as the medium expectancy group to which it belongs.
- Even when compared in terms of percentage of GDP spent on healthcare, the US spends a much higher percentage than any group—17.4 per cent compared to 11.5 per cent by the highest life expectancy group and 8.7 per cent by its peer group.
- The US spends 204 per cent of Canada's expenses in healthcare and achieves 96 per cent of its life expectancy.
- The US is neck and neck with Poland in life expectancy (78.8 vs 78.5 years) but spends ten times more. When compared on the basis of percentage GDP, Poland spends 6.5 per cent of its GDP on healthcare while the US spends 17.4 per cent.

Quality of Healthcare

The data presented above paint a dismal picture of US healthcare, yet some argue that the quality of healthcare in America is superior to that of any other country in the world. They argue, for example, that if you want to get an MRI in Canada, you might have to wait for two months, while in the US, you will only have to wait one week. They argue that you might have to wait twelve to twenty-four hours in an emergency room of a UK hospital before a doctor will see you, while in the US, you will only have to wait three to six hours. The quality argument, although valid to a certain extent, doesn't result in the ultimate measurable objective of healthcare spending: improvement in life expectancy. US healthcare, when considered in terms of spending, is a colossal failure.

Analysing the Causes of Runaway Expenses in US Healthcare

When I had a simple toothache, I found myself at the mercy of an overlapping, overly complicated system that delivered grossly ineffective care slowly and expensively. It was a bureaucratic nightmare, largely created by my dentist, the specialist he recommended, and my dental insurance. Call it what you want, but I wouldn't call it quality care. The following major factors contribute to high costs in the US.

Government Control

Medicare and Medicaid are two of the most expensive government programmes in the US. According to the Centers for Medicare and Medicaid Services (CMS), in 2020 (note that the data in the table are for 2019), the US spent $4.1 trillion (19.7 per cent of GDP) or $12,242 per capita on healthcare. Of this amount, $829.5 billion (3.99 per cent of GDP) and $671.2 billion (3.22 per cent of GDP) went to Medicare and Medicaid, respectively. Together, the two government-run programmes cost the US $1.5 trillion (7.2 per cent of GDP) or $4,545 per capita.

The Food and Drug Administration (FDA) is largely responsible for the low life expectancy in the US. The FDA's take-no-risk culture has prevented American access to many life-saving drugs that are legal in other advanced economies. Consider the following example. On Thursday, 5 May 2022, the FDA warned people against taking the Johnson & Johnson COVID-19 vaccine at a time when an estimated 100 million new infections loomed in the coming months. Why? A report just released indicated that one in 3.23 million adults who took the J&J vaccine developed a rare blood clot. By March 2022, a total of 17 million people had taken the J&J vaccine. Among them, nine had died of a blood clot. If the FDA had possessed similar data before, it wouldn't have approved the J&J vaccine. According to data compiled by Worldometer, among ten advanced economies, the death rate from COVID-19 ranged from 2,000 to 7,000 per million as of 30 April 2020. The FDA, in other words, was willing to sacrifice 2,000 lives to save 0.3 people from a rare blood clot. Compare this to death rates in the US from car accidents in 2021: 129 per million.[10] Such examples abound. The US would be better off if people could decide for themselves what risk-to-benefit ratio is acceptable. The FDA's approval process also contributes to the high cost of drugs in the US.

10 https://www.nhtsa.gov

Medical Tort Law

In the US today, we can hardly turn on the TV without seeing ads by large law firms encouraging people to sue drug companies, hospitals, makers of healthcare devices, and doctors for damage—real or perceived—caused by their products or practices. In many cases, the law firms will file lawsuits on flimsy or even false grounds with the hope that the sued party will settle out of court to avoid a protracted legal fight.

A July–August 2004 article in the *Journal of Medical Practice Management* estimated that uncapped medical malpractice litigation added $97.5 billion to hospital and physician services.[11] Many physicians, unable to carry the high cost of malpractice insurance, leave medical practice.

Like my dentist, doctors and hospitals often conduct redundant or multiple tests before treatment to protect against negligence claims. According to an article entitled "Health and life insurance as an alternative to malpractice tort law", "Tort law could be counterproductive in medicine, encouraging costly defensive practices that harm some patients, restricting access to care in some settings and discouraging innovation."[12] In December 2010, Senator John Ensign (Republican-Nevada) estimated unnecessary tests cost between $100 billion and $250 billion (0.7 to 1.6 per cent of 2010 GDP) in the US annually. Most are ordered because of the fear of lawsuits. As I learned during my dental emergency, such expenses, far from being stand-alone costs, necessitate additional visits to hospitals and doctors' offices that are even more costly than the tests.

---

11 July–Aug 2004, 20(1): 44–51.

12 *BCM Health Service Res.*, Walton, 2 June 2010, 10:150.

If we can reduce government intervention and medical liability, healthcare costs will drop accordingly, and citizens can use the amount saved for other expenses.

Birth Control and Abortion Rights

One of the pillars of the new economic framework is equal rights, including the right to experience and enjoy sex irrespective of a person's gender. This means a woman has the right *not* to become pregnant from sex. Since a man has the freedom to have sex without the burden of becoming pregnant, a woman must also have the right to have sex without being forced to carry a child. This right must be balanced with the right to life of the foetus if the foetus can legitimately attain the status of a person.

My extended family experienced first-hand the perils of denying women the same sexual freedom accorded to men. In 1960, my wife Srimati's granduncle lived in Regent Park, Kolkata. He was a judge, and his home, a recently built six-bedroom, two-storey house, featured white masonry and verandahs with waist-high railings on both floors, front and back. The tiled floors were laid out in a red mosaic pattern, the doors were made of mahogany wood, and the windows had been fitted with shutters, iron bars securing those on the ground floor. Each floor boasted a kitchen, a large seating room, and two bathrooms. The concrete roof, fenced in by waist-high railings, could be used for large gatherings and for dining outside. The entire compound was protected by eight-foot-high masonry walls. Visitors entered through a red iron gate, on the other side of which stretched a drive wide enough to accommodate at least four cars. Countless fruit trees and flowering plants decorated the courtyard, and the mango trees grew so tall that their ripe fruit could be plucked from the rear verandah during mango season.

Few homes were situated nearby. But following the Hindu–Muslim communal riots that occurred when pre-Independence India was divided into secular India and Muslim Pakistan—a condition under which India received its independence—Hindus began to migrate from East Pakistan to West Bengal, particularly to Kolkata and its suburbs. When building his home, Srimati's grand-uncle had anticipated that some of his relatives in East Pakistan might come to live with his family. True enough, Srimati's own grandfather, a renowned advocate of the Dhaka High Court, and her grandmother came to stay with her grand-uncle. Another guest was Srimati's divorced aunt and her teenage daughter.

A kind and decent man, Srimati's grand-uncle treated his guests with the utmost love and respect. The family members who stayed with him always felt at home in his house, which became a popular gathering place for relatives on weekends. Srimati and her siblings spent every free hour they had there. Even today she speaks fondly of her memories of his home.

When the aunt's daughter began attending college, her grand-uncle hired two tutors for her—one to help her with her academic studies and the other to provide music lessons. The music teacher, a handsome young man in his late twenties with a sweet voice and amiable demeanour, was always greeted with smiles from the residents of the house when he arrived, and the aunt's daughter grew fond of him. The two would close the door of the music room and commence the next lesson. One fine morning, the aunt noticed her daughter was nauseous. She was pregnant. The aunt broke down in tears as if the entire world had come crashing down upon her. If the scandal of her daughter's premarital pregnancy became known in their conservative family, the entire community would isolate them.

To manage the situation, Srimati's grand-uncle barred the music teacher from entering the house and arranged for the aunt to take her daughter to a hill station near Darjeeling on the pretext that her doctor had recommended she take a hilltop vacation to treat lung problems. While the aunt and her daughter were at the hill station, Srimati's grand-uncle arranged for a secret abortion to be performed on the girl. The two women returned after the daughter had recovered from the trauma, but the daughter's life would never be the same. She missed a semester of college and sank into depression, all the while longing to see her beloved music teacher again. She was married away to a successfully employed man who lived in the US. When the couple left India to live in the US, they cut off all communications with their relatives back home.

By the time Srimati and I visited her grand-uncle's home last in the 1970s, her grand-uncle and grand-aunt had passed away. Her grandfather had moved away with his son, who was a wing commander in the Indian Air Force in New Delhi. The aunt remained, and the grand-uncle's eldest son and his daughter moved into the house. It was my first visit to the house, but Srimati's relatives treated me as if I'd been a family member all my life. I was moved, particularly when the aunt told me that she dearly missed her only daughter. She asked me if I could inquire about her when I returned to the US and, if successful in locating her, tell her to call her mother.

After I returned to the US, I used my various contacts to find the girl's husband and then asked my secretary to call him and tell him that her boss wanted to talk to him, confident that the ploy would prevent him from suspecting that someone from Kolkata was trying to contact him. When he answered, I identified myself and shared the purpose of my call.

"Your mother-in-law is always sad," I said, "and would greatly appreciate it if her daughter would call her at least once."

"I will convey your message to my wife," the man said in a polite tone.

His wife never called her mother, and he refused to respond to my future entreaties.

The aunt died in 2010 in loving care of her relatives. She never reconnected with her only daughter. The brief romantic encounter, the secret abortion that followed, and the scar left behind by societal pressure ruined not only a mother–daughter relationship; it plunged each woman into deep despair. One longed to see her daughter, and the other never forgave her mother for tearing her away from the love of her life.

*

Abortion and birth control are intertwined and play an integral role in healthcare. As we have already shown, healthcare consumes a huge chunk of national GDP. Our new economic framework can't gain broad-based approval if it ignores abortion and birth control. Abortion, of course, is a contentious issue that divides people not only in the US but all over the world. Before we present our position, let's take a moment to summarize the nature of the issue. Reproductive rights can be argued on legal/constitutional, religious, political, utilitarian, and medical grounds—all of which are superseded by moral consideration.

Legal and Constitutional Viewpoints

In its landmark *Roe v. Wade* decision, the US Supreme Court declared on 22 January 1973 that abortion is a legal right of all women. The decision was based on an interpretation of the fourteenth amendment of the constitution, Section I of which states, "No State shall make or enforce any law which shall abridge the privileges or immunities of citizens of the United States; nor shall any State deprive any *person* life, liberty, or property, without due process of law; nor deny any *person* within its jurisdiction the equal protection of the laws" [italics mine]. In applying the fourteenth amendment to decide the case, the majority opinion held that the Constitution didn't consider a foetus a person until it was born. A person's age, the majority argued, is counted from their date of birth and not from a date during their mother's pregnancy. The majority interpreted the "privacy right" enshrined in the constitution's fourteenth amendment, defined broadly to include a woman's right to determine whether or not to terminate her pregnancy.

The *Roe v. Wade* decision remained a contentious issue among legal scholars for decades. Justice Antonin Scalia, for instance, called taking advantage of the right-to-privacy clause "utterly idiotic".[13] A leaked Supreme Court draft in 2022 suggested that the Supreme Court of the United States (SCOTUS) was poised to overturn the law, by then nearly fifty years old. And sure enough, on 24 June 2022, in *Dobbs v. Jackson Women's Health Organization*, SCOTUS reversed a lower court ruling and, by a slim 5–4 majority, overturned

13 https://rewirenewsgroup.com/2012/09/18/scalia-thinks-roe-is-utterly-idiotic

Roe v. Wade. In the decision, the majority turned abortion rights over to the states, arguing that abortion isn't "deeply rooted" in US history and therefore can't be considered a constitutional right. After the ruling, states scrambled to codify abortion rights, or the lack thereof, with some reverting to decades-old laws that had been in place before *Roe v. Wade*.

Religious Viewpoints

The world's four major religions—Christianity, Islam, Hinduism, and Buddhism—generally oppose abortion and the practice of contraception. Personhood, they argue, begins at the moment of conception. According to ProCon.org, the position of each major religion can be summarized as follows:

Christianity's official position notwithstanding, its congregations often take a more liberal view of abortion. Thus, although the Catholic and Lutheran Churches oppose abortion, more of their members believe abortion should be legal (51 per cent to 45 per cent among Lutherans, and 48 per cent to 45 per cent among Catholics). Furthermore, the United Methodist Church, the Presbyterian Church, and the Unitarian Universalist Association of Congregations are officially pro-choice.

In Islam, multiple verses in the Quran state that life begins with the seed at conception. The Hindu text of *Kaushitaki Upanishad* condemns abortion and considers it the equivalent of killing one's parents. Buddhism rejects abortion at any time because it involves the deliberate destruction of a life.

Political Viewpoints

Pro-life groups align with the religious view that the unborn, at all stages of pregnancy, is a person. Thus abortion is considered the equivalent of killing a child.

Pro-choice groups argue that every woman should have control over her body. They consider abortion a women's rights issue—up to the point of birth of the child. Although some pro-choice advocates adopt the extreme view that a woman has a right to abortion as long as the foetus is in her womb, others are ready to accept a foetal viability test to determine when abortion should be a woman's right. The test hinges on the ability of the foetus to survive outside the womb.

From Gallup to Pew Research, most major polling outfits in the US show that a majority of Americans, about 60 per cent to 40 per cent, believe abortion should be "mostly or always" legal.[14] Pro-life groups have found a home in the Republican Party, while pro-choice groups typically align with Democrats. In the wake of *Dobbs v. Jackson Women's Health Organization*, red states (Republican-leaning states) are endeavouring to restrict and even criminalize abortion, while blue states (Democratic-leaning states) are working to codify and even expand reproductive rights.

Europe in general takes a less radical and more permissive view of abortion. The UK and the Netherlands, the most permissive of European nations, allow abortion up to twenty-four weeks into pregnancy and at taxpayers' expense. In Sweden, abortion is allowed on demand up to eighteen weeks into a pregnancy. In France, the limit is fourteen weeks; in Italy ninety days (thirteen weeks); in Germany, Denmark, and Belgium

14 https://fivethirtyeight.com/features/americans-views-on-abortion-are-pretty-stagnant-their-views-on-the-supreme-court-are-not/

twelve weeks; and in Portugal ten weeks. Poland and a handful of other Catholic nations ban abortion unless the mother's life is at risk.

Utilitarian Viewpoints

According to the Congressional Budget Office (CBO), a ban on all pregnancies after twenty weeks of gestation will increase the federal deficit by $225 million over nine years due to additional births and an increased need for Medicare coverage. In a peer-reviewed article in the *Quarterly Journal of Economics*, Steven D. Levitt concluded that abortion reduces crime because "women who have abortions are those at risk to give birth to children who would engage in criminal activities".

Medical Viewpoints

Many physicians argue that a foetus's personhood is predicated on its ability to experience pain. Dr Maureen Condic, a professor of neurobiology at the University of Utah School of Medicine, argues that the source of most primitive responses to pain is the spinal reflex and that this reflex is developed after eight weeks of gestation. Bernard N. Nathanson, the late abortion doctor, apparently gave up practising abortion when he saw in an ultrasound a twelve-week-old foetus open its mouth in what he called a "silent scream".[15]

15 "Fetal Images: The Power of Visual Culture in the Politics of Reproduction", *Feminist Studies*. 13(2), 1987: 263–90.

Dr K.J.S. Anand, professor of paediatrics at the University of Tennessee, contends that a foetus will feel pain during an abortion only when it is beyond twenty weeks of gestation. Britain's Royal College of Obstetricians and Gynaecologists opined that "the cortex is necessary for pain perception" and that the "cortex does not become functional until at least the 26th week of the fetus". According to the American College of Obstetricians and Gynecologists, "There is no legitimate scientific information that supports the statement that a fetus experiences pain."

The New Economic Framework and a Woman's Reproductive Rights

As already argued, women are entitled to the same rights as men, including the right to enjoy and experience sex without being burdened with pregnancy. Thus our new framework will provide every woman of childbearing age access to free birth control. The money will come from the common pool of funds left over *after* common services have been provided and *before* the remainder is distributed evenly among the population. In this respect, our framework differs from religious edicts that bar contraception. We consider contraception to be morally acceptable since it doesn't interfere with the rights of others.

But what about unintended pregnancies? Here we must consider not only the rights of the mother but those of the foetus. As we have observed, aside from extreme pro-choice groups, most people make room for foetal rights, although opinions vary widely as to when such rights begin. To retain credibility, our new framework must find a universal answer to this question.

Let's briefly review those propositions that are morally unacceptable.

1. "My body, my right", the argument of some extreme pro-choice groups, is an untenable position. It's an animalistic answer to a human question. It's no more justifiable than "my shelter, my right", which could be used to kill undesired babies. Humans are not just individuals; we belong to society and can't survive without it. And humans are more than animals; we serve a higher purpose in life than satiating our appetites. No right, including a woman's right to make her own reproductive choices, can come without responsibilities. If procreation perpetuates the human race, the female body plays an indispensable role in that process. A woman's right to abortion must be judged in view of her necessary role in procreation and her responsibility not only to herself but to society. These two interests must be balanced against one another.
2. The idea that personhood begins at birth may suffice as a legal definition, but it's not supported by logic or science. Birth, like puberty, is merely a stage in the continuum from conception to maturation and death. Consider two scenarios. In the first, a pregnant woman is medically induced to deliver her baby at thirty-two weeks. Nobody would argue that a person hasn't been born or that such a person doesn't have the same rights as any other. In the second, the mother is allowed a full thirty-six weeks of pregnancy before delivering naturally. If personhood begins at birth, that same

foetus that became a person when delivered at thirty-two weeks remains a non-person for four more weeks when delivered at thirty-six weeks. Debtosh, our oldest son, was born four weeks premature, but he grew up to graduate from MIT and is now president of PMC Group NA. Raj, our second son, was also born two weeks premature. He graduated magna cum laude from Harvard, became a professor at Carnegie Mellon University, has been a prolific inventor, and is president of PMC Group International.

3. The foetal viability test—namely, the ability of the foetus to survive outside the womb—is a flawed criterion because no baby, even one born full-term, can truly survive on its own once out of the womb. Every newborn needs support from its mother and multiple interventions by its paediatrician. Indeed, a lower infant mortality rate and better infant care have increased life expectancy. My wife and I know of a couple that gave birth to twins after eighteen weeks of gestation. Each twin weighed less than one-and-a-half pounds at birth and was kept in an incubator for several months. They are now healthy, grown children. Denying them incubator support would have been akin to denying a critically sick patient life support.
4. The attempt by physicians to define personhood as the ability to experience pain is also untenable, for no provable method exists to determine foetal pain.

In our new framework, we draw a distinction between life (living matter) and a person. Just as a cell or the DNA in a cell is living matter but not a person, an aggregate of cells—even a foetus—can be a living aggregate but not a person.

We take the scientifically supportable and non-controversial view that life is a continuum from conception to maturity. Birth is a stage in this continuum, just as puberty or menopause are phases in a woman's life. It's our position that a foetus becomes a person when the foetus develops its first nerve cell, the cell that is the essential component of the brain. The brain is essential to our personhood. It enables us to think, learn, and invent. It's also the organ that makes us feel pain. Until a foetus develops nerve cells, it's just a vessel preparing to support the onset of a brain, i.e., the appearance of nerve cells. This event—the appearance of brain cells in the foetus—occurs six weeks into gestation and can be experimentally observed. Brain cells boast unique morphologies that are different from those of other cells in the body and are thus readily identifiable. Scientists should be able to establish standardized and reproducible test methods to detect nerve cells in a foetus. We take the safe and incontestable position that personhood begins when brain cells can be detected. If for whatever reason a woman fails to stop a pregnancy by using contraceptive devices, she should be entitled to a physician-supervised abortion within six weeks (or when the nerve cells start to develop) of conception, free of cost.

But whose right prevails when we must choose between saving the mother or the unborn? In such rare instances, the mother will receive preference, for she is a fully functional person, while the foetus is still developing.

Concluding Remarks

Our new economic framework entitles every woman to free contraceptives and a free abortion until six weeks of pregnancy. Six weeks is enough time for a woman to decide if she wants to carry her pregnancy forward. The right to abortion during the first six weeks of pregnancy will also satisfy the equal rights requirement, which Justice Sandra Day O'Connor referred to when she wrote, "The ability of women to participate equally in the economic and social life of the Nation has been facilitated by their ability to control their reproductive lives."[16]

Adopting our proposed arrangement would save lives. According to the World Health Organization, unsafe abortions cause 68,000 maternal deaths worldwide every year. But every right comes with responsibilities. Access to free contraception and time-limited abortion are rights that must not be abused. If history is any guide, most men and women will exercise restraint while practising sex, but some people will use free access to abortion as a means of contraception. According to the Centers for Disease Control and Prevention, 45 per cent of abortions in 2014 were undergone by women who had had one or more previous abortions and 8.6 per cent were undergone by women who had had three or more abortions. Such practices can be discouraged by imposing increasingly steep financial penalties on women who seek numerous abortions. However, our position is that an abortion before the foetus develops nerve cells should not be a criminal offence.

Prioritizing in order of abstention, contraception, and time-restricted abortion makes it possible to build a compromise between groups with opposing views. But as we discuss women's health in terms of contraception and abortion rights, we must not lose sight of the fact that, for

16 See 1992 decision, *Planned Parenthood v. Casey.*

many women, motherhood is the most fulfilling experience in life. Countless loving couples, meanwhile, long to be parents. In America alone, two million couples cannot have children of their own and are looking to adopt.[17] So if for whatever reason a woman were to keep a child deep into an unwanted pregnancy, she would always be able to find someone eager to adopt.

17 https://www.americanadoptions.com/pregnant/wanting_adoption_families

9

Brave New World Dream

We have explored our new economic framework and the scientific principles that support it, but what would it look like in the real world? If the US, for example, adopted our new framework, how would life change for the average American citizen? What would it be like to live in a country whose economic laws were derived using a process that mirrored nature?

By working with the well-established laws of nature, we can create a new economic framework capable of creating wealth and distributing fairly. As explored in the preceding chapters, our new system will rely on the following twenty pillars:

1. **The laws of nature**. We have arrived at our new economic framework by using established scientific principles enshrined in the universal scientific laws of thermodynamics and, to a limited extent, the law of Boltzmann distribution and Darwin's law of evolution.

The product of such a new arrangement also harnesses the edicts of ethics.

2. **Minimal government**. The government will enforce and administrate the principles laid out in the new framework, but no branch of government will be allowed to create new procedures that contradict the new system or bypass its edicts. The argument that an elected government by a democratic process represents the will of the people is grossly inaccurate. Democracy, although better than autocracy, is still a flawed system; it imposes the will of the majority on everyone and encroaches on individual freedom as a result.
3. **Judicial oversight**. The administrative government will be subject to constant review by a special branch of the judiciary whose function will be to enforce implementation and preservation of the new framework.
4. **National income to replace welfare**. All social welfare programs will be abolished and replaced by equitable and rights-based distribution of the common share of the national income to every citizen. This will eliminate what Sen calls "abject poverty" in his welfare economics.
5. **Free education**. All forms of education—from preschool to undergraduate, master's, and doctoral studies—will be free and will be paid for by a significant part of the consumption-based taxes (see item no. 13).
6. **Optimal inequality**. Once the fair share of the national income is distributed among all citizens equitably, the remaining amount will be distributed to generate a healthy "inequality" among entrepreneurs and people willing to work. Polarity created by inequality of income incentivizes work and is critical for wealth generation.

7. **No unions**. All unions will be abolished. Employees will be free to decide where and how they want to work.
8. **No tenure**. Along with teachers' unions, teachers' tenure will be eliminated. Free education is a right of every citizen, but tenure and teachers' unions interfere with the hiring of the best teachers available.
9. **Same financing rules for all businesses**. If a business is creditworthy, it must have access to borrowed money at the same interest rate, whether it's a huge corporation or a small family-owned business. Likewise, when it comes to borrowing, the same debt:equity ratio should be required for every business, no matter its size.
10. **Nobody is too big to fail**. No corporation should become so big that it's given special treatment or commands extraordinary power.
11. **No monopoly or horizontal integration**. Since thermodynamics doesn't provide any benefit to monopoly, similar economic rules must apply. Corporations that exceed certain sizes must be broken up into smaller pieces. The maximum size of each piece will be determined by the size of the economy and the nature of the industry.
12. **No income tax**. No federal income taxes will be collected, which will necessitate abolishing the Internal Revenue Service.
13. **Consumption tax**. Instead of federal income taxes, the new system will rely on consumption-based taxes to fund projects of common interest and to allocate equitable cash distributions to every citizen.
14. **No inheritance tax**. The right to private property means no inheritance taxes. Wealth concentration in the hands of a few will be avoided due to the following factors: (i)

longevity limitation; (ii) dilution of inheritance through distribution to heirs; (iii) elimination of monopoly and size limitations of any commercial enterprise; (iv) distribution of a significant portion of national wealth as common property equitably to all citizens in the form of cash and funding projects of common interest; (v) encouragement of entrepreneurship and availability of free education; (vi) a moral and religious awakening in all people; (vii) encouragement of philanthropy. When every citizen feels they have received their fair share of the national wealth based on sound logic, not individual opinions, discontent about inequality will naturally disappear. See Book 4 for more on items (vi) and (vii).

15. **Independent reserve currency**. The US dollar will no longer serve as the world's reserve currency and will be replaced by an independent reserve currency, which will be anchored to a basket of products and services.
16. **No Medicare or Medicaid, and no mandated healthcare programmes**. Individuals will carry health insurance that meets their personal needs. Minimum coverage will be required so that no one becomes a public liability.
17. **Free healthcare emergency services**. All hospitals will be authorized to provide emergency medical services to all citizens and will be reimbursed by a common national fund.
18. **Free contraception**. All women of childbearing age will be entitled to free contraception.
19. **Time-limited free abortion**. Accredited medical facilities will be authorized to perform abortion at the request of any woman until the foetus begins developing nerve cells. This period will be approximately six weeks

from conception, but the exact time will be established through research.

20. **A movement**. The new framework will be implemented through a movement, not a violent revolution or slow evolution. It will be sparked by a group of steadfast intellectuals, and will spread like a chain reaction.

The above is only an outline. Many of the tenets of our new framework can't yet be imagined—at least not until independent scholars have a chance to explore the details in depth. As mentioned in Chapter 7, the details are limitless, which means future scientists-turned-economists will have to help us fill in the blanks. But that doesn't mean we can't begin pondering the possibilities. What follows is pure speculation. We are going to use our imagination to create six hypothetical examples of life in America after our new economic framework has been adopted.

Amari

Amari grew up on a farm in rural upstate New York, studied agriculture at Cornell University in nearby Ithaca, and eventually went to work for Company X, a multinational corporation headquartered in Minnetonka, Minnesota. He lost his job when, as part of the new economic framework, the special branch of the federal judiciary tasked with enforcement deemed Company X a monopoly and broke it into several smaller companies.

Ever a risk-taker, Amari could have gone to work for one of the smaller offshoots but instead decided to move back to his hometown of Wappingers Falls, New York, and start his own business. Despite lacking the financial clout and outsized economy of scale of the corporation that used to employ him, he had no problem securing a modest business loan and buying a property, thanks to the new economic framework. Determined to change agribusiness, Amari has created an experiment of sorts in the rolling hills outside his hometown. Part small family farm, part laboratory, Amari's new forty-acre operation employs six people while exploring the cutting edge of organic farming, biodiversity, and pest management.

Amari is part of a new generation of entrepreneurs and innovators who, empowered by the new system, are able to take big risks without fear of financial ruin. If his new enterprise fails, he won't starve or lose his home; he will just move on to the next challenge. Entrepreneurial success requires prudent risk, and such success can be defined statistically. And perhaps not surprisingly, it boasts a directional arrow. When people don't have to worry about losing their security, they take more risks, and those risks translate into more national income, i.e., more GDP. Because the new framework encourages risk-taking, the national income is raising the poverty floor.

Rosa

Rosa is in her mid-fifties and lives in Seattle, Washington. She and her husband bought their home twenty-five years ago, before real estate prices skyrocketed up and down the west coast. She is only a decade away from retirement but has just lost her job downtown at the regional office of Centers for Medicare and Medicaid Services (CMS). She wasn't fired;

her job has been eliminated now that CMS and other federal welfare programmes have been disbanded as part of the new economic framework, which renders such aid unnecessary.

Although Rosa has a bachelor's degree in actuary science and has always loved maths, she has been burned out at her job for a few years now. Thus, she is not that sad to see CMS and other federal programmes terminated. In the old world, she would have been too old to reinvest in her education and would have been forced to file for unemployment while she looked for a similar position elsewhere. But filing for unemployment is unnecessary, thanks to the national income, which is enough to provide the basic necessities, including food, transportation, utilities, and even a modest rent, for a family of four. And anyone can continue with their education without fear of crippling tuition fees. College, like high school, is free.

With countless opportunities available to her, Rosa decides to earn a master's degree in teaching at the University of Washington (UW). She works as a volunteer tutor at Ballard High in her spare time and looks forward to teaching full-time. The UW campus isn't far from her home in the Ballard neighbourhood, where she lives with her youngest son, now a senior in high school. Her husband passed away two years ago, and her other two children have already moved out and started their respective careers.

At the UW, Rosa isn't the only middle-aged student. Plenty of other seasoned adults have decided to go back to school now that education is free. She fits in well with her classmates and enjoys her classes. Well, most of them. One of her professors, an older gentleman on the eve of retirement, seems to have taken a romantic interest in her. She makes it clear she is not interested in his advances, but he continues to press her, even insinuating that her grade depends on her cooperation. In the old world, the professor might have been protected by tenure. Indeed, rumours at the school suggest the professor has a history of such behaviour but has never faced administrative consequences. But when Rosa brings a complaint to the head of the department, the professor is summarily fired. No more students will fall victim to his advances. He was a lousy teacher to boot, Rosa observes, and didn't know his subject.

Rosa is type 1 diabetic. The price of insulin has gone through the roof in recent years, and even with the national income, Rosa has worried about how she will continue to pay for her prescription. Fortunately, ever since the FDA streamlined its drug-approval process, drug prices have dropped. In the case of insulin, a new start-up company recently won financing from a bank and, thanks to its innovative methods, has been able to offer insulin at a fraction of the price of the old providers. Now the competition is scrambling to catch up, and the price of insulin has plummeted as a result.

Conor

Conor is a twenty-year-old high-school dropout who, until recently, was trapped in a cycle of poverty and abuse. He was raised by his single mother, a drug addict with mental health issues, and unable to move out of their Gary, Indiana, apartment due to the price of everything: food, transportation, housing. He was working two menial jobs but was still unable to make both ends meet, even with the help of food stamps. That was before the movement changed everything. Conor has always been good with his hands and likes to take things apart and put them back together, especially electronic devices. He started tinkering with radios when he was eight years old and eventually became known as Mr Fix It around the apartment. He could repair a lamp, a garbage disposal, an old stereo—whatever needed fixing.

Thanks to the new national income, Conor is able to move out, and thanks to the free education available to all, he goes to community college to earn his high school diploma and a two-year trade degree. He eventually lands a job as an electrician at an offshoot of Amazon, which was broken up after the special judicial branch declared it a monopoly. Conor's company specializes in music gear—guitar amps, keyboards, recording hardware—and needed an in-house electrician to test and repair products.

One day while at work, Conor feels a stabbing pain in his side and goes home, thinking he has indigestion or the flu. When the pain worsens, he drives across town to the emergency room at Saint Catherine Hospital and learns his appendix is about to burst. His appendectomy and short stay at the hospital are paid for by the common fund, and soon he is back to work fixing electronic gear.

His mother, meanwhile, no longer needs welfare of any kind, thanks to the national income. In fact, between her job and the national income, she has just enough monthly income to pay for addiction treatment and mental health services. After going to night school, she lands a decent job as a legal assistant and notices that she is able to save money faster than ever, since she only pays taxes on consumption (the IRS has been abolished and, along with it, income tax and estate taxes). She eventually saves up enough money to visit Ireland, where her grandparents were born. Due to the new reserve currency, such trips are easier to finance these days, since no one has to worry about fluctuations in the dollar.

Sita

Sita is a stay-at-home mom in her early forties and lives in Athens, Georgia. She and her husband are almost ready to send the kids off to college when she becomes pregnant. The couple had been using free, government-supplied contraceptives, but a faulty condom led to what Sita and her husband came to think of as their "miracle baby".

Only a year or two away from perimenopause, Sita is excited to become a mother once again. But twelve weeks into her pregnancy, she begins experiencing alarming symptoms. When she visits her ob-gyn near Bishop Park, she learns that her pregnancy is ectopic. The fertilized egg has attached itself to the fallopian tube instead of the uterus and thus has no hope of survival. She has no choice but to seek an abortion, which is provided free by the government because her health is at risk and the pregnancy is not viable.

Afterwards, Sita is inspired to start a blog and share her experiences. She soon gains a niche audience and becomes a bit of an expert on ectopic pregnancies. Now Sita is advocating on a host of pregnancy-related issues. She has a bachelor's degree in sociology and decides to enrol at the Terry College of Business at the University of Georgia to earn an MBA, with a plan to start a non-profit. But before she can get the non-profit up and running, she is hired by Piedmont Athens Regional Hospital to do community outreach. Happily, Sita finds that the low-income neighbourhoods she is tasked with helping are changing, thanks to the new economic framework. More people are going to school, starting businesses, and enjoying affluent lifestyles. Sita is happy to realize that in a few years she will no longer be needed and will be out of a job—just in time for retirement. By now, she no longer pays social security, but her national income will more than suffice as a retirement plan.

Minh

No corporation is too big to fail in the new economic framework, and when the special branch of the judiciary let one of the country's largest software companies go under, Minh lost her job as a data engineer. Minh, who has been a workaholic ever since graduating cum laude from Brown University in Providence, Rhode Island, decided to stay in the industry and start her own company in Silicon Valley.

Minh belongs to a growing number of young, up-and-coming professionals whose incomes are climbing as fast as their social status. Yes, she is richer than most of her friends, family, and neighbours, and yes, she and her colleagues have benefited from several pillars of the new economic framework. They pay no income tax and couldn't form a union even if they wanted to (all unions, including government ones, have been abolished). And they are driving optimal inequality—the kind that encourages innovation, entrepreneurship, and hard work without stratifying privilege and success. After all, a certain amount of inequality is healthy, for without the polarity created by inequality of income, our new framework would fail to incentivize work, which is critical for wealth generation.

Every time the national income grows, it's because of people like Minh. She and others like her are increasing the country's GDP, which in turn is making it possible for other less educated, less wealthy people to follow in her footsteps.

Jeff

As someone who never wanted to go to college or trade school, Jeff has nevertheless always had a strong work ethic. He joined the Local 1138 Carpenters Union in Toledo, Ohio, as an apprentice right after graduating from high school and worked his way up to foreman of a mid-sized construction company. When the US adopted the new economic framework, he was alarmed to see his union disband. It had always ensured competitive wages, solid benefits, and a steady progression in the trade.

But his fears proved unfounded. Along with no longer paying union dues or income tax of any kind, he has been able to negotiate health insurance prices in the open market, and thanks to tort reform, his monthly premium is actually less than it was when he belonged to the union.

Theresa, Jeff's wife, recently suffered a debilitating stroke and can no longer work. In the old system, that would have meant losing half their family's income. Moreover, they would have been hard-pressed to afford in-house care and rehabilitation. But their national income means they can continue to pay down their mortgage, keep their growing kids fed and clothed, and even save a little money every month. Theresa's prognosis for a full recovery is good, and she has decided to stay home with the kids, who will benefit greatly from having a parent waiting for them every afternoon when they return from school. In the old system, Jeff and Theresa would have been forced to face some hard decisions, including potentially selling their home and downsizing.

*

The six hypothetical scenarios above illustrate how some people will fare in our new system. Not everyone will prosper, but the vast majority of people will do better under this new framework than they did before.

Economics, of course, isn't just about developing the best universal economic model; it also features a political dimension, which means it requires the support of the people. Changing the status quo is difficult. Our new framework will face objections from mainstream economists and obstruction from politicians and existing political institutions. Only a sustained people's movement will bring about such a fundamental transformation.

My hope is that this book incites a middle-class movement to bring about major changes in economic arrangements nationally and worldwide. Such a movement can succeed through the ballot box and without violence but will require a massive educational initiative to convince everyday citizens that the time for change is now. Such an educational programme will demonstrate that capitalism, while a creator of massive wealth, has become an immoral force, and that communism and socialism, the two most popular alternatives, are impotent when it comes to wealth creation. Without wealth creation, equitable distribution becomes an empty gesture. While capitalism makes a few people rich and some people poor, communism and socialism make everyone poor, aside from a privileged few.

Concluding Remarks

The allure of the American dream still captivates the popular imagination. Politicians and the ultra-rich, in a transparent effort to protect their own interests, point to success stories while proclaiming that here—and only here—anybody can achieve their goals if they work hard enough. But we've already debunked the idea of American exceptionalism. Yes, America is one of the best places in the world to work and live, but only because so many other countries are built on terrible political and social arrangements. Advantages that depend on the weaknesses of others are not sustainable.

The US must lead by example and adopt a new economic framework. It's time we embrace a brave new dream—one that can come true in every corner of the globe, not just in America.

Humanity wins if everyone wins.

APPENDIX 1

Some Historical Dates, Books 1 to 4

Geological and Evolutional Events

Event	Years ago
Big Bang—origin of the universe	13,800,000,000
Our galaxy	10,000,000,000
Our solar system	5,000,000,000
Early beginning of Earth—formation of continents	4,500,000,000
First life appeared on earth	4,000,000,000
Appearance of plants	2,500,000,000
Appearance of soft-bodied animals	1,500,000,000
Appearance of the first bird forms	180,000,000
Extinction of dinosaurs	135,000,000

Appearance of mammals and primates	67,000,000
Appearance of Hominids	4,000,000
Appearance of Homo sapiens	200,000
Appearance of modern human	40,000
Agriculture	9,000
Age of Hinduism	3,700
Age of Judaism	3,300
Age of Buddhism	2,500
Age of Christianity	2,000
Age of Islam	1,400

The Size of the Universe

The diameter of the universe is about 93 billion light years. The light year is a measure of distance, not time. One light year equals six trillion miles, the distance travelled by light in one year. Therefore, the diameter of the universe is 558,000,000,000,000,000,000,000 miles, or to put it simply, 558 x 10^{21} miles, or 898 x 10^{21} kilometres.

APPENDIX 2

Historical Dates of People and Events Mentioned in the Memoir

Person or Event	Date(s)	Comment
Socrates	470–399 BCE	Philosopher
Aristotle	384–322 BCE	Philosopher
Thomas Hobbles	1588–1679	Philosopher
Robert Boyle	1621–1691	Physicist: Inventor of Boyle's Law
Baruch Spinoza	1632–1677	A Dutch philosopher of Portuguese-Jewish origin
John Locke	1632–1704	Philosopher and physician
David Hume	1711–1777	Philosopher and historian
Jean-Jacques Rousseau	1712–1778	Philosopher and writer
Immanuel Kant	1724–1804	Philosopher

Declaration of US independence	4 July 1776	
First Amendment to the US Constitution	15 December 1791	The Bill of Rights
Most recent Amendment to the US Constitution	7 May 1992	The 27th, on Senators' and Representatives' salary
Adam Smith	1723–1790	Father of Capitalism. Famous writings: *The Theory of Moral Sentiment* (1759); *An Inquiry into the Nature and the Causes of the Wealth of Nations* (1776–1778)
Marquis de Condorcet	1743–1794	Philosopher and social reformer
Jacques Charles	1746–1823	Formulator of Charles's Law (1780)
Jeremy Bentham	1748–1792	Philosopher and jurist
Mary Wollstonecraft	1759–1797	Philosopher and writer
Thomas Robert Malthus	1766–1834	Economist; Famous writing: *Principles of Political Economy* (1820)
David Ricardo	1772–1823	Political economist; Famous writing: *On Principles of Political Economy and Taxation*

Jean-Baptiste Say	1767–1832	Economist; Famous writing: *Traite d'Economie Politique*
John Stuart Mill	1806–1873	Philosopher and political economist; Famous Writing: *Principles of Political Economy* (1848)
Abraham Lincoln	1809–1865	16th President of the United States
Charles Darwin	1809–1882	Naturalist and geologist; Writing: *On the Origin of Species* (1859)
Bruno Bauer	1809–1882	Philosopher
Karl Marx	1818–1883	Father of Communism. Famous writings: *The Communist Manifesto* (1848) and *Das Capital* (1867)
Rutherford B. Hayes	1822–1893	19th President of the United States
Laws of Thermodynamics	1824–1860	The empirical and fundamental laws of physics that govern conservation of mass and energy; direction of flow of energy; generation of work from flow of energy; and directions of chemical reactions.

Friedrich Nietzsche	1844–1900	Philosopher. Called God "The Father of Evil"
The Communist Manifesto (see also Karl Marx)	February 1848	Authors: Karl Max and Friedrich Engels
John Dewey	1859–1952	Philosopher
Vladimir Lenin	1870–1924	Head of the Soviet Union (1917), (1922–1924)
Albert Einstein	1879– 1955	Special Theory of Relativity 1905; General Theory of Relativity 1915
Rabindranath Tagore	1861–1941	Poet, Nobel Prize in literature 1913
Mohandas Karamchand Gandhi	1869–1948	Humanitarian. India's freedom fighter, called "Father of the Nation"
John Maynard Keynes	1883–1946	Economist
Adolf Hitler	1889–1945	Führer of Germany 1933–1945
Subhas Chandra Bose	1897–1945	India's freedom fighter. Famously known as *Netaji*
Roy F. Harrod	1900–1978	Co-inventor of the Harrod-Domar Economic Growth Theory
Albert Camus	1913–1960	Writer and philosopher; Nobel Prize in Literature 1957

Milton Friedman	1912–2006	Economist; Nobel Prize in economics 1976
Introduction of Federal Income Tax in the United States	3 February 1913	
Creation of the Federal Reserve Bank of the United States (FED)	23 December 1913	
Evsey David Domar	1914–1997	Co-inventor of the Harrod-Domar Economic Growth Theory
Edward Denison	1915–1992	A pioneer in the measurement of the US Gross National Product
Paul Samuelson	1915–2009	Economist; Nobel Prize in economics 1970
Overthrow of tsarist regime in Russia by Lenin-led revolution	7 November 1917; as per old calendar, 25 October	
Dissolution of Dollar's dependence on Gold Reserve in the US	1968	

Elimination of the dollar's convertibility to gold	1971	
John Rawls	1921–2002	Philosopher; Famous work *A Theory of Justice* (1985)
Amartya Sen	1933–	Welfare Economist; Nobel Prize in economics 1998
Robert Solow	1924–	MIT Economist; Nobel Prize in economics 1987
World Bank	Established July 1944	HQ: Washington DC
International Monetary Fund (IMF)	Established 27 December 1945	HQ: Washington DC

APPENDIX 3

Summaries of Books 1, 2, and 4

BOOK 1: ***The Bright Side of Adversity: An Autobiography of a First-generation Immigrant to the US from India*** **(Om Books International, 2024)**

This captivating autobiography tells the story of a multifaceted first-generation immigrant to the US from India who rose from a tumultuous childhood to achieve prominence in diverse fields as a scientist, inventor, educator, executive, entrepreneur, and philanthropist. He established one of the fastest-growing chemical and pharmaceutical companies in the world and chronicled it in *The Makings of PMC Group: A Corporation with a Soul*. After declaring capitalism morally bankrupt and socialism financially impotent, he developed a new economic framework called *Wealth of People*.

He made a convincing case why science and spirituality can peacefully coexist in the same mind, developed his own epistemology to decipher truth from falsities in religions, and argued that human life has a special purpose to serve in this universe. An eternal optimist, he shows in *Highest Reality: A Treatise on Religion, Truth, Morality, and the Purpose of Life* that our ability to discover new things is as vast as the secrets of the universe and that there are no problems that human ingenuity cannot solve.

The primary focus of this biography, however, is not the life of the author or his accomplishments. The message is that life unfolds in the midst of adversity, and when we embrace adversity as a strength, it becomes a stepping stone to success. Similarly, when we face uncertainty with courage, a journey becomes an adventure full of excitement, awe, beauty, and fulfilment. The autobiography serves as a medium to bring these messages to life.

The fifteen chapters in the book cover the length of the author's life from birth to age eighty-three, the year he finished writing the manuscript. However, he covers only the first fifty-four years of his life in detail and the next twenty-eight years in summary. This latter period is chronicled in detail in three separate books that belong to a four-book memoir series. Chapters 1 through 12 follow a chronological sequence. The remaining three chapters cover topics that do not belong to chronological classification; they are based on the author's experiences throughout his life.

BOOK 2: *The Makings of PMC Group: A Corporation with a Soul* (Leadstart, 2024)

The year 1994 presented a dilemma to me. At the time I was the chief technical officer of PPG industries reporting directly to the chairman of the board. The dilemma was whether to launch a campaign for the chairman's job, which was becoming vacant at PPG and for which I had been shortlisted or form my own company. I opted for the latter and started PMC Group. My main reason for forming PMC Group was a firm belief that a corporation must have a soul, which corporate America was in danger of losing. Once I made up my mind and decided to form PMC Group, I resigned from PPG and bought one of its subsidiaries, the Polymer Products Company, which at the time boasted a revenue of only $16 million. From such a modest base, I built PMC Group at an accelerated rate.

As the business community recognized my success at PMC Group, writers began to approach me with ideas for a biography, and I realized that I wasn't interested in such ideas. We already had biographies and memoirs of industrial giants, such as *Iacocca*, Jack Welch's *Jack, Straight from the Gut,* and *Sam Walton: Made in America*. In the years since, we've had Walter Isaacson's *Steve Jobs*, Robert Iger's *The Ride of a Lifetime, Bloomberg by Bloomberg,* and many others. I felt that merely retelling the stories of my goals and successes would add little to that literature.

As I concentrated on building PMC Group companies, it became one of the fastest-growing chemical and pharmaceutical companies in the world. Between 1995 and 2022, the annual revenue of PMC Group grew ninety times, from $16 million to more than $1 billion. We achieved leading positions in many industry sectors and established manufacturing facilities in the United States, Europe, South Korea, and India. Currently, we employ more than 2,000 people.

Before I started PMC Group, I wrote down the mission of the corporation that I envisioned. "PMC Group's vision," I wrote, "would be to build a success model for twenty-first-century corporations that can grow rapidly, create jobs, promote social responsibilities, and generate the profits necessary to perform these functions well." In our model of a corporation with a soul, top- and bottom-line corporate growth would work in tandem with each other and with the creation of jobs and the discharge of social responsibilities. The purpose of PMC Group would be to embody and carry forward the dreams and aspirations outlined in its vision.

In 1997, I presented my vision of PMC Group to the US Commercial Development Association's annual banquet as their keynote speaker. Most of the corporate leaders in attendance praised my vision, but no one adopted the values that underpinned my company. By 2019, however, a similar group at the Business Round Table meeting that August debated the purpose of a corporation, and 181 of 188 attending CEOs adopted values that nearly matched those of PMC Group. So, I think the time has finally come for my memoir. I believe that all the success and satisfaction I've enjoyed have come from my enduring passion for discerning scientific truth and the ethics of human behaviour. By sharing this passion and the knowledge it brought to me with as many people as possible, I hope to spread the success and satisfaction I have known. I know of no better way to strengthen the foundation of an abundant, fair, and sustainable life for all.

I founded PMC Group on principles that we rarely see in corporations, such as loyalty to the communities in which we operate. Our products enhance the quality of life of people everywhere, and our business units invest generously in their communities. This is especially true of education, for it ensures moral and prosperous people.

BOOK 4: *Highest Reality: A Treatise on Religion, Truth, Morality, and the Purpose of Life* (Prabhat Prakashan, 2024)

Life is a journey. It's also a learning experience. And it's not just a learning experience; it's about reflecting on what we learn. And it's not just about reflecting on what we learn; it's about discovering new things that go beyond how the physical world works. It also concerns non-physical things—the *spiritual* things. It's about discovering how the physical world interacts with our emotional world. It's about probing the nature of truth. It is about pondering about religions—the good and the bad in them. It's about understanding the importance of helping others and of philanthropic activities. It's also about pondering the purpose of life. This book, the last volume of my four-volume memoir series, is about all of the above. It brings everything together by relating each idea to my own inquiries and to the inquiries of those who have contemplated the same matters in the past.

As we journey through life, we accumulate varied experiences that contribute to our world views. Our experiences often take us from one pole of reality to another. Adam Smith, the father of the capitalist order of economics, teaches us that if we take care of our self-interest, an "invisible hand" will take care of the collective interest of the rest. But in countries where citizens follow their self-interest with zest, they become corrupt and immoral. As children, we were taught to love our country, but when we love it with fervent passion, we pave the way for tyrants like Adolf Hitler. We were also taught not to accept injustice, but as the quote often attributed to Gandhi goes, "An eye for an eye leaves the whole world blind." We find that science has done great things for us, but if we use our science without moral constraints, we will destroy ourselves. Many religions teach that theirs is the only true religion and that all others are false or even evil. When we follow such advice, the result is jihads and crusades that kill millions.

No wonder we get confused. I've gone through such confusion, and swung from one belief to another until I established my own world view, which balances science with morality, materialism with spirituality, and self-interest with interest of others—always trying to distinguish a process from the product of a process. The process must follow the laws of science, but morality must rule the product.

When we were born, we had no religion, values, or biases. We acquired those from our families, cultures, and the environment in which we spent our early years. Children born in a Muslim family grow up to be Muslims. When a Christian family raises an infant born to Muslim parents, the child grows up to be a Christian. The same is true for almost every other religion and sect. In a sense, we are born as a "clean slate" that eventually accumulates characteristics from our native culture and environment. As we grow older, we develop the ability to reason and examine our predilections through the prism of our judgement. Some of us apply this judgement and accept some predilections while rejecting others. But many among us remain confined in them—willingly and happily so—for life.

Born into a Hindu family, I followed with abiding faith the practices of Hinduism that in our conservative family included a formal religious festivity almost every month. As the saying goes, a Hindu performs thirteen religious ceremonies in twelve months. My family's ceremonies involved worshiping various deities—God in human images, both male and female. We prayed to these deities, asking them to grant us every favour possible: to give us knowledge and make us successful as students, to keep our family healthy and safe, to give us good fortune and wealth, to protect us from snake bites, and so forth.

In addition, every morning we would pray before our family goddess, Lakshmi, the goddess of good fortune and wealth. If any misfortune struck the family or if one of us fell sick, I would prostrate myself before our family deity. If I was not home, I would kneel before an imaginary image of Vishnu (Hinduism's supreme protector God) seated on a lotus flower. When the misfortunes disappeared, as they usually did, I thought my prayers had worked, and my religious faith deepened. I became a strong believer in the power of the deities we worshipped.

Hindus consider religious activities an act of sacrifice for the good of the family and society. My unfailing devotion to religion and my faith in the power of the divine became so intense that at one point in my life I thought about abandoning everything material and becoming a sanyasi (Hindu monk) in the hope that I would do much good for society in that capacity by connecting directly with God, although I was unsure what that good would be. Since I didn't know how to become a devoted sanyasi, I sought a guru—a successful sanyasi—who could help me achieve my aspiration, which endured until I completed my master's degree and began conducting research for my doctoral degree.

My blind faith in God and everything religious came to an abrupt halt when I met a sanyasi, who, as rumour had it, was a God-sent saviour but turned out to be a fraud. After that experience, I began questioning my religious beliefs. I decided to test whether God really existed as I believed He did. I thought if I could please God by worshipping Him, I could also annoy Him by disrespecting Him. So, I stopped worshipping and dared God to stop me from pursuing my doctorate degree. When I earned my doctorate degree with flying colours, I thought my so-called experiment proved that my faith in God was a mistake. Of course, as a scientist, I should have known that a negative result doesn't prove the opposite. Yet this "experiment" shook my belief in God. I became agnostic—someone who neither admits nor denies the existence of God.

Although an agnostic, I continued attending public religious ceremonies like the Durga Puja but viewed them as cultural programmes rather than religious ones. Later, when our children and then our grandchildren were born, my wife and I performed their *annaprasana* (a Hindu rice-eating ceremony) at the age of one, *hate khari* (marking the beginning of literacy), and for my grandson, the *upanayana* (a sacred thread ceremony)—all as cultural observances. My children and grandchildren remember these ceremonies fondly, but they don't practise religion, at least not in the way I did when I was their age.

Although I left the practice of Hindu religious rites, I remained a Hindu—a Hindu by birth. More than 80 per cent of the world's population belongs to some form of religion, and almost 98 per cent of that group belong to one of the four major religions: Christianity, Islam, Hinduism, and Buddhism. This situation has persisted more or less unchanged for generations. My studies revealed that even some of the most renowned scientists had faith in God or some divine power.

Being an agnostic, I felt helpless and frustrated on some occasions. When I was distressed, I wished I could pray to some supreme power but only became more distressed when I realized I didn't believe in any supreme power. I turned to studying the major religions, hoping to find some form of truth in them. If such a truth existed, I reasoned, it should be common to all religions. These studies led me to devise my theory of truth. I theorized that religious truths can be true only if (i) diverse groups of people accept them as true, (ii) they survive almost unchanged from generation to generation over a long expanse of time, and (iii) science cannot contradict them. I found that the core message of all religions was the same, although they differed in their respective rituals. I also concluded that most religions harbour both truths and falsehoods, with the falsehoods evident as the root of religious hatred and violence.

As a successful entrepreneur, I realized that fulfilment in life doesn't come from personal success alone. It comes from promoting both self-interest and the interests of others, with the first finding its expression of contentment in the second. I explore these concepts in Chapters 8 and 9, "Beyond Self-Interest" and "The Paritosh and Srimati Chakrabarti Ashram".

I close the book with a chapter on the purpose of life, using examples from science, art, and philosophy to explore the concept that the grandest of all existences is nothingness and that nothingness is also the womb of all realities. All realities emerge as pairs of opposites from nothingness, and they end up again as nothingness upon their collapse. Our ability to create reality as pairs of opposites—our scientific, artistic, and philosophical advances and the fact that these realities can accumulate from generation to generation—gives humanity the power to fully understand some day the purpose that lies behind the existence of the universe. When humanity reaches that goal, we will have succeeded in fulfilling our purpose, which until then should be to do everything in our power to keep humanity alive and united at peace with itself.

Finally, as someone who has practised science for most of my life, I can attest that nothing in this book is based on my personal beliefs alone. The rigour of sound logic and/or the process of science supports everything, including the chapter on belief as a province unto itself.

Bibliography

(Consolidated for Books 1 to 4)

Ali, Ahmed. 1993. *Al-Quran: A Contemporary Translation*. Princeton University Press, Princeton, New Jersey.

Armstrong, Karen. 1993. *A History of God*. Ballantine Books, New York.

Atkins, Peter, Julio de Paula, and James Keeler. 2018. *Atkin's Physical Chemistry:* 11th Ed. Oxford University Press, Oxford, UK.

Atkinson, Brooks, Ed. 2000. *The Essential Writings of Ralph Waldo Emerson*. The Modern Library, New York, NY.

Barnes, Jean-Paul, Transl. and Intro. 2001. *Being and Nothingness* by Jean-Paul Sartre. Citadel Press, New York, NY.

Bartlett, John. 1980. *Bartlett's Familiar Quotations*. Little Brown & Company, London, England.

Bose, Sugata. 2011. *His Majesty's Opponent: Subhas Chandra Bose and India's Struggle Against Empire*. The Belknap Press of Harvard University Press, Cambridge, Massachusetts.

Cannan, Edwin. 1994. *Adam Smith: The Wealth of Nations*. Random House, The Modern Library Edition, New York.

Chopra, Deepak and Rudolph E. Tanzi. 2012. *Super Brain*. Ebury Publishing, London.

Clark, Ronald, W. 1971. *Einstein: The Life and Times*. Avon Books, New York, NY.

Dewey, John. 1989. *Freedom and Culture*. Prometheus Books, Buffalo, New York.

Dickens, Charles. 1981. *Great Expectations*. Bantam Books, New York, NY.

Domar, Evsey. 1946. 'Capital Expansion, Rate of Growth, and Employment'. *Econometrica*, 14 (2): 137–47.

Edgerton, Franklin (Translation). 1993. *The Bhagavad Gita*. Harvard University Press, Cambridge, Massachusetts.

Einstein, Albert. Translation by Alan Harris. 1979. *The World as I See It*. Citadel Press, Secaucus, New Jersey.

Frost Jr, S.E. 1989. *The Teachings of the Great Philosophers*. Doubleday, New York, NY.

Galbraith, John K. 1987. *Economics in Perspective—A Critical History*. Houghton Mifflin Company, Boston, Massachusetts.

Galloway, Scott. 2020. *Post Corona—From Crisis to Opportunity*. Penguin Press, London.

Gangopadhyay, Sunil. Ed. 1999. *Smarak Grantha*. Swaraswati Press, Kolkata.

Gardner, Marin. 1997. *Great Essays in Science*. Oxford University Press, Oxford, England.

Garraty, John A. and Peter Gay. 1972. *The Columbia History of the World*. Harper & Row Publishers, New York, NY.

Greenspan, Alan and Adrian Wooldridge. 2018. *Capitalism in America: A History*. Penguin Press, New York, NY.

Halpern, Paul. 2020. *Synchronicity: The Epic Quest to Understanding the Quantum Nature of Cause and Effect*. Basic Books, New York, NY.

Hannah-Jones, Nicole. Ed. 2021. *The 1619 Project*. One World (Random House), New York, NY.

Harari, Yuval Noah. 2015. *Sapiens: A Brief History of Humankind*. Harper Collins Publishers, New York, NY.

———. 2017. *Homo Deus: A Brief History of Tomorrow*. Harper Perennial, New York, NY.

———. 2018. *21 Lessons for the 21st Century*. Spiegel & Grau, Random House, New York, NY.

Harrod, Roy F. 1939. 'An Essay in Dynamic Theory'. *The Economic Journal*, 49(193): 14–33.

Hesse, Hermann, 1951. *Siddhartha*. Bantam Books, New York, NY.

International Religious Foundation. 1995. *World Scripture: A Comparative Anthology of Sacred Texts*. Paragon House, St Paul, Minnesota.

James, Lawrence. 1994. *The Rise and Fall of the British Empire*. St Martin's Griffin, New York.

Johnson, Boris. 2014. *The Churchill Factor: How One Man Made History*. Riverhead Books, New York, NY.

Kaufmann, Walter. 1989. *The Genealogy of Morals: Friedrich Nietzsche*. Vintage Books, New York, NY.

Keay, John. 2000. *India: A History*. Grove Press, New York, NY.

Kelley, Kevin W. Ed. 1988. *The Home Planet*. Mir Publishers, Moscow.

Kevles, Daniel J. 1986. *In the Name of Eugenics: Genetics and the Uses of Human Heredity*. University of California Press, Berkley, CA.

Kershaw, Ian. 1998. *Hitler, 1889-1936*. W.W. Norton & Company, New York, NY.

Klamer, Arjo. 1983. *Conversations with Economists*. Rowman and Littlefield, Savage, Maryland.

Kukathas, Chandran and Philip Pettit. 1990. *Rawls: A Theory of Justice and Its Critics*. Stanford University Press, Stanford, California.

Kyokai, Bukkyo Bendo. 1986. *The Teaching of Buddha*. 445th Ed. Kosaido Printing, Tokyo, Japan.

Little, Arthur D. 1994. *An Exchange of Knowledge Among Leading Practitioners in Product and Technology Management: Best of the Best*. An Arthur D. Little Colloquium. Cambridge, MA.

Lock, Peter. 2006. *Routledge Companion to the Crusades*. eBook ISBN 0415-39312-4.

Max Muller, F (Translation). 1962. *The Upanishads: Part I*. Dover Publications, New York, NY.

McCloskey, Donald. 1985. *The Rhetoric of Economics*. The University of Wisconsin Press, Madison, Wisconsin.

———. 1989. *Formalism in Economics, Rhetorically Speaking*. Xerox.

Meacham, Jon. 2018. *The Soul of America: Battle for Our Better Angels*. Random House, New York, NY.

Morgan, Michael L. Ed. 1992. *Classics of Moral and Political Theory*. Hackett Publishing Company, Indianapolis, Indiana.

Muller, Richard. 2016. *The Physics of Time*. W.W. Norton & Company, New York, NY.

Newman, Melvin S. Ed. 1963. *Steric Effects in Organic Chemistry*. John Wiley & Sons, Inc., New York, NY.

Ritter, Lawrence S. and William L. Silber. 1984. *Money*, Fifth Edition. Basic Books of Harper Collins, New York, NY.

Roger, Charles Barclay. 5 October 2020. 'Amartya Sen and the Idea of Justice'. At https://www.opendemocracy.net/en/amartya-sen-and-idea-of-justice/

Ruhe, Peter. 2001. *Gandhi*. Phaidon Press Inc. New York, NY.

Samuelson, Paul. 1970. *Economics*, Eighth Edition, McGraw Hill, New York, NY.

Schacht, Richard. 1992. *Nietzsche*. Routledge, New York, NY.

Sen, Amartya. 1988. *On Ethics & Economics*. Blackwell Publishing, Malden, Massachusetts.

———. 1992. *Inequality Re-examined*. Harvard University Press, Cambridge, Massachusetts.

———. 2000. *Development as Freedom*. Anchor Books (Random House), New York, NY.

———. 2009. *The Idea of Justice*. The Belknap Press, Harvard University Press, Cambridge, Massachusetts.

Sinclair, Gavin. 1997. *All Things Work for Good: A Book of Encouragement for People with Cancer, Their Family and Friends*. The Positive Press, Gainesville, Florida.

Solow, Robert M. 1987. 'Growth Theory and After'. The Nobel Prize Lecture, 8 December 1987.

———. 1994. 'Perspective on Growth Theory'. *Journal of Economic Perspectives*, 8 (1): 45–54.

Sowell, Thomas. 1977. *Classical Economics Reconsidered*. Princeton University Press, Princeton, New Jersey.

Swami Vidyatmananda, Ed. 1972. *What Religion Is: In the Words of Swami Vivekananda*. Advaita Ashrama Publications, Kolkata.

Thoreau, Henry David. *The Wisdom of Thoreau*. Kensington Publishing, New York, Citadel Publication 1967.

Updegrove, Mark, K. 2017. *The Last Republicans*. HarperCollins Publishers, New York, NY.

Wilkerson, Isabelle. 2010. *The Warmth of Other Suns*. Random House, New York, NY.

———. 2020. *Caste: The Origins of Our Discontents*. Random House, New York, NY.

Witherspoon, W. Roger. 1985. *Martin Luther King Jr: To the Mountain Top*. Doubleday & Company Inc., New York, NY.

Yunus, Muhammad. 1999. *Banker to the Poor: Micro-Lending and the Battle Against World Poverty*. Public Affairs, New York, NY.

Index

11 September attack, 75

A

activation energy, 163–164, 221
Affordable Caare Act, 237
Afghan people, 73–74
Afghanistan, 73
    per capita GDP, 76
    population, 76
    Taliban rule, 75
Akhtar, 229–230, 232
al-Qaeda, 75
Alibaba Group Holding, 118
Amazon.com, 90–92
American War of Independence (1775–83), 35–37
Apple, 93
Archimedes Principle, 125
asset-light strategy, 100
Avogadro's number, 152

B

banks, 209
Battle of Trafalgar (1805), 38
Begum, Sufiya, 28–30
Bentham, Jeremy, 62, 82
Bezos, Jeff, 102
Bill of Rights, 68
birth control and abortion rights, 199, 243–256, 260–261, 266
  Dobbs v. Jackson Women's Health Organization, 247–248
  medical viewpoints, 250–251
  political viewpoints, 249–250
  religious viewpoints, 248
  Roe v. Wade decision, 247–248
  utilitarian viewpoints, 250
Black Tuesday, 40
Boehlje, Michael, xix
Bolsonaro, Jair, 226
Boltzmann constant, 152
Boltzmann formula, 139–140
Boltzmann law of distribution of energy, 169–172
Boltzmann's law of wealth distribution, 205–206, 215
Bonaparte, Napoleon, 38
Bose House, 73
Bose, Subhas Chandra, 73, 83
boundaries of economic thought, 32
Boyle, Robert, 150–151
Boyle's law, 151–152
Bretton Woods Agreement, 111
The Bright Side of Adversity: An Autobiography of a First-generation Immigrant to the US from India, 284–285
Britain's economic ambitions, 35–40
British East India Company, 52–54

Buddhism, 35
Bush, George W., 225

C
capital account payment, 18
capitalism, 31, 79–80, 103, 112, 115–116, 126–127, 179, 195, xxii–xxiii
  case of US national wealth, 79
  clearing mechanism, 80
  economic failure of, 80–81
  immorality of, 104–115, 190, xxiii–xxiv
  injustices within, 83
  mistreatment of labour, 94–100
  role of capital, 86–90
  tech businesses' exploitation of, 100–103
Carnot cycle, 157–159, 162, 164–165
  adiabatic compression, 161–162
  adiabatic expansion, 160
  economic equivalent of, 184–185
  isothermal compression, 160
  isothermal expansion, 159–160
Carnot, Sadi, 158
  Reflections on the Motive Power of Fire, 161
Carter, Jimmy, 106
Celsius scale (centigrade scale), 138
chain reaction in education, 2, 7
Chakrabarti Foundation scholarships, 7
Charles, Jacques, 150–151
Charles's law, 151–152
chemical energy, 133–134, 162–163
chemical thermodynamics, 163

China, 77–78
  as manufacturing hub, 216
  mix of communism and capitalism, 117–118
classical economics, 51–55
Clinton, Bill, 106
Clive, Robert, 36
closed systems, 141, 168
combustion, 162
common ownership, 196
common property, 196
common services
  abortion, 199
  contraception, 199
  defence, 198
  education, 196–198
  emergency healthcare, 199
  environment, 198
  infrastructure, 198
  other services, 199
communism, 31, 50, 55–57, 77–78, 126, 227
  elimination of private property, 78
  in Russia, 118–119
  protection of sick companies, 80
Condorcet, Marquis de, 82
conservation of energy, 132–135, 215
conservation of mass, 131–132, 134–135
  chemical change, 132
  physical change, 132
conservative justices, 68
Consider a Spherical Cow (Harte), 124
consumption tax, 202–203, 259
consumption tax on products and services, 202–203

Contractarians, 81
contractionary monetary policy, 13
conversion of mass into energy, 134–135, 145
credit and credit rating, 21
Cuba, 77
current account payment, 18

D
Darwin, Charles, 27, 211
principle of "survival of the fittest," 128
theory of evolution, 172–174
Declaration of Independence, 68, 114
demand-side macroeconomic theory, 13
Denison, Edward, 85, 101
Dewey, John, 95
DNA, 173, 211
Domar, Evsey David, 84
Dow Jones Industrial Average, 218

E
Earnings Before Interest, Depreciation, Tax, and Amortization (EBIDTA), 88–89
economic Darwinism, xxiii
economic equivalent terms
of Carnot cycle, 184–185
of energy, 181–182
of enthalpy, 182
of entropy and energy barrier, 192–194
of first law of thermodynamics, 183
of Gibbs free energy, 182–183
of internal energy, 182

of second law of thermodynamics, 184–185
of temperature, 180
economic growth, 115–116
economic polarity, 77, 79, 258
economy of scale, 188–189
Edward VII, 39
efficiency
equation of Carnot engine, 190
of single-stage machine, 187–188
polarity *vs*, 185–186
wages of labourer *vs*, 190–192
Einsteinian physics, 134, 145
mass–energy equivalence equation ($E = mc^2$), 134–135, 145, 147, 218, 223
electrical energy, 133
electrolysis, 162
electromagnetic energy, 133
emergency care, 236
endothermic reaction, 166
energy
economic equivalent of, 181–182
energy–work relationship, 152–153
Engels, Friedrich, 39, 44
The Communist Manifesto, 68
enthalpy, 163, 165–168
economic equivalent of, 182
entrepreneurship, 213–214
entropy, 136, 139–141
equality principle in inheritance, 211–213
equitable distribution without wealth creation, xxii
Europe, 40–41

excess economic output, distribution of, 203–205
exchange rate equilibrium, 19, 215–216
exothermic reaction, 166–168
expansionary monetary policy, 13

F
Facebook, 92–93, 102
Federal Open Market Committee (FOMC), 20–21
Federal Reserve Act, 10
Federal Reserve-MIT-Penn Model (FMP Model), 14
FedEx, 91
financial account payment, 18
financing rules for businesses, 259
first law of thermodynamics, 131–135, 146–147
  economic equivalent of, 183
Fisher, Irving, 12
foreign money exchange rates, 19, 215–216
  fixed, 20, 217
  floating, 19–20, 215
France
  labour productivity, 119–120
  socialist values, 119
France's economy, 35, 37–38
Franco-Prussian War 1871, 41
Franklin, Benjamin, 42
free contraception, 260
free education, 258
Friedman, Milton, 13, 96–97

G
Galbraith, John Kenneth, 31
Gandhi, Mahatma, 83

gas laws, 150–154, 169–170
Gautama Buddha, 35
genetic inheritance, 211–213
geological and evolutional events, timeline, 276–277
George, Lloyd, 46
Gibbs free energy, 163, 168–169
    economic equivalent of, 182–183
gold standard, 16–17, 109–110, 215–217
    amount of gold held by nations, 16–17
Google, 92
Grameen Bank, 8, 29–31, 219–220
Great Recession of 2008, 25, 97
Gross Domestic Product (GDP), 10, 12
Gross National Product (GNP), 10–11
    calculation, 115
    influence on stocks and bond markets, 22

H

Harrod, Roy F., 84
Harrod–Domar Model, 84–86
healthcare costs of different countries, 237–239
healthcare emergency services, 260
heat energy, 138
heat transfer, 140
heat transfers, 161
Highest Reality: A Treatise on Religion, Truth, Morality, and the Purpose of Life, 287–292
historical dates of people and events, timeline, 278–283
Hobbes, Thomas, 63, 81
    Leviathan, 81
Hume, David, 42
Hutcheson, Francis, 64, 80–81

I

income tax, 200–203
independent reserve currency, 260
Indian Association for the Cultivation of Science (IACS), 229–232
industrial capitalism, 50
Industrial Revolution, 53
inflation and interest rates, 20–21
inheritance tax, 205–206, 259–260
inorganic world, 128
internal energy, 163–167
  economic equivalent of, 182
internal revenue service (IRS), 200–203
international balance of payment of a country, 17–19
International Monetary Fund (IMF), 19–20
International Specialty Products (ISP), 1
Iron Law of Wages, 95
isolated systems, 141

J

Jack Ma, 118
Johnson & Johnson COVID-19 vaccine, 241
judiciary, 68, 258

K

Kabuliwala, 71–73
Kant, Immanuel, 63, 81
Kekulé, Dr Friedrich August, 148
Kelvin scale, 138–139
Keynes, John Maynard, 13, 31, 34, 40, 45–47, 55, 69–70, 108, 111, 130, xxv
  A Treatise on Money, 46

A Treatise on Probability, 46
deficit spending, 108
education, 45
Indian Currency and Finance, 46
official career, 46
recognitions, 46
The General Theory of Employment, Interest, and Money, 47, 58–59
The Means to Prosperity, 47
Keynesian economics, 13–14, 50, 57–59
government spending, benefits of, 58–59
top-down macroeconomic prescription, 58
kinetic energy, 133, 146
King George's War (1744–48), 35
King Jr, Martin Luther, 83
KKR Private Equity, 74
Krugman, Paul, 225

L

Laden, Osama bin, 75–76
Laos, 77–78
Lavoisier, Antoine, 131
lawn maintenance business, 94
laws of nature, 257–258
laws of thermodynamics, 127–142
Boltzmann formula, 139–140
closed, isolated, or open systems, 141
conservation of mass and energy, 131–135
entropy, 136, 139–141
first law, 131–135
second law, 135–137
spontaneous and non-spontaneous process, 142

temperature, 136, 138–139
third law, 137
Lehman Brothers, 25, 88
Lenin, Vladimir, 69
Letiche, John M., 54
liberal justices, 68
life expectancy, 239
Locke, John, 63, 81
Lopokova, Lydia, 47
Louis XVI, 38

M
Machiavelli's *The Prince,* 34
Madoff, Bernie, 105, 113
Mahabharata, 90–91
The Makings of PMC Group: A Corporation with a Soul, 285–287
Malthus, Thomas Robert, 52, 55, 65, 95, 99, 195
An Essay on the Principle of Population, 53–54
Mandela, Nelson, 179
Mao Zedong, 117
Markowitz, Harry, 97
Marx, Karl, 34–35, 39, 41, 43–45, 82, 98, xxi, xxiv
Critique of Hegel's Philosophy of Right, 57
Das Kapital, 31, 44
education, 43–44
elimination of private property, 56
Marxism, 45
parents, 43
struggle between bourgeoisie and proletariat, 56
The Communist Manifesto, 44, 56, 68, xxiv
mathematical models, 97–98
maximum efficiency of a heat engine, 161

McCloskey, Donald, 96
mechanical energy, 133
Medicaid, 10, 237, 240–241, 260
medical malpractice litigation, 242
Medicare, 10, 237, 240–241, 260
meiosis, 212
Melville's *Billy Bud*, 34
mercantilism, 52
Merton, Robert, 97
microchips, 101–102
microcredits, 30
microfinance, 30
Military Retirement Fund, 112
Mill, John Stuart, 12, 52, 65, 80, 95, 195
  Principles of Political Economy, 54
Milton, John, 39
minimal government, 208–209, 258
  corruption and, 215
mining rights, 18
mitosis, 212–213
Modi, Prime Minister, 26
monetary policies, 11
  gold standard and, 16–17
money, 87
  definition, 9–10
  supply, 10
money supply (M1, M2, and M3), 10–11, 18
  connection between gold and, 17
  liquidity of, 10–12
  monetarists' assumption, 12–14
  velocity of, 11–13
monopolies, 78, 90–94, 185–186, 259

forward and backward integrations, 186–188
polarity *vs* efficiency, 185–186
moral economy, 190–192
morality-based approach to welfare economics, 59–60
Mordashov, Alexey, 119
Mukhopadhyay, Ramkumar, 48
Conversations with JOV, 48–50
maan-kachu trade, 3–6

N
Nair, Aravind, 167
nation's economic system, 31
national economics, 67–70
natural processes
controlled process, 222–224
explosive process, 222
slow process, 221–222
New Deal program, 59
New York Stock Exchange, 218
Nine Years' War (1688–97), 35
niti and *nyaya* (jurisprudence), 82–83
non-spontaneous processes, 142
North Korea, 77
Nozick, Robert, 61–62
criticism of Rawls's theory, 61–62
nuclear energy, 135
nuclear power, 129

O
Omar, Mullah, 75–76
open systems, 141
optimal inequality, 258

organic chemistry, 148–149
organic world, 128
Organization of Economic Cooperation and Development (OECD), 104
overriding principle of morality, 192–194

P

pendulum theory, 145
Pep Boys, 94
Personal Consumption Expenditures (PCE), 10
phenotype, 212
photochemical reaction, 162
Plato's *Republic,* 34
PMC Group, 8, 25, 117, 119
PMC Group of Companies, 73
  business acquisitions, 73–74
PMC Rubber Chemicals India Private Limited, 229
polarity *vs* efficiency, 185–189
political economy, 31, 113, 118
  social changes in, 224
Ponzi scheme, 105–106, 108, 113
Ponzi, Charles, 105
potential energy, 133–134
poverty alleviation, 2
PPG Industries, 150
president's economic policy, 15–16
  Biden administration, 15–16
  Eisenhower administration, 15
  Johnson administration, 15
  Kennedy administration, 15
  Keynesian policy, 15
  Obama administration, 15

Reagan administration, 15
supply-side monetarist policy, 15
Trump–Pence administration, 15–16
pressure–volume work (PV work), 153–154
private property, right to, 205–206
private-equity-funded monopolies, 94
Procter & Gamble, 92
Purdue's economics department, xix–xx
Putin, Vladimir, 119

Q
quality of healthcare, 240
quants (quantitative analysts), 25

R
racism in America, 179
Raman, Dr C.V., 229
Rawls, John, 80, 95, 194
A Theory of Justice, 60–62
contractual arrangement between rational people, 61
on fairness, 60
OP theory, 61–62
principles of justice, 60
Reagan, Ronald, 69
realization-focused group, 82–84
Rhodes, Frank H. T., 33–34
Ricardo, David, 12, 52, 65, 95, 99, 195
Iron Law of Wages, 52
On Principles of Political Economy and Taxation, 52, 190
Ritter, Lawrence, 9
Robinson, Eugene, 225
Roosevelt, Franklin D., 59, 69, 110

Rousseau, Jean-Jacques, 63, 81
Royal Farms, 94
Russia, 227
  communism in, 118–119
  state capitalism, 118–119
Russian Revolution (1917), 56, 58

S

Samuelson, Paul, 96–97
Sanders, Bernie, 112
Sartwell, Crispin, 225–226
Say, Jean-Baptiste, 54
  Say's Law, 55
  Traite d'Economie Politique, 54
Scholes, Myron, 97
Schrodinger's equation, 219
Scott, Henry, 42
Scripps Research Institute, 82
second law of thermodynamics, 135–137, 150
  economic equivalent of, 184–185
securitization of mortgages, 25
Sen, Amartya, 31, 34–35, 62, 76, 82, 95
  career, 66
  Development as Freedom, 66–67
  economic theory, 65–66
  ethics in capitalism, 64
  interpretation of *The Wealth of Nations,* 54
  morality, 65
  rationality, 63–64
  recognition of capitalism, 65
  Social Choice Theory, 62–67
  The Idea of Justice, 63

Seven Years War (1756–63), 35, 37
sick companies
  capitalism's approach, 207
  communist and socialist's approach, 207
  definition, 207
  effect on national wealth, 208
Silber, William, 9
Sinclair, Dr Gavin, xix–xxii
single-stage process, 186–187
Siraj ud-Daulah, 36
Smith, Adam, 27, 31, 34–35, 41–43, 79, 81, 156, xxi
  "invisible hand", 51
  basic tenets, 52
  economic theories, 42
  General Economic Theory, 57
  parents, 41
  principle of laissez-faire, 51
  The Theory of Moral Sentiments, 42, 64
  The Wealth of Nations, 31, 37, 42, 51, 64, 68
  title of Doctor of Laws (LLD), 42
Smith–Ricardo–Mill–Malthus Doctrines, 51–55
Social Choice Theory, 62–67
social contract theory, 81
social Darwinism, 174, xxiii
Social Security, 10
Social Security Trust Fund, 112
social welfare programmes, 200
socialism, 55–57, 77–78, 126, 227
  protection of sick companies, 80
socialist countries, 77
socio-economic climates, 33–34
Solow, Robert, 13, 85–86, 101

growth theory of economics, 191
role of technology on economic growth, 191
technological changes, 103
view on economics, 96
Soviet Union, 77
spontaneous processes, 142
St Louis Fed Model, 14
state capitalism, 118
statistical laws, 130
stock market bubbles, 23–24
stock market crashes, 26–27
stocks and bonds, 22–25
factors influencing, 23–25
institutional investors, 24
pendulum effect, 23
reaction to speculation, 24
subprime mortgages, 25
Surendra Paul Lecture, 230

T

technological changes, 103
technology on economic growth, 191, 203
temperature, 138–139
economic equivalent of, 180
thermal energy, 133
third law of thermodynamics, 137
Timchenko, Gennady, 119
total factor productivity, 196
Townshend, Charles, 42
Transcendental Idealism, 81
Transcendental Institutionalists, 81
transfer payments, 10

transition state, 163
TruGreen, 94

U
UK's economy, 227
unions, 259
universal molar gas constant, 152
universe, size of, 277
UPS, 91
US
  capitalism, 84
  distribution of wealth, 114–115
  dollar, 18
  economic framework, hypothetical examples, 261–269
  economic growth, 85
  economy, 109–110
  financial structure, 112–113
  GNP, 85–86
  national debt, 106–107, 112
  spending power, 108
US healthcare
  birth control and abortion rights, 243–254
  cost of drugs, 241
  government control, 240–241
  medical tort law, 242–243
  practice of contraception, 248
  Roe v. Wade decision, 247–248

V
Vietnam, 77
virtues, 213–214
Voltaire, 42

W

Wall Street, 23, 25, 100–102, 218
Wall Street Journal, 117, 226
Walmart, 92
War of Austrian Succession (1740–48), 35
War of Spanish Succession (1701–14), 35
Wawa, 94
wealth creation or wealth distribution, 194–195
  Boltzmann's law of distribution, 205–206, 215
  doctrine of inheritance right, 210–211
  national economy, 210
White, Harry Dexter, 111
Williams, Bernard, 63, 80
Wollstonecraft, Mary, 82
woman's reproductive rights, 243–256
work
  agents and, 156–157
  commentary on, 154–156
  pressure–volume work (PV work), 153–154
World Bank, 19–20
World War I (1914–18), 39

Y

Yunus, Dr Muhammad, 8, 29–30, 219–220, xxv

Z

Zoellick, Robert, 216
Zuckerberg, Mark, 93, 102